AF788822

Marketing Modernity

Marketing modernity traces the development of consumer culture in Italy from the 1920s to the present day. In so doing, Adam Arvidsson argues that the culture of consumption we see in Italy today has its direct roots in the social vision articulated by the advertising industry in the years following the First World War. He then goes on to discuss how that vision was further elaborated by advertising's interaction with subsequent major actors in twentieth-century Italy: Fascism, post-war mass political parties and the counter-culture of the 1960s and 1970s. Based on a wide range of primary sources, this fascinating book takes an innovative historical approach to the study of advertising and consumption.

Adam Arvidsson is Assistant Professor in the Department of Film and Media at the University of Copenhagen.

Studies in Consumption and Markets

Edited by Colin Campbell
Department of Sociology, University of York, UK
and Alladi Venkatesh
Graduate School of Management, University of California, Irvine, USA

Consumption has become a major focus of research and scholarship in the social sciences and humanities. Increasingly perceived as central to any successful understanding of the modern world, the meaning of the individual and collective consumption of goods is now a crucial issue at the heart of numerous contemporary debates on personal identity, the social and cultural structure of postmodern societies, and the historical development of modern industrial society. This new series will publish work on consumption-related topics across a number of disciplines.

Titles in this series include:

The Dynamics of Advertising
Barry Richards, Iain MacRury and Jackie Botterill

Ordinary Consumption
Edited by Jukka Gronow and Alan Warde

The Changing Consumer: Markets and Meanings
Edited by Steven Miles, Alison Anderson and Kevin Meethan

Food and Cultural Studies
Bob Ashley, Joanne Hollows, Steve Jones and Ben Taylor

Marketing Modernity: Italian Advertising from Fascism to Postmodernity
Adam Arvidsson

Marketing Modernity

Italian advertising from Fascism to postmodernity

Adam Arvidsson

Routledge
Taylor & Francis Group
LONDON AND NEW YORK

First published 2003
by Routledge
2 Park Square, Milton Park, Abingdon, Oxon, OX14 4RN

Simultaneously published in the USA and Canada
by Routledge
270 Madison Ave, New York NY 10016

Routledge is an imprint of the Taylor & Francis Group

Transferred to Digital Printing 2005

© 2003 Adam Arvidsson

Typeset in Garamond by RefineCatch Limited, Bungay, Suffolk

All rights reserved. No part of this book may be reprinted or reproduced or utilized in any form or by any electronic, mechanical, or other means, now known or hereafter invented, including photocopying and recording, or in any information storage or retrieval system, without permission in writing from the publishers.

British Library Cataloguing in Publication Data
A catalogue record for this book is available from the British Library

Library of Congress Cataloging in Publication Data
A catalog record for this book has been requested

ISBN 0–415–27044–8

Printed and bound by Antony Rowe Ltd, Eastbourne

To my mother, Birgit Arvidsson

Contents

Illustrations

Figures

Tables

Acknowledgements

This book began as a PhD project at the European University Institute in Florence. I am deeply thankful to my two supervisors, Gianfranco Poggi and Luisa Passerini, for their guidance and support. The external members of my exam committee, Victoria de Grazia and Peppino Ortoleva, also made vital contributions to the completion of that project. I would also like to thank Bianca Beccalli, John Brewer, Enrica Capusotti, Gina Castillo, David Ellwood, Simonetta Falasca-Zamponi, Nando Fasce, Claudio Fogu, Nicolas Guhilot, Caterina Paolucci, Margaret Somers, Bo Stråt and Erik Tängerstad for their comments and suggestions. Gianpaolo Capisani shared his wide knowledge on Italian popular culture with me, and Cecilia Conti taught me what there is to know about Italian housewives. In reworking the manuscript I have benefited from suggestions and advice from my former colleagues at the University of East Anglia, Tim Dant, Judith Metha and Roberta Sassatelli. I have also profited from presenting and discussing my work at a number of conferences and workshops, at the European University, the Centro di studi Euro-Americani, Piero Bairati at the University of Turin and through the Italian society for contemporary history (Società italiana di storia contemporanea, SISCO). I thank those institutions and, in particular, Maurizio Vaudagna at the centro Bairati, for inviting me. People within the world of Italian advertising and market research let themselves be interviewed by me, sometimes repeatedly. I am particularly grateful to Francesco Alberoni and Gianpaolo Fabris. I have conducted most of my research at the Biblioteca Nazionale in Florence, the Biblioteca Comunale in Milan and the Circolo Giuridico in Siena. The Archivio Storico Barilla in Parma, the Fondazione Piaggio at Pontedera, the Centro Documentazione Rai in Turin and the Special Collections Library at Duke University have all let me benefit from their collections and archives. (Fondazione Piaggio, Archivio Storico Barilla and the Biblioteca Nazionale have also generously granted me permission to reproduce a number of images.) I thank the personnel of all those institutions. Most of the research behind this book was conducted during the four pleasurable years I spent as a researcher at the European University Institute. I am grateful for having had the opportunity to be part of that vibrant intellectual community. The mistakes and errors that will inevitably follow are my own responsibility.

Part I

From Fascism to Fordism

1 Introduction

Autumn 2001 at my local Sainsbury's supermarket had an Italian theme. According to *The Observer*'s food columnist, Nigel Slater, who wrote the copy for the accompanying campaign brochure, the purpose was to introduce Brits to the rich regional variety of Italian food, beyond the now familiar vocabulary of 'pizza, pasta, espresso'. Such lesser-known regional dishes are authentic, we were assured, but 'none of this means that Italian food is stuck in a time-warp', Nigel Slater admitted, showing his awareness of the 'floating' or 'contested' status of culture and identity. 'It is simply that they [Italians] have a respect for their traditions that other countries may have lost'. Soon, Slater hoped, this 'love of good food will be as much ours as theirs'.[1]

It is not just that Italian food tastes good. As stressed throughout Sainsbury's publicity drive, it stands for something that Brits, or at least Brits of the middle class, *Observer*, Sainsbury's, New Labour kind, appreciate: authenticity, tradition, a sense of quality and, of course, individual creativity. (Sainsbury's was eager to point this out: to cook an authentic Italian pasta meal it is not enough to mix the ready-made pasta with the ready-made sauce. One must also 'get creative, raid the fridge', add something of one's own.) Italy is not just another more or less exotic 'Other' to consume, as in the case of Sainsbury's range of Thai, Japanese or African food; it is an ideal to imitate. Indeed, at the 'Italian' bar, Café Nero, that has opened in the market square a couple of hundred yards from my local Sainsbury's branch, the main selling pitch is the make-believe Italian environment. Employers are even instructed in how to 'behave Italian' behind the counter and there is a tendency to hire only dark-haired staff. To those of us who remember Nino Manfredi's immigrant worker in the 1973 film *Pane e cioccolata*, trying desperately to colour his hair blond, such inverted cultural hierarchies are definitely quaint. As late as the mid-1980s Italian friends would routinely suffer racist slurs and sometimes violence when inter-railing to London. Today their attackers are probably at home cooking up a *Stracotto al Chianti*.

The international image of Italy has definitely changed since the 1980s. This is not only because the country has progressed from relative poverty to relative prosperity, demonstrated in 1988, when the Italian economy overtook the British in GNP per capita. And it is not only because the country has become a destination for migration rather than a point of departure. (Both of these statements are true with some modifications: northern Italy has 'always' been relatively prosperous, or at least since the late 1950's 'economic miracle'. Parts of southern Italy are still poor. A lot of Italians still migrate, particularly from the south.) And it is not only because Berlusconi and his Forza Italia party have shown that in Italy, like in the rest of the West, advertising, spin and careful marketing carry more political weight than old-fashioned ideologies. There is also something else. The international image of Italy, an Italian fashion scholar writes, is no longer a matter of 'madolines, pasta and straw-clad wine flasks (*fiaschi*)', but of high-quality stylish labels, like 'Ferrari, Armani and San Pellegrino table water'.[2] (Incidentally, the mandolines, pasta and *fiaschi* are the same objects that Mussolini used to invoke in describing the dreaded *Italietta* of the preceding liberal years, stuck in underdevelopment and provincialism.) Italy has become a locus for the style-conscious postmodern consumer culture that we all belong to. (And this signifying relation has a global validity. In the posh four-star Bangkok hotel that my airline supplied me with, there was of course an Italian restaurant, and a Prada store in the nearby mall.)

A similarly transformed self-image has been common to Italian observers as well, at least since the mid-1980s. 'In the last couple of years', influential semiologist Alberto Abruzzese wrote in 1988, advertising and consumer culture has made 'the aesthetic dimension of human existence' more important than before. This has led to a new general awareness and appreciation of personal appearance and of 'the look'.[3] In an essay with the telling title 'From Ideologies to Gregarious Individualism', prominent sociologist Franco Ferrarotti did not hesitate to describe the Italy of the late 1980s as a fully-fledged consumer society, where consumption, as many Anglo-Saxon writers on the postmodern have kept stressing, had become the central social institution, comparable to the factory in Gramsci's classic account of an emerging 'Fordist' late capitalism.[4] Consumerism, Ferrarotti argued, had now fully taken up its function as a 'surrogate for social integration'. This had led to a 'fragmentation of formal ideological schemes, both to the right and to the left'; to the 'rise of short-term needs connected to the interests, but also the diversified tastes of differentiated social groups'; this occurred 'independently or beyond what is commonly called public interest'. To Ferrarotti, the 'gregarious individualism' that followed meant the end of the political as the central locus for the formation of personal and social identity.[5] (In Italy this latter role of the political has been particularly powerful, at least if we believe Almond and Verba's study from the late 1950s. Italians, they argued, 'regard their party not as an electoral contestant but as a church or a way of life'.)[6]

Similarly, in 1995 Giuseppe DeRita, head of the influential polling company Censis, described the trends unearthed by the previous 20 years of polling as a development from a society marked by a fairly simple structure of aspirations and interests to a general state of differentiation and 'politeism'. This, he argued, was driven by the progressive affirmation of mass consumption.[7] This narrative is common enough to readers of contemporary social theory. Before, we lived in a class society where each cleavage generated its own values that would eventually find a political expression and that would, in turn, articulate a collective identity. Today we live in a consumer society and politics is if not irrelevant, then a fluid space of unstable social formations that come and go.[8] Usually, this progression is from a politically centred 'modern' society to a commercially decentred 'postmodern' society, and consequently from structure and production to culture and consumption, as the most important field of sociological analysis is simply taken for granted. It has become something of a Grand Narrative of contemporary social theory, and is often invoked as an explanatory factor in itself.[9] This narrative also contains a theory of subjectivity.[10] In modern society we were determined by our position in a well-defined social structure, where identities are more or less given. In postmodern society we are 'set free' from social structure and condemned to reflexively construct our own identities through, predominately, consumer choices. We have, as Anthony Giddens has put it, 'no choice but to choose'.[11] Precisely because of the common-sense status of this narrative it is very rare to see attempts at a more detailed explanation of how this transition has come about. Clearly, if we go back half a century, consumer goods were generally not regarded as conducive to a reflexive process of identity construction. Instead, social theory regarded mass consumption as a source of conformity, 'one-dimensionality', standardization and the end of individuality in general.[12] How, then, did consumer goods become a medium for the reflexive construction of identity? How did consumer culture go from denying our ability to choose to compelling us constantly to make lifestyle choices? The chapters that follow will address that question. They will look at arguably the most important actor in the formation of consumer culture, of a system of meanings that make goods conducive to one form of subjectivity or another: the advertising industry. I will argue that this conception of goods as tools for the reflexive construction of subjectivity has resulted from the ways the advertising industry has responded to the challenges presented by the modernization process.

The main proclaimed purpose of advertising is to sell goods (perhaps the real, unofficial purpose is rather to sell advertising). In order to do so, goods have somehow to be inserted into the social life of potential consumers: a legitimate space has to be created for them. (At least if we take a Weberian view of the social actor as someone who has more or less meaningful and coherent motives for what he or she does. A behaviourist could of course argue differently.) In its attempts at doing this, advertising thus comes to engage more or less directly with the social. It becomes a kind of sociological, or socio-technical practice. In Italy the development of advertising and a modern consumer culture has coincided with an extremely rapid development from a predominantly agrarian to a 'post-industrial' society. This means that advertising has had to engage with and mediate a whole series of kinks and contradictions resulting from this turbulent modernization process. My argument is that the form of subjectivity that contemporary consumer culture carries has come out of these efforts at mediation.

Consumer culture

> Advertising ministers the spiritual side of trade. It is a great power that has been entrusted to your keeping which charges you with the highest responsibility of inspiring and ennobling the commercial world. It is part of the greater work of regeneration and redemption of mankind.[13]

A key tenet of sociological thought, from the classics and on, is the double nature of modernity. On the one hand, the modernization process destroys old meaning systems. Capitalism reduces it all to the cold and neutral reality of the commodity form. The spread of instrumental rationality disenchants the world. The individual is left to face the reality of life without the veil of myth or tradition: Marx and Engels put this well in the Communist Manifesto.[14] On the other hand, modern society depends on its ability to recreate a meaningful sense of community. Durkheim understood this well. Life without any kind of myth is not worth living, and an entirely meaningless society will eventually collapse under its own anomic tendencies. (Which was precisely what Durkheim feared would happen.) Consequently, the modernization process gives rise to a series of institutions in which the naked reality of a disenchanted life is re-presented as a coherent, ordered and meaningful totality, and where the amorality of brute facts is given a renewed ethical dimension. The disenchantment of modernization is accompanied by its re-enchantment.[15] The institutions that engage in this 'self-representation of society' (to use Niklas Luhmann's term) construct a model of the social.[16] They present it as a place were a certain moral, ontological and epistemological order prevails, and where the individual has a particular place. Many different instruments are employed in constructing such a model of the social. Social theory is one important tool, but so are statistics, moral philosophy, psychology, medicine and theology (religion also is not declining in modern society, but rather on the rise). Usually some mix of these different tools is employed. Many actors are involved in this self-representation of society. An obvious candidate is the state (or its 'ideological apparatus'); others are churches or sects, the media, political parties and movements and, yes, the advertising industry. That the state has been a central actor in the self-representation of modern society; and that it has employed a whole variety of techniques to that purpose, both 'science' and 'ideology', is hardly a disputed issue. But what about advertising?

In Marx's rendering the commodity form is empty. What is meaningful from the point of view of the individual, use-value, is meaningless from the point of view of commodity exchange. Commodification turns quality into quantity. Of course, this is not an empirical description of how consumer capitalism works. Since capitalism began to take the consumer side of the equation seriously, somewhere in the nineteenth century, it has been crucial to give meaning to commodities, to generate a consumer culture. Take the case of the US, not the earliest, but the best-studied example in this respect. There the emergence of new mass distribution systems that followed the economic transformations in the wake of the Civil War made it increasingly important to give potentially anonymous commodities a meaningful place. When the local grocer was no longer there to create trust and give the commodity a place in human society, the commodity had come to carry such meanings by itself. As has been more recently argued, it was this need to create meaning in the face of potentially anonymous forms of distribution, rather than the need to sell off forcefully a surplus accumulated through new mass production systems, that provided the main opening for American advertising.[17] At first, advertising would make use of the shared symbolic resources (or the 'commercial vernacular' to use Lears's term) of popular culture. Products would be linked to images of royalty, to colonialist images of Africans or Native Americans, to famous buildings or to the often invented personal identity of the manufacturer.[18] Soon, however, commodities would begin to embody meanings that referred back to a particular consumer culture, reproduced and elaborated in advertising-financed media like weekly magazines, radio and cinema, and populated by people, or better, 'forms of personhood' that were first and foremost defined as consumers.[19] During the twentieth century this consumer culture has grown to become one of the most important forms for the self-representation of society.[20] Advertising is 'capitalist realism', as Michael Schudson claims. It is there that the idealized mythology of life in capitalist society is mainly articulated.[21] (We are all familiar with this: in advertising, breakfast cereals taste great, family dinners are actually fun, parents and children *interact*, etc.) By presenting objects as part of this realist mythology advertising connects them to a model of life that is already presented as desirable by its very presence in the discourse.[22] This link to a desirable ideal thus justifies the presence of goods; it provides a legitimate reason why anyone would ever desire, crave or need a particular object. Advertising thus supplies us with a set of arguments and guidelines, or, more abstractly, values, which can be invoked to justify our behaviour as consumers. It gives us what we can call a 'consumer ethic'.[23] Now this consumer ethic need not necessarily have a great influence on actual purchases and uses of goods. A large body of research – market research as well as more recent sociological research – has shown that people are not passive recipients of advertising and, as the advertising profession has known for a long time, a wide range of other factors influence actual purchasing decisions. (Hence a wide range of other subtle and not-so-subtle methods are employed to influence consumers, like sophisticated shelving systems in supermarkets.)[24]

What people do as consumers, however, tends to diverge quite widely from what they say they do. As Daniel Miller has shown, shopping activity and the models used to make sense of or legitimize that activity are two quite different things: along with shopping there is a 'discourse on shopping' that 'generalizes the normative statements that are made about shopping in the abstract'.[25] My suggestion is that in modern society consumer culture may be an important reference for such a normative discourse on consumption. The consumer ethic that prevails there thus has a greater impact on thinking than on doing. It can influence how people conceptualize their subjectivity as consumers, or as members of society in general before it impacts directly on their everyday practice. Consumers, and in some cases people in general, can mobilize the ethical models of consumer culture to justify their own practices. In advertising, a particular consumer subjectivity is invoked in order to justify the position of a product on the market ('ecologically conscious consumers need ecologically conscious soap, therefore we are pleased to offer . . .'). Consumers can use the same models to justify their needs, desires or strategies of selfhood (after all, I think as I browse the ales of my local Sainsbury's, life is, as its upmarket product line tells me, about 'being good to yourself'). Rather than being agents of 'strong socialization' that 'constitutes' or 'determines' the subjectivity of consumers, advertising and consumer culture are best seen as resources that can be invoked in people's own self-determination. Here lies also the most important role of advertising and consumer culture, at least for my purposes. It provides a symbolic resource that can be invoked and, as the impact of advertising and consumer culture has grown, tends to be invoked, in situations very different from that of consumers on the market. One particular feature of postmodern society, for example, is that the symbolic resources of consumer culture are invoked in political discourse as well: from the framing of electoral campaigns, to the arguments over rights and duties that concern the welfare state.[26]

The argument ahead

The main purpose of this book is to describe the role of the advertising industry in promoting and shaping the development of mass consumption in Italy, and to argue that the contemporary postmodern form of subjectivity has its origins in these efforts. While my purpose is not to make generalizable claims about the nature of advertising and mass consumption in general, my narrative will easily invite comparisons with the better-known Anglo-Saxon story. Let me, then, begin with a brief note on the particularity of the Italian experience.

While virtually all European countries saw substantial economic growth and important social transformations in the post-war years, the Italian case was in many ways exceptional. Italy progressed from a 'semi-peripheral' position in the mid-1950s to a situation close to the European average in the mid-1970s.[27] True, there had been steps towards industrialization and mass consumption before, as chapters 2–4 will show in more detail, but these had been almost exclusively limited to the northern 'industrial triangle'. The period of growth that began with the 'economic miracle' of the late 1950s, however, had effects that spread over the whole country. While differences in income between the north and the south remained substantial, the discrepancies in access to basic consumer goods were radically diminished, as the diagram on car ownership below illustrates. In addition, the social structure of the country changed considerably. With internal migration, industrialization and urbanization there was a rapid shift from agriculture to industrial and service employment. As many scholars have pointed out, Italian development in the post-war years produced a rapid transformation of a predominately agrarian society where most people lived by local traditions, to a 'post-industrial' society where most people would to an increasing extent acquire their values and aspirations from a common consumer culture.[28] Indeed, the rapidity of this transformation – some 30 years from one pole on the scale to the other – has made many intellectuals and other observers speak about a revolutionary transformation. Pier Paolo Pasolini, most famously perhaps, spoke of a nationwide 'anthropological revolution' set in motion by consumer goods, which was in the process of transforming a 'pre-industrial, peasant Italy' steeped in 'clerical values' into one dominated by the 'hedonist ideology of consumption' and by 'an American-style philosophy of tolerance'.[29]

The feeling that the impact of consumer culture set in motion something of a revolutionary development was also triggered by the traditionally weak sense of national identity that has characterized Italy. While in countries like Britain or France consumer culture would meet and interact with a pre-existing strong sense of national identity, this was not the case in Italy. Indeed, attempts to promote a modern national identity were marked by an

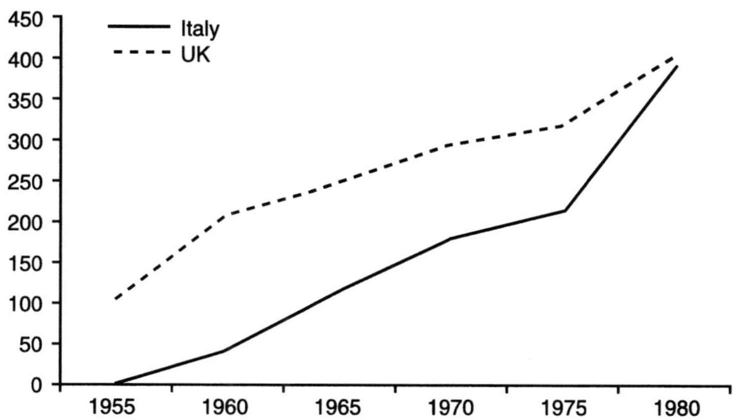

Figure 1.1 Television sets per 1,000 people, Italy and the UK.

From a position with roughly half the per capita GNP of the UK in the mid-1950s ($516 as against $1,189 in 1955) Italy caught up by the early 1970s. Propelled by the 'second economic miracle' of the late 1980s the Italian economy overtook the British. This catching up is also evident from the distribution of television sets. (Source: Unesco, *Statistics on Radio and Television*, passim.)

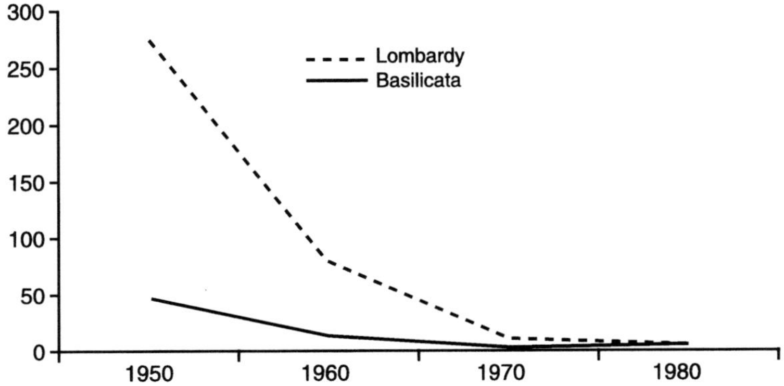

Figure 1.2 Number of people for every car in circulation, Lombardy and Basilicata.

Comparing Italy's data on car ownership from its most prosperous region, Lombardy, with one of the poorest regions in the south it is obvious how the post-war boom has reduced the initially very wide gap in popular access to consumer goods: in 1950 Lombardy had almost six times as many car owners as Basilicata (48 people for every car in circulation vs. 276 people/car). In 1980 the difference (although still substantial) was around 70 per cent (3 people for every car in circulation in Lombardy, 5 people/car in Basilicata). (Source: Quirino, P., 'I consumi in Italia dall'Unità a oggi', ed. Omano, R., *Storia dell'economia italiana*, vol. III, *L'età contemporanea*, Turin: Einaudi 1991, p. 239.

inability on the part of the state to transform the country in any depth (see chapter 2). Up until the Fascist regime, there was no 'nationalization of the masses', and most people remained closer to local traditions and solidarities than to the state and the nation.[30] The ultra-nationalism of the Fascist regime was in many ways a response to this historical split between the state and society. Its ambition was to modernize and nationalize the country by subsuming all social life under the totalitarian control of the state. While these attempts were efficient to some extent, most scholars would agree that the larger part of the southern rural population remained outside the reach of Fascist attempts at nation-making. The mass parties that emerged after the war, the Christian Democrats (DC), and the Communists (PCI), made similar attempts at constructing nationwide political identities, and both claimed to be the rightful heirs of the original nationalism of the unification movement, the Risorgimento.

What really united the country, however, was consumer culture, particularly when spread through the new medium of television. Not only did television promote the widespread use of Italian (before most people had been speaking local dialects), but it also promoted a sense of belonging to a modern 'imagined community' of, at least potential, consumers. The democratic appeal of television, sociologists Francesco Alberoni and Guido Baglioni argued, made at least the younger generations identify with the values and aspirations of a modern consumer society long before they had the material means to participate therein. This 'anticipatory socialization', they concluded, was an important pull factor behind internal migrations.[31] Mass consumption and television succeeded in in-depth transformation of the social fabric, which the state apparatus had hitherto been unable to set in motion. To quote Giorgio Bocca, a journalist who wrote extensively on the transformations set about by the late 1950s 'miracle':

> What neither the Pope, nor the divine emperor of Alighieri, the Machiavellian prince, Cavour's piemontese bureaucracy nor Mussolini's *federali* ever managed to do is now being done by consumer society and its oracle, television: soon Italians will have the same habits and ideals from the Alps to Sicily; they will dress, think, eat and have fun in the same way.[32]

That consumer culture has occupied this position has meant that advertising has had to confront the contradictions of modernity in more direct ways than what might have been the case in other contexts.

The first part of the book will trace the first development of advertising and consumer culture, up until the Second World War. Chapter 2 will provide an overview of Italian economic development from the unification and onwards, with a particular view to the emergence of the first preconditions for mass consumption: industrial production, a national market and a nationwide media system. Chapter 3 will highlight the conflict between consumer culture and the cultural politics of the Fascist regime. It will describe the efforts on the part of the regime to subsume a nascent mass consumption under its totalitarian project and to create a Fascist consumer culture with nationalistic connotations. At the same time, however, as chapter 4 shows, American ideas on how mass consumption should be organized were influencing the debates of the emerging advertising profession. During the 1930s they came to formulate a model of mass consumption based on the notion of the consumer as someone chiefly guided by private desires, rather than by the collective concerns of the nation.

The second part of the book will describe the emergence of mass consumption in the post-war years. Chapter 5 shows how the privatist model now promoted by an Americanized advertising industry influenced the discourse on modernization in the post-war years. Centred on the persona of the 'housewife', American-style consumer culture came to dominate advertising and the media. There it formed a model of modern life that had a vast impact on the everyday aspirations of Italians. The same model of modernity also came to influence intellectual representations of the modernization process, where the transformations under way were read as part of a homogenizing process of 'Americanization'. This self-representation, I argue, also had an important impact on the political discourse on modernity, in particular on the part of the Christian Democrats. American consumer culture and American marketing techniques, however, also came with a social project. In the immediate future, the advertising profession argued, advertising and consumer goods would come to serve as the main medium for social integration, and they would create a modern morality that permitted a freer and more individualized pursuit of self-realization. Chapter 6 traces the discussions around this new model within the advertising and marketing profession. Looking at the representation of women consumers, it shows how this new image of the 'individualized consumer' came to impact advertising and women's magazines. A new research method, Motivation Research, was crucial to this process. In chapter 7 I describe how this process continued through the crisis and reconstruction of the 1970s. The advertising industry now had acquired the means to engage directly with the social transformation occurring. The chapter shows how advertising translated the new values and aspirations to emerging with the breakdown of an older 'Fordist' model in the late 1960s, to the postmodern lifestyle consumer culture that came to dominate Italian public culture during the 1980s. Chapter 8 traces the outline of contemporary postmodern consumer culture in Italy. Looking back at the political response to the cultural and social transformations set in motion by the crisis of Fordism, it seeks to explain why consumer culture met with so few alternatives in the quest for cultural hegemony in the 1980s. I end by summarizing the argument and drawing some more general theoretical conclusions.

2 From unification to the Fascist takeover

The first developments of mass consumption

On an ideal typical level, we can identify two ways of 'organizing modernity' with respect to mass consumption, once again to use Wagner's terminology: the American model and the European model.[1] From the 1920s onwards, mass consumption, as rendered meaningful by advertising and consumer culture, was arguably the core component of North American national identity.[2] One need only think of President Eisenhower, who, in seeking to encapsulate the essence of 'America' in 1947, turned his patriotic fervour to the virtues of consumer goods – 'ice boxes, radios, cars' – or of the generosity of American GIs in Europe distributing tinned corned beef and chewing gum as part of American goodwill diplomacy.[3] In the European model, on the other hand, modernity is chiefly organized around the state. People are construed first as citizens and then as consumers, and mass consumption is made meaningful within the framework of a politically grounded national culture (or at least this is attempted).[4] Beginning in the first post-war years these different ways of organizing modernity began to clash and interact as American consumer culture made inroads in Europe. These interactions between the 'European Way' and the 'American Way' defines much of the early history of advertising and consumer culture in Italy as well. Or, more precisely, in Italy the Fascist regime made a sustained attempt to promote a 'European' model of mass consumption. These efforts, however, had to confront, among other things, the legacy from the liberal years.

One of the most pressing problems for the Italian unification movement was to create a national identity to fit the newly formed state: to 'make Italians', having once 'made Italy', as the classic phrase goes (attributable to one of the movement's central thinkers, Massimo D'Azeglio). Even though characterizations of nineteenth-century Italy as a 'state without a nation', once popular with historians, have now come under some revision, it remains safe to say that the preconditions for any kind of nationwide mobilization of the masses in post-unification Italy were very scarce.[5] National politics remained a very distant reality in the lives of most Italians. The suffrage amounted to 2 per cent of the population in 1861 (of these only 50 per cent used their right to vote) and expanded to 7 per cent in 1876, when it was decided that further expansions would accompany increases in literacy. This was a low figure by European standards.[6] In addition, political elites were predominantly regional in their orientation and solidarities. Italian unification had in practice been a 'Piedmontization' of Italy; that is, an imposition of the structure of the Piedmontese state on the rest of the peninsula, without much regard for cultural difference or local efficiency. Along with an originally strong sense of geographical identification, this produced a loosely integrated political elite who tended to regard the state apparatus as something to which they had very few commitments. This in turn led to a strong predominance of local over national interests in parliamentary politics.

In addition, Italy was sharply divided between north and south. This division tended to become more marked as the process of modernization went on. While agriculture in the north was commercialized at an early stage and oriented towards a European market, that of the south remained characterized by large units (*latifondi*), mostly run by absentee landlords with, generally, little interest in raising productivity or undertaking modernizing reforms. Content with skimming off enough surplus to continue their traditional lifestyle, they viewed change and modernization with suspicion. The institutional structure of the southern economy thus remained underdeveloped with respect to the north. This initial discrepancy was further strengthened during the first decades after unification. The unified state bought southern consensus for northern developmental policies by neglecting to fulfil the promises of land reform that went back to the Risorgimento. This 'deal' between north and south was further consolidated in a kind of Italian 'iron and rye' alliance with the protectionist policies of the late 1880s. Here, southern agricultural interests were protected from the competition from American grain, and northern industry received an increasing boost from public spending. In addition, northern industrialization had very few effects on the southern economy, as trade between the north and the south remained marginal. (Instead the industrializing north was more closely connected to central Europe.)[7] According to economic historian Valerio Castronovo, the initial difference in per capita income between north and south fluctuated around 20 per cent in the 1860s. In the 1890s, however, a northern agricultural worker had almost twice the buying power of his southern comrade.[8] Whereas the north became part of the European core at an early stage, the south remained at the periphery, exporting labour and labour intensive agricultural products. Even in the north, however, standards of living were much lower than for Europe in general, not to speak of Great Britain. In 1861 93 per cent of overall national consumer spending was directed at covering primary needs like food, clothing and housing.

Although this figure hides important differences between the north and the south, as well as between comparatively wealthy pockets like Tuscany and the rest of the north, it is reasonable to suppose that the overall majority of Italians had little time for other things than the dreary pursuit of basic necessities (apart from wine, which, as the government-sponsored inquiry Inchiesta Jacini from 1879 showed, was consumed in great quantities in popular *osterie*).[9] Most of these rather modest needs were, furthermore, met through local, or at the most regional distribution systems, often involving complex networks of small wholesalers, retailers and travelling salesmen. There was virtually no national market until the development of the railways in the 1880s, and even then it remained rather feeble. (Indeed, the fragmented nature of the Italian distribution system remains one of its key characteristics to this day.)[10] The prohibitive cost of newspapers (5–10 centesimi in the 1870s as compared to an average daily wage of 2 centesimi), and the low literacy rates (25 per cent on average in the 1860s, reaching above 35 per cent in the four most prosperous northern regions of Piedmont, Lombardy, Veneto and Liguria, and dropping below 15 per cent south of Rome)[11] would at any rate exclude most people from participating in the public sphere. Those who did, found it locally fragmented and with little focus on national concerns. There were 555 different papers circulating in 1873. Most of them catered to the constituencies of local notables.[12] None of them had a national circulation until the 1880s. To the extent that there was a national public sphere in the first decades after the unification this was restricted to the literary magazines that came out of Florence, which were read and discussed in the elegant bourgeois cafés that flourished even in provincial cities, and to the bourgeois women's magazines that began to circulate in the 1870s (to supply the basis for a national feminist movement in the last years of the century).[13]

To satisfy their consumer cravings the wealthier bourgeoisie looked primarily to big cities, whether traditional centres, like Naples, for squandering agricultural surplus, or more cosmopolitan places like Milan and Florence, as well as, of course, Paris. In the big cities there was an ample supply of tailors and artisans ready to copy the latest models of Parisian fashion, together with a less expensive market for ready-made clothing that catered to the emulative desires of the often not-so-wealthy professional classes. During the 1870s Milan began to establish modern institutions for shopping, catering to bourgeois tastes and to the small but growing urban middle class. A decisive step was the construction of a central European-style arcade, Galleria Vittorio Emanuele, in Piazza del Duomo in 1867. In 1870 the Bocconi brothers opened their department store, Magazzini Bocconi, inspired by the success of French examples. They moved to Piazza del Duomo in 1877, changed their name to Aux villes d'Italie, and began to distribute their wares all over the peninsula through mail-order catalogues. Naples followed suit with the construction of Galleria Umberto I in Piazza Plebiscito and with the Mele department store that opened in 1889.[14] While still off limits for most of the population, these department stores would cater to a growing middle class market and supply clothes, furniture, tea, spices and other exotic foodstuffs, and trinkets to crowd the now fashionable bourgeois *salotto* (living room). The first three decades after unification thus saw the modest emergence of a series of institutions whereby the professional classes could imitate what they regarded to be a cosmopolitan bourgeois taste. The construction of such an emulative consumer culture would proceed further with industrialization.[15]

With the construction of the railways in the 1880s and with the industrialization that followed in the 1890s the social fabric of the peninsula changed significantly. Ensuing urbanization created a growing urban working class, and a middle class of employees and professionals, at least in the emerging northern 'industrial triangle' of Turin, Genoa and Milan. The urban middle class formed a market for the growing editorial industry that produced popular cheap novels and books on manners, etiquette and home management. They participated in the diffusion of a national cuisine through widespread cooking manuals like that of Artusi. They participated in sports and new kinds of leisure pursuits, first bicycle riding and later football.[16] The urban middle classes also made up a market for new illustrated weekly magazines with a national diffusion, like *Illustrazione italiana* (founded in 1875). Like the contemporary American penny press, these magazines combined a human interest with infotainment and stories on the wonders of science and industry, and served as a backdrop for the popularization of new consumer goods, like patent medicines, bicycles and kitchen equipment. These middle-class consumers also provided a first target for branded goods. Industrials like Borsalino, Cinzano and Campari would now hire the services of artists like Hohenstein, Cappiello, de Carolis and Metlicovitz who were inspired by the French school of Toulouse-Lautrec. Following a Veblenesque logic of emulation, these advertising artists would depict products as part of elegant scenes from an imagined bourgeois lifeworld to give them a sign value of social superiority, thought to be attractive to the middle classes.[17]

Industrialization, however, also created the preconditions for the emergence of a consumer culture that was not based on the principle of emulating a bourgeois habitus, but that rather catered to an emerging mass market. During the early years of the century the conditions of the working class improved somewhat. By 1910 GDP per capita in the more prosperous industrial triangle was roughly on the level of France and Germany, if not England. In the first decade of the twentieth century national consumption grew two to three times as fast as population growth, a development considerably biased in favour of the industrial triangle. As this trickled down, a relatively wide stratum of (comparatively) affluent workers emerged. They could now afford to eat better, improve their hygiene, prolong the education of their children, buy some modern kitchen utensils and perhaps even a bicycle or a sewing machine (Singer targeted the Italian market heavily in the 1910s).[18] They even had some time over for more participation in social affairs. These comparatively affluent workers would form the main basis of the growing socialist movement. With its newspaper *Avanti*, founded in 1896 as Italy's first paper with a truly national circulation, and with its dense network of popular universities and people's houses (*Case del popolo*), Italian socialism formed civil society, mainly in the north. To this should be added the cooperative consumers' movement that expanded rapidly beginning in the 1890s to comprise

Figure 2.1 Bourgeois elegance at the café. Poster by Hohenstein for Campari, c. 1900. (Courtesy of the Biblioteca Nazionale, Florence.)

some 2,700 associations in 1902, also mostly concentrated in the north, in Lombardy, Emilia and Tuscany.[19] The urban middle class, and to some extent also the more 'affluent' working class were a target for the expansion of the Press. Beginning in the 1880s the two main Milan newspapers *Corriere della sera* and *il Secolo* began to make efforts to reach a more popular market. Inspired by the example of the American 'penny press', Dario Papa, editor of *Corriere della sera*, emphasized that in order to expand the readership it was necessary to abandon the academic, literary style that had hitherto prevailed in Italian journalism, and make the paper into something that could capture popular interest. Following this initiative, *Corriere della sera* introduced a crime and sensations page (what is known in Italy as *cronaca nera*). It invested in new printing equipment, subscribed to international telegraphic networks and started to extend its financial reliance on advertising. *Il Secolo* followed suit, and in the 1890s the two papers were in fierce competition, each investing in new technology and expanding its network of correspondents. In the mid-1890s each paper put out about 100,000 copies, to be compared to the 30,000 copies of *il Secolo* in 1866, then Italy's largest newspaper. By the early 1900s *Corriere* had doubled its output to 200,000 copies. Catering to new kinds of readers, *Corriere* also started selling a Sunday magazine, *Domenica del corriere*, in 1898; in 1901 they added *La Letteratura*, a popular literary supplement; in 1903 *il Romanzo menisle* (the Monthly Novel); and in *1908 il Corriere dei piccoli*, a children's newspaper.[20] These new supplements catered in part to the increasing need to attract advertising revenue.

As the large northern papers expanded their circulation nationwide and established themselves as the main medium for the middle classes (this was particularly true of *Domenica del corriere*), Italy acquired a medium for the national diffusion of consumer culture. With the possible exception of Bocconi's and Mele's mail-order catalogues this had been virtually absent before. Branded goods could now achieve a national recognition and become a common cultural reference. This was the case, for example, with the toothpaste Kaliklor launched by means of a contest where the winning slogan 'A smile tells all my virtues' (*A dir le mie virtù basta un sorriso*) soon became a national cliché. Along with the first emergence of such modern forms of publicity, the Italian distributive sector began to change. Even if it maintained its reliance on a complex network of wholesalers and retailers, markets and travelling salesmen, and even if most objects of everyday use were sold by the pound, some modern structures of distribution began to evolve in the wake of the First World War. In 1917 the prestigious department store Magazzini Bocconi in Milan changed its name to Rinascente and became a proponent of middle-class consumption, different in ethic from the preceding bourgeois model (see chapter 3). By 1922 Rinascente had 38 branches in different cities all across the country. With the beginning of branding and packaging of some items for everyday use (pasta, bouillon cubes, canned foods, imported American soaps and toothpastes), the phenomenology of middle-class shopping changed to some extent.[21]

Through these transformations, the urban middle classes encountered a series of institutions that allowed their habitus-formation to refer not to inherited traditions, but, as Lucetta Scaraffia argues, rather to the more free-floating 'world of symbols, language and communication' that made up public culture.[22] To be sure, the new middle class had a number of qualities that made it seem fit to be the carrying strata of such a modern form of acculturation. Most importantly, state employees and white-collar workers owed their position to education and formal merits. They were isolated from the inherited popular culture of the traditional urban *petit bourgeoisie*, important not only as a source of class habitus, but also as a medium for the transfer of economic and cultural capital.[23] Rather, they turned to public culture for their habitus formation: either, as in the case of the formation of male identities, to the professional ethic of the state administration, or to the expanding media system. In the weekly press and the growing supply of cook-books, etiquette books and other kinds of instructive manuals middle-class women in particular found a wide range of instructions on how to live a proper middle-class life.[24] Consumer culture would also tie into this emerging mediated middle-class lifeworld, mainly the domestic film-star system, or *divismo*. This concentrated around the growing Italian film industry and its first *dive* (diva), Lydia Borelli, but not exclusively: writers, musicians and poets would also be transformed into public personalities whose phrases and mannerisms, like those of la Borelli, were quickly imitated or reiterated in middle-class social life.[25] These stars would also frequently endorse products. Thus, flamboyant poet-flyer-superstar Gabriele D'Annunzio came up with the name for the new Bocconi department store, Rinascente, and offered his services to the biscuit factory Saiwa; Giacomo Puccini endorsed the toothpaste Odol; and Guido da Verona, a popular author of middle-brow fiction, composed poems in honour of Rinascente.

The carrying stratum of urban middle-class consumers grew more solid during the Fascist 'twenty years', or *ventennio*. In part this resulted from the ongoing growth of intermediate professions like clerks, salesmen and secretaries. In part it was a result of the regime's efforts to pamper its middle-class supporters, in particular through the expansion of the state apparatus. Even though the Italian economy fared fairly poorly during the years of the regime as the effects of the depression combined with imposed protectionist policies and, towards the end, the war effort, the middle class constituted the carrying stratum for an expanding consumer market.[26] This was particularly prevalent during the 1930s. Then the market for films and popular music developed along with the weekly magazines that also began to differentiate their approach to meet the expectations of different targets. Branding, advertising and national distribution all asserted their importance, as did the new chain stores selling inexpensive goods, Standa and Upim. There was also an emerging urban youth culture dedicated mainly to Hollywood films and to American consumer goods and practices like cocktails, nightclubs and cosmetics (such as Lux soap and Pond's skin cream).[27]

If the extent to which the Italian middle class actually did come to rely on the free-floating imaginary of an increasingly commercialized media system can be debated (in particular for the 1910s and 1920s), such a scenario, or at least fears of its impending realization, did, however, influence the concerns of social commentators even before the war. To modernist intellectuals like Giuseppe Prezzolini the middle class appeared to embody the fluidity and moral relativism that he saw as inherent in modernity. This, their weightlessness and unreliability, he argued in his *The Art of Persuasion* (*L'Arte di persuadere*) of 1907, came from their involvement with modern commerce and modern media: they were used to the continuous changes of fashion and their words were just like their cheap imitation suits, 'false but useful'. According to Arturo Lancelotti, a journalist who was to write extensively on advertising and propaganda in the inter-war years, the middle-class person was motivated by a quest for public fame, or just a drive to impress and be seen, rather than by any stable values or ideals.[28] Such fears of the middle class turning into consumers, abandoning their commitment to tradition or to national unity for the rapidly changing fads of consumer culture, increased with the influence of American consumer culture in the post-war years. Driven mainly by cinema, Americanization seemed to be in the process of imposing a homogenous 'international commodity culture' to which intellectuals and the avant-garde reacted with increasing aversion. (During 1926 and 1936 the share of films shown in Italy that had American origins remained fairly stable – around 75 per cent.)[29] Even if the Italian situation was far too fragmented to speak of an overall affirmation of consumer culture, certain groups, like the northern urban middle classes, now found themselves deeply immersed in a cultural universe organized around the media system, rather than around traditional distinctions of status and geography.

The process of political unification was, however, still lagging. This was particularly prominent in the wake of the First World War when the old-style mediation efforts of the Giolitti governments proved unable to ride out the social crisis that had followed the war. (And one might add the inability of the Socialist Party to coordinate the revolutionary effervescence of the 'red years' of the early 1920s.) One of the key promises of the Fascist regime that took over in 1922 was that it would redeem the historical discrepancy between the state and society that had characterized most of Italian history hitherto. As reflected throughout its basic texts, the main claim to legitimacy of the Fascist state was its ability to complete the process of modernizing nation-making that had begun with unification, and unite all Italians under one single national consciousness as expressed in the state. This involved the staging of something of an 'anthropological revolution' through the intervention in and reorganization of everyday life. A series of measures, from architecture to mass rallies and mass organizations, all aimed to make the inhabitants of the peninsula Italian in a modern, Fascist kind of way.[30]

The regime made use of the media system and of the forms of mass publicity it had fostered (Mussolini's own rise to fame was largely dependent on the newspaper he founded in 1914 with the support of northern industrialists, *il Popolo d'Italia*). With varying degrees of success it promoted the spread of radio sets, a revitalization of the now dormant Italian film industry (which, however, never quite came off) and managed, quite successfully, to take control of the Press through censorship and, sometimes, the direct invention of Mussolini's Press office.[31] For the regime, consumer culture and the free-floating, unstable identities it seemed to promote among the middle classes – its dearest constituency – were clearly a problematic obstacle to this totalitarian effort. This was particularly true in relation to the supposed disintegrating effects of American consumer culture. If viewing the development of Fascist cultural politics as primarily a response to the threat of consumer culture is perhaps a slight exaggeration, this was no doubt an important factor.[32] At the same time, however, the regime recognized the benefits of goods in simplifying life and putting in motion a process of modernization that was conducive to national unity. Modern consumer culture was viewed both as a problem and as a resource. The following chapter will look more closely at these debates.

3 Bourgeois into Fascists?

Mass consumption and the regime

When, in 1939, the Italian cosmetics company Gi.vi.emme decided to revitalize its declining brand of toothpaste Erba (once a market leader) they hired Dino Villani, one of the early pioneers of American advertising techniques in Italy. Villani had just proven his worth in constructing a national market for Motta's Panettone. Using advertising, sponsored radio shows and even theatre groups, he made Motta's originally Milanese cake part of middle-class Christmas fare all over Italy. Villani quickly understood that the key to expanding the market for Erba was to reposition its slightly dated image and target the younger generation, where new consumers could be found to replace an older clientele who were gradually dying off. To capture the youth market, however, the product had to be given a new image, different from that traditionally presented to an older generation of consumers. Such connotations of novelty were, in fact, essential, Villani maintained: 'young people look for novelties and consider the kinds of products that their parents use antiquated'.[1] As the Motta experience had taught, the best way to achieve such connotations of novelty was by aligning the product with the new symbolic universe that had developed around the women's magazines, the film industry and the popular music industry.

To give Erba a strong presence in this new pop culture Villani went with the emphasis on beauty and looks on the part of American advertisements that targeted young women. He arranged a beauty contest.[2] Here, however, Villani and Gi.vi.emme faced their first problem: the special laws on public security of 1939 had explicitly forbidden any kind of female beauty contests. This was well in line with an attitude towards the public representation of women that was now becoming increasingly pronounced. Fertility and motherly qualities were to prevail over vanity and beauty. The Ministry for Popular Culture had made strong statements against publications containing pictures of women with dogs (an 'artificial' diversion from the motherly role), and it sought to influence women's magazines in their choice of fashion models, indicating the regime's preference for long hair and rounded figures.[3] Villani's solution was to launch a contest for 'the most beautiful smile', which was formally open also to men and children. (While most of the advertisements that followed would publish one or two pictures of smiling children, men were very rare indeed.)[4] The 'most beautiful smile' stood the chance of winning 5,000 lire together with a whole range of other articles, such as clothes, shoes, sheets, plates and cutlery, offered by the growing number of companies that sponsored the contest. While the premium amounted to roughly half a decent annual middle-class salary, it was modest in advertising terms. (A couple of years earlier, Villani had hidden 200,000 lire in a Motta Panettone.) Villani hoped, however, that either the chance to appear in the glamorous finals held at Salsomaggiore, or at least to get one's picture published in one of the advertisements that ran in Mondadori's new and popular American-style weekly magazines, the news magazine *Tempo* (modelled on *Newsweek*) and the women's magazine *Grazia* (self-consciously styled on *Harper's Bazaar*), would be attractive. Participants were thus offered the chance to become something of a celebrity, to have their 15 minutes of fame as one of the visible personalities of a new, commercially mediated public culture. (As to the practical consequences of this, finalists did receive a great amount of mail, in particular from soldiers, and some were offered minor parts in films. But the spoils of victory were small compared to those of the Miss Italia contest in the post-war years.) The advertisements were supported by radio shows, by a popular official campaign song and by itinerant 'smile festivals' that toured the seaside during the summer. Together these initiatives made the contest into a national concern, capable of holding the attention of an audience that came from many different social classes (even the king himself followed it), popular enough to irritate the authorities, whom Villani placated with a series of nationalistic gestures.

While Villani gives little weight in his memoirs to the sales results of the campaign, he takes obvious pride in its success as a commercial spectacle: the impact his campaign made on pop culture at the time. It is also in this respect that his initiative remains most illuminating, for at least two reasons.

First, already in the 1930s, Villani's approach to mass marketing was based on an implicit notion of goods as carriers of complex cultural meanings, and not just as things defined by their uses. (After all, brushing teeth and dental hygiene was not the focus of the campaign.) The task of advertising was to create such meaning complexes and, possibly, to involve the public as spectators and participants. This kind of approach presupposed an audience capable of appreciating the spectacle of commercial culture, and that could translate the attraction of the product image into actual consumer demand. It also presupposed an acceptance of such fabricated meaning complexes. As Walter Benjamin would say, this meant a public for which the sense of authenticity and 'aura' was disappearing, and where meaning complexes like a product image or even personal identity could be constructed with varying degrees of freedom. According to Villani's colleagues in the Italian advertising trade, this condition of fluidity and contingency did prevail among middle-class consumers, in particular the younger generation, who had grown up with mass media and mass culture. For these young consumers, goods were, among

Figure 3.1 '5,000 lire for a smile.' The product as apolitical enjoyment. (Courtesy of Archivio Storico Barilla, Parma.)

other things, tools for dreaming up an identity. To quote the advertising psychologist Adolfo Pellegrini (see Chapter 4), writing in 1938:

> The larger part of this anonymous public . . . believes easily in all that it has dreamed or desired. . . . Some dream of being a character in a novel,

just because they have a bag covered in luggage stickers, smoke an aromatic cigarette or sip an exotic brand of liquor. Most of all, people want to think of their own life as beautiful, a desire that is not difficult to fulfil.[5]

Second, it is telling that Villani chose not to align his product with themes from Fascist mass culture. After all, the regime had invested an increasing amount of resources in the construction of a 'political spectacle' able to cater precisely to the sensibilities of such a modern mass audience.[6] Instead of appealing to potential consumers as Fascists, who were presumably moved by their political and moral commitments to the nation, Villani catered to the apolitical sensibilities of an American-style consumer culture that had developed within Fascism itself. His campaign catered to a generation of women who used cosmetics and perfume; who wore fashion clothes and silk stockings; who smoked in public and used the provocative mannerisms of the Hollywood stars (the more vulnerable and languid example of the Italian *dive* was by now out of fashion) to create an attractive appearance to be publicly presented: flaunted, so to speak, in the face of the male gaze. They lived within what Victoria de Grazia identifies as an 'unabashedly secular, cosmopolitan, commercial culture [that] was the real pace-setter in forming a new girl peer culture', through, mainly, the new forms of consumption and the new techniques of self-presentation it enabled. (If this was mostly an urban phenomenon, de Grazia shows how it attracted young rural women as well.)[7] Its reference was the cosmopolitan modernity that featured in Hollywood films and in the domestic 'white telephone' variety: a world where symbolically charged 'international' terms like 'cocktail', 'drink', 'smoking', 'whisky', 'cheque', 'hotel', together with modernist interiors, connoted a dislocation that contrasted sharply with Fascist obsessions with territory. (In order not to provoke the regime, many of these films were set in Budapest, which featured as a kind of non-place of modernity.)

This cosmopolitan consumer culture was further elaborated in the new American-style women's magazines, like *Grazia*, *Gioia* and *Lei* (from 1937, *Annabella*) that targeted young middle-class women. These magazines contained a large amount of advertising, escapist fiction about the rich and famous and, most importantly, a whole series of advice on how to bridge the obvious gap: how to dress elegantly on a modest salary; how to achieve a film-star physique through diet and exercise; how to flirt and generally appear more exciting to male admirers; how to become 'a modern girl', as *Lei* advertised. Within this cultural framework, relatively cheap American consumer goods, soap and cosmetics like Lux, Pond's and Max Factor, together with domestic imitations like Diaderma, could work as tools for the construction of forms of femininity rather different from those presented as desirable by the regime. As presented in the women's magazines these goods could allow at least the possibility of symbolically evading the demands and duties of Fascist middle-class womanhood. In this context, American style consumer culture permitted a kind of dreamscape for the imaginary construction of a personal *différence* that could never be entirely subsumed under the constituted order.[8]

This American-style, cosmopolitan consumer culture would never overtly challenge Fascism. In the women's magazines 'Fascist' and 'American' symbols would coexist rather promiscuously: Mussolini would sit next to Douglas Fairbanks on the same page. The initiatives of the regime would be given attention and taken seriously, and the morale of most escapist fiction, like most 'white telephone' films, would be well in line with the regime's urges not to venture beyond one's proper place. (We remember Vittorio de Sica and Assia Norris in *il Signor Max* (1937) who find true happiness, not in the contrived atmosphere of the Grand Hotel but at the local *dopolavoro* (national afterwork organization), where, however, the same kind of jazz is played). But Fascism never managed to colonize this commercial universe, where the main

Figure 3.2 A secular cosmopolitan peer culture. Diaderma promises to fit all fashions (featured in *Lei*, 1935). (Courtesy of the Biblioteca Nazionale, Florence.)

orientation remained a blatantly apolitical pursuit of beauty, love and the kind of superficial personal independence that mass consumption could give. This apolitical pocket within the (if 'imperfect') totalitarian enterprise became increasingly difficult to tolerate during the 1930s as the regime began serious attempts to 'go to the people'. With Achille Starace as party chairman, American-style cosmopolitan consumer culture was targeted in a series of rather uncoordinated measures. Women were discouraged from wearing trousers (a sign of personal independence since the previous century), dancing and in particular 'Negro dances' like the rumba and foxtrot were targeted as threats to the moral and mental health of the population; cocktails and the general atmosphere of the nightclub emerged as a threat to Fascist masculinity.[9] With the growth of policies to stimulate demographic expansion during the 1930s the products of this cosmopolitan consumer culture began to be targeted as threats to fertility. The short hair, thin frames and androgynous demeanour of 'modern girls' was construed as a moral and aesthetic abhorrence, as part of a new female figure, the artificial and deformed 'crisis woman' (*donna crisi*). Instead, the true and natural fate of women was motherhood, to which the use of cosmetics, cocktails, cigarettes and silk stockings was directly antithetical. Similar claims even achieved a scientific status as demographers began to argue for the correlation between 'the artifices of exercise or creams' and the loss of fertility.[10] The journal of the Fascist women's organization, *Donna Fascista*, summarized this opposition between motherhood, on the one hand, and cosmetics and female empowerment, on the other, in 1935 (the article had originally been published in the paper founded by Mussolini, *il Popolo d'Italia*, earlier the same year):

> The creams and cosmetics that elegant and fashionable women use, as well as the famous 'women's rights' – for those who instead of giving birth want a public life that is almost even more repugnant – have given us a new kind of woman where it difficult to find any differences from the stronger sex. A woman whose smile is painted with lapis, whose eyes express the so-called modern malaise, the dissatisfaction of someone who doesn't know that life begins and ends [!] in her womb. The dissatisfaction of the modern woman, bored, boring and stupid.[11]

Most of these initiatives were neither new nor particular to Fascism (the Catholics had a long tradition of making demons out of things like the tango or cosmetics). The regime's totalitarian ambitions, however, gave them a new dimension.

The ambiguities of America

Despite rhetoric about crisis women and moral decay, the greatest danger associated with mass consumption was less a matter of individual morals than of social unity, at least as far as Mussolini's attitude went. Within a project for the organization of modernity that had promised, as he concluded in his 'ascension day speech' in 1927, to transform the country thoroughly, 'not only its face but more than anything else, its soul', American-style cosmopolitan consumer culture risked diverting the attention of the masses from their new political destiny.[12] According to Falasca-Zamponi, mass consumption came to stand for an alien and threatening individualism. As she argues, 'the multiplications of desires and temptations, as the necessary result of an enlarged spectrum of options, would threaten to reintroduce individualistic principles into a society that was being organized around totalitarian premises'.[13] At the same time, however, Mussolini clearly considered this individualism a matter of appearances only. On the market the consumer would choose among false differences that encouraged a sense of personal uniqueness that served only to hide the most profound conformism. American consumer culture was thus conducive to the assembly of a profoundly inauthentic personality. Its 'individualism' was antithetical to the true individualism championed by Fascism, the vitalistic 'I don't give a damn' (*me ne frego* – the motto of the Fascist *squadristi*), of the strong masculine individual who could put himself above morality and conventions. The true threat of American-style consumer culture was thus not primarily its individualism – which was in any case just a façade – but the privatism and passivity it encouraged. In his *The Doctrine of Fascism* Mussolini emphasized his distance from the 'materialist conception of happiness' that this kind of consumer culture promoted, which he argued was a necessary foundation for the ideology of liberalism (as well as socialism): 'Fascism', he maintained, 'denies the materialistic conception of "happiness" as possible . . . it denies, that is, the equation "well being = happiness", which would turn men into animals who would think only about one thing: to be fed, fattened, reduced, that is, to vegetative life purely and simply.'[14]

The example of what could happen if one followed this path was, of course, America: in America, mass consumption, and the promiscuous blurring of essential difference and character that it had encouraged, had created an entirely new kind of human being, the Yankee. The Yankee did not fit any of the categories usually used to understand or classify people: to European observers 'he' had no race, but was a mixture of many races; 'he' had no class, no tradition and almost no gender – American women were androgynous and American men boyish. Instead 'he' was moulded and shaped by mass culture, by the 'cinema, jazz music, radios, YMCAs, girlie magazines' and above all 'thousands and thousands of standardized products', which now seemed to be expanding all over the world.[15] His passions, aspirations and very life were standardized. 'He' was a Babitt, to use a stereotype borrowed from a Sinclair Lewis novel, and had virtually no thoughts or desires that he could genuinely call his own, no true commitments, and no morality. Through mass consumption and the standardization it entailed, the US had become a purely 'technical society', a 'beef-civilization' (*civiltà della bistecca*) marked by wealth but no values: the Americans were a 'people of engineers', their lives filled with comfort without meaning or scope, individualism without any real choice, and conformism without social unity.[16] Such ideas were not entirely new: they had emerged with the first manifestations of American industrial power in the early 1900s (in Italy most markedly in the case of the futurists and the Florentine avant-garde of Prezzolini, Papini and the other intellectuals gathered around the journals *la Voce* and *Leonardo*).[17] As American commercial culture expanded abroad in the wake of the First World War, similar forms of anti-Americanism flourished as a response, in Italy as well as elsewhere. An expanding mass consumption came to stand for a threatening Americanization, which in turn represented the modern menace of a social order that had become entirely fluid, subject to the fluctuations of fashion and the media, rather than being firmly anchored in territory, nation or other transcendent values.

The problem, however, was that America also imposed itself in other less ephemeral ways. Mussolini's promised reform of the 'soul of the country' aimed not only to restore a national identity thought to have been squandered by the misrule of the liberal years, but also to modernize. Fascist nationalism was, as Emilio Gentile shows, about the symbolic rebirth of a new and modern Italy.[18] While Italian Fascism might be too complex and contradictory an assembly to be easily labelled with Herf's term 'reactionary modernism' (not all reactionaries were modernizers and not all modernizers were at the same time reactionaries, like, for example, the futurists), most currents would agree that industrial mass production and accompanying mass consumption was the only possible path ahead.[19] Here, again, most agreed that the American path was the most promising. It was obvious that American superiority rested less on the Yankee national character than on the American model of social organization: mass production for mass consumption. While few American systems of mass production, like Taylorism, were implemented in Italian industry in the inter-war years (with the exception of the FIAT Lignotto works: 'a new great factory built the American way', where production began in 1921),[20] most would argue that measures in that direction had to be taken. Indeed, the most vociferous of these groups of modernizers, the so-called 'revisionist' faction that gathered around Giusseppe Bottai and the journal he edited, *Critica Fascista* (Fascist Critique), argued that such principles of scientific management should be extended throughout the whole of society. This current gathered engineers, accountants, economists – in short, a rising managerial class of 'technicians' employed in private companies or in the 'competence committees' that formed within the state administrations – as well as architects and business leaders who saw Fascism as an opportunity to modernize and 'rationalize' the social system.[21] These technicians or 'organizers', as they sometimes called themselves, found common ground in the corporativist projects, in voluntary associations like GAR (Gruppo Amici Razionalizzazione – Friends of Rationalization),[22] and, not least, in *L'Ufficio moderno*, a journal dedicated to advertising, business administration and scientific management.

At this time 'American methods' meant chiefly Taylorism or 'scientific management' (the two terms were used interchangeably). These ideas had been in the air since the 1910s. F.W. Taylor's *Principles of Scientific Management* had been translated in 1919, but before that overviews were published in *L'Impresa moderna*, Italy's first journal of business administration (and a predecessor of *L'Ufficio moderno*), founded in 1914. With the foundation of a state institute for scientific management, with a substantial range of initiatives and publications (Ente nazionale italiana organizzazione scientifica, Enios) in 1926 and the imposed revaluation of the lira in the following year, the so-called 'Quota 90' that triggered a more pressing need to rationalize production and distribution, their popularity was renewed.[23] Taylorism had a particularly central status in the project for a coporativist social order, dear to Bottai and the revisionists. Corporativism, perhaps the only original social model to come out of Italian Fascism (although precedents can be found in both social democratic and Catholic political thought), entailed the overall organization of production in branchwide corporations. There, capital and labour would come together as 'producers', realizing their common interests. The corporations would be regulated by the Ministry of the Corporations (headed by Bottai from 1929 to 1932) and would find their political expression in the national council of the Corporations, that replaced the parliament as the national representative body in 1939. Although coporativism was institutionalized and commonly accepted in rhetoric, its practical impact was at best patchy. Most importantly, corporativism met with passive resistance from Italian big capital that was not particularly anxious to hand over control of the means of production to any external managerial elites. (Consequently, when the state did intervene heavily in the economy in the wake of the depression, the process was largely guided by the newly formed state-holding company IRI (Istituto per la ricostruzione industriale) and not by the corporations.) To its proponents, however, corporativism seemed to offer a possibility for an overall rationalization of production as well as an occasion to foster social solidarity and overcome class conflict. Here Taylorism seemed to provide the best solutions. It promised a rational alternative to the traditional paternalistic structure of Italian industry with its unscientific reliance on practical experience or 'empiricism' (*empirismo*).

With the accompanying discipline of psycho-technics, preoccupied with the measurement of individual performance and potential, Taylorism also contained the promise off a better 'integration' of the working class into the productive machinery. It showed a practical way of overcoming the 'secular antagonism' between labour and capital by making the former a mere 'moment' of the production process.[24] As Roberto Tremelloni, an economist with socialist origins who wrote extensively of scientific management in the 1920s, put it at a conference on scientific management in Milan in 1928, 'in the past man came first; in the future, the system will come first'. With a more rational organization it was hoped that workers would also 'put the system first', and realize that rather than being antagonists, machines and management were, in fact, the workers' 'invisible slaves'. Such 'slaves' would help make their labour cheap, although their wages were high. The argument put forth in journals like *L'Ufficio moderno* and in *Critica Fascista* was that American methods were necessary if Italy wanted to keep up, and if enough prosperity were to be generated to realize the corporativist project of overcoming class conflict.[25] Poets, writers and literati did nothing but complain about 'America', about Babitts and standardization, but for the revisionists and the 'technicians' these ideas seemed far less threatening. Indeed,

> there are already too many lawyers and literati. Italy needs engineers, physicists, chemists, mathematicians, agronomists, and, above all, organizers. . . . Accountants can calmly ignore Guido di Verona's novels as long as they keep in touch with the developments of modern methods of accountancy. Science instead of literature! In today's society, each man has a precise function to fulfil and he must concentrate on that. Standardize! Specialize! Let us value the teachings of Taylorism, as interpreted and adjusted to Latin conditions![26]

Although these emerging 'technicians' would embrace a cosmopolitan culture of modernity where rationalization was a key component (the Swedish model and the Myrdals' writings were frequent points of reference in *Critica Fascista*), they remained within a nationalist discourse where it was essential to keep redrawing the boundary between 'Italy' and 'America'. The last sentence of the quote above is particularly significant in this respect. One key argument on the part of the proponents of Taylorism and the standardization of production, headed by Bottai himself, was that the negative, dehumanizing aspects associated with these methods in the US were not necessarily intrinsic to these methods themselves, but that this rather depended on the larger social framework. In Italy such dehumanizing consequences could be avoided as long as these methods were not used in a way that was 'contrary to our character and our interests'.[27] In the US Taylorism no doubt dehumanized workers, but this was above all the result of the worker's existence outside the factory, where the 'false individualism' of mass consumption denied them any possibility for a fuller life – where they were indoctrinated by 'sports and empty hedonism'.[28] In Fascism, on the other hand, the worker would acquire a new, richer meaning to life, on the factory floor as well as in his whole social existence, by being part of a larger totality: the nation as expressed in the state. The 'Atomism in all its manifestations' that had characterized liberal Italy was now finished, and the presence of the state should no longer be felt 'just through the police, but in the organic capacities that manifest themselves in the nation'.[29] To achieve this it was necessary that the other side of the equation, reproduction, social life and consumption be taken in serious consideration.

Here, as well, Taylor-inspired methods of standardization were seen to have a great potential. In the field of mass consumption they could 'reduce the excessive variety of production' that derived from a semi-industrialized, partly artisan, but above all insufficiently integrated, economy in favour of standardized goods at acessible prices. As one editorial in *L'Ufficio moderno* pointed out, 'we have a thousand different models of Italian cars' (a slight exaggeration, no doubt), that differ 'only by their colour'. But there was no standardized car, mass produced and reasonably priced.[30] Standardization would thus contribute to making modern consumer goods accessible to the whole population. To differ from the American example, however, standardized mass consumption needed to be accompanied by a non-individualistic ethic of consumption. Modern consumer goods had to be made to foster a sense of collective belonging and social integration. In acquiring and using modern standardized products, the individual should be made to feel part of a national modernity that had transcended the pronounced regional and class divisions of the liberal period. As a Fascist it was thus fully possible to embrace mass consumption, even enthusiastically so. Emilio Cederaschi, manager of UPI (Unione Pubblicitaria Italiana), the advertising company in charge of most of the official campaigns of the regime, depicted his vision of a standardized utopia in 1937:

> Mass man, and today that means everybody . . ., is for, and he is right in being for, all that makes life easier and more practical, from the standardized radio, to the mass produced car, from the perfectly organized cruise trip, to the rational house, from the mass produced suit to mass produced ideas – everything of course of the highest quality.[31]

Modern mass consumption did not necessarily lead to social fragmentation. If consumption was given a different overall organization, it could foster social solidarity and national unity.

Consumer culture and Fascist mass organizations

The most coherent attempts at fostering such a Fascist consumer culture occurred within the mass organizations, in particular the national 'after work' organization OND (Opera nazionale dopolavoro) that was dedicated to the reform of worker leisure, and the Fascist women's organization, the Fasci femminili, which worked towards the overall rationalization of household work. The OND was created to meet the 'problem' of worker leisure that came with legislation on the eight-hour working day and to create and diffuse a new kind of national, unified and rationally organized worker leisure. The ideas behind the OND were in this respect very similar to those of the Fascist 'organizers' more generally. (And its founder, the engineer Mario Giani, gained a great deal of inspiration from Taylorist scientific management. OND was to be to leisure what scientific management was to work, a kind of 'Taylorization of leisure'.) This new organized culture would also serve as an antidote to the negative consequences of standardization in the workplace, enabling the worker to find 'happiness' and satisfaction in his or her free time. It would promote 'individual self-betterment' instead of the class struggle. And, it was hoped, it would be supported by new nationally common patterns of consumption. The introduction of new modern objects in everyday life would promote new, modern ideas.

Consequently the OND promoted a series of measures to facilitate popular access to modern consumer goods. It functioned as a savings agency and worked as a guarantor for instalment schemes for more costly consumer goods, like radios. The OND arranged a series of shows, like the 1927 exhibition on the home and on rational furniture, where the otherwise prohibitively expensive products of Italian rationalist designers like Giò Ponti could be viewed. A number of manufacturers would target their products, like clocks, radios and cigarettes particularly at the *dopolavoro* market, and use the organization and its publication *Gente nostra* as one of their chief marketing outlets. The OND membership card also gave discounts and special offers from a number of outlets (the organization made more than 15,000 agreements in this respect). Overall the consumption-ethic furthered by the OND was rational, frugal and anti-hedonistic. The exhibition of rational furniture promised objects that had been designed with an 'attention to price, artistic taste, solidity and practicality' and to maximize 'the sense of well-being of the popular classes at the least possible cost'.[32]

Similarly, a 1927 advertisement for Rinascente, which announced the department store's cooperation with the *dopolavoro*, stressed its devotion to a new, popular (rather than bourgeois and elitist) consumer ethic. The new, favourable scheme for instalment payments now supplied was aimed 'certainly not to those favoured by fortune, who do not have to worry about life's necessities . . . but the other classes, those who often have difficulties in paying in cash for what they need'. These instalment plans could be used to purchase Italian products, notably furniture. After the exhibition in 1927 Rinascente had opened a department for Italian design. This would not only help to spread an Italian design that, as Giò Ponti had stressed, was tailored to the Italian climate and character, but it would also aid the 'coming together of producers and consumers' and give an 'Italian character to our industry'.[33] Rinascente further announced that their initiative would help to 'protect mothers and children' (a team dear to the now accelerating demographic policies), to 'safeguard the family' and to stimulate the 'love of work and of life in general'.[34]

While the OND was originally intended as a workers' leisure organization, it became, in practice, a middle-class thing. (In 1926, 20 per cent of all workers were *dopolavoro* members, as against 80 per cent of all civil servants.)[35] For the middle classes, it seems, the OND had some influence on the development of modern consumer habits, if nothing else through its popular forms of leisure consumption, like the 'popular trains' and organized weekend excursions, in which the nation itself, with its natural and artistic treasures, would be offered as an object for consumption.[36] The general fate of the

OND's attempts to standardize and unify leisure and consumption more generally were, however, as de Grazia illustrates, victims of a kind of colonization from below. An existing middle-class habitus made its mark on the organization, to the point that '*dopolavoro* culture' came to stand for the kind of lowbrow human interest mixture popularized after the war by publications like *Reader's Digest*, or to the intellectual snob, quite simply 'trash'. Given this, it is difficult to say how far attempts to create a national consumer culture actually managed to overcome the privatist *petit bourgeois* tastes that Mussolini had identified as Fascism's main adversary in this field.

The Fasci femminili also devoted attention to the organization of mass consumption. As a continuation of the independent Movimento femminile fascista (subsumed under party leadership in 1926), which in turn had roots that went back to the bourgeois feminism of the pre-war years, the Fasci femminili became one of the few openings for women intellectuals within the Fascist state apparatus. Their *raison d'être* was home economics. This discipline had grown out of Taylorist methods of scientific management and developed with the American consumer appliances revolution in the 1920s.[37] Its main thrust was the necessity to replace 'old housewives tales' with modern rational methods. Initially the Fasci femminili were rather successful in their attempts to promote home economics, made an obligatory subject for girls' secondary education in 1928. In 1927 the fourth international conference on home economics was held in Rome, together with the third international conference on scientific management (where there were several panels on home economics). Home economics, with its promise to reduce and rationalize housework, had originally carried a slightly emancipating prospect. As it was presented by the Fasci femminili, however, such implications tended to be downplayed. Instead, the Fasci femminili stressed its potential contribution to the process of national modernization. This contribution consisted not only in the simplification of everyday life, but also in promoting a new, rational and nationally unified way of organizing domestic life. As Mariuccia Salvati has argued, home economics was presented as conducive, both to a rationalization and to a nationalization of the masses.[38] In her editorials in *Casa e lavoro*, an influential journal devoted to home economics and published by Enios, the editor, Maria Diez Gasca, would underline this dual function. According to her, widespread schooling in home economics was necessary in order to provide an overall rationalization of private consumption, as Italian housewives generally lacked the necessary knowledge to make informed decisions about purchasing modern consumer goods. They would often let themselves be influenced by irrational factors, like the name of the product, its foreign origins (which connoted higher status) or the arguments of salesmen.[39] This was not the only potential benefit of home economics. Indeed, as Diez Gasca wrote in one of her editorials, 'The teaching of home economics should not occur only for technical reasons. . . . It does not aim to transform the home into a miniature factory.' Equally important was its contribution to 'protecting the spirit of the family' against 'the fashionable and fascinating danger of so-called individual liberty'. Against this, home economics could help to reinforce the virtues of the family and of traditional femininity, but not in a traditional way, which would in any case succumb to the assault of modern life, but in a modern, Fascist way. By teaching home economics on a mass level, 'the regime forms an army (*esercito*) of Italian women, powerful, strong in their faith, gifted with the simplest of manners and with an irresistible capacity for sacrifice, frugal and masters of any virtue, with courage and healthy customs'.[40] According to an article in the organ of the Fasci femminili, *Donna Fascista*, home economics, together with rationally designed furniture and modern kitchens, would allow the modern woman to make the home both into a 'haven in a heartless world' and into the primary 'moral fortress of the nation'.[41]

The effects of these campaigns were, however, rather limited. Home economics did influence a middle-class habitus, in particular through its spread to more widely diffused publications like *Cucina italiana*, a popular cooking magazine that was first published in 1929. Its influence outside the middle class was scarce, primarily as the construction of popular housing was not a priority of the regime (in particular, after the start of the demographic campaigns when it seemed that urban dwelling was downright antithetical to demographic growth, and 'ruralization' was encouraged instead). Apart from the bigger cities (where the diffusion of gas stoves proved a case in point) the domestic environments where home economics could make sense were simply absent.[42] Even as part of a middle-class habitus, it is probable that most of its political connotations were lost.

If we look at *Cucina italiana* we do find a distinct presence of propagandistic and explicitly political material, in particular after the proclamation of autarchy. Such 'political' material was, however, generally confined to articles and editorials, while the more instructive material, descriptions of how to behave as an ideal, rational housewife and columns on cooking and good manners, were virtually unmarked by the concerns of the regime. What we see there is rather a conservative middle-class orientation to the pleasures of private life, mixed up with exiting novelties from America, like drinking cocktails before dinner or preparing the favourite dishes of Hollywood film stars.

While it was essential that housewives be schooled in home economics and related disciplines 'chemistry, hygiene, administration, paediatrics', this knowledge did not so much serve to maintain a strong moral foundation of the nation, as to further the private happiness of the family. In order to do so, the housewife required not so much discipline and a spirit of sacrifice, as the ability to be elegant and presentable when entertaining and, above all, to be loving and seductive when alone with her husband.[43] Apart perhaps from its nationalistic overtones, there was nothing unique about the way in which home economics was campaigned for in Italy. In Sweden one finds a very similar emphasis on a nationally unified domestic culture of rational methods and modern domestic appliances. There, also, the rational housewife, in charge both of the domestic budget and of her own mental faculties while out shopping was habitually pitched against the irrational woman consumer whom it was thought that advertising, and in particular American consumer culture, would produce.[44] Rather than making a realistic contribution to any original Fascist project of mass consumption, the Fasci femminili as well as the OND mostly made use of the Fascist discursive universe in order to legitimize their claims and position. This conclusion is valid for the advertising profession as well.

Fascist advertising

For the small but rather vociferous group of modern advertising professionals, or 'advertising technicians' (*tecnici pubblicitari*) as they called themselves (chapter 4), the prospect of aligning the promotion of mass consumption with the Fascist project of nationalizing the masses was certainly promising. It offered a powerful opportunity to legitimize their activity and professional competence in a highly suspicious, if not downright adverse, environment. (Trade journals from 1910 and onwards were full of arguments – to be presented to potential clients, presumably – as to why on earth anyone would need the services of an 'advertising technician' who did not even produce any advertisements himself, but rather coordinated the campaign.) Their suggestion in this field was the 'collective advertising campaign'. Collective campaigns (again an American invention, the examples of Sunkist oranges and of Californian wine and raisins were frequently cited) had many advantages over ordinary advertising. First, cooperation between different producers would promote an industry-wide solidarity in line with the corporativist vision. Second, collective campaigns advertising beer, coffee, rice or bananas would contribute to standardization, the reduction of the 'excessive diversity' of goods that stood at the heart of the Fascist version of mass consumerism. Most importantly, however, collective campaigns by their unified effort would mobilize an advertising effort strong enough to influence consumer behaviour. This was particularly important in the context of national self-sufficiency, or 'autarchy'.[45]

According to the highly politicized organ of the National Fascist Syndicate of Advertising Agencies, *La pubblicità d'Italia*, that made the connection between collective campaigns and autarchy its major concern from the first issue, the contribution of advertising in this field was essential. To realize a truly self-sufficient national economy it was not enough to boost production. If Italian industry were to fight off foreign competition and wasteful domestic rivalries successfully, a massive advertising effort was needed to 'enter into the spirit, the tastes and the habits' of Italians, in order to make them prefer national products, but also to make them prefer those national products that best suited the needs of autarchic economic development, such as rice, beer and artificial fibres like lanital, rayon and cafioc, and, of equal importance, to direct demand away from brands to products, thus limiting unnecessary rivalries among domestic producers.[46] Under Fascism advertising should thus be used to impose the demands of the nation on the individual. Like the worker, the individual consumer should be turned into a 'moment' of the national economy. Indeed, when used collectively rather than in the private interest:

> Advertising should be considered a science of government, in so far as it is a way to move the masses in a determined direction, creating an irresistible suggestion in order to reach a specified goal. Effectively advertising has an overwhelming power, enough to found new cities, states and religions.[47]

Enthusiasts thus suggested that collective campaigns be 'made the distinctive mark of Italian advertising'. (Although they would agree that both the Americans and the Germans were further ahead in their field.) They also argued that their scope be extended beyond the field of consumption to combat, for example, the seemingly pressing problem of demographic decline.[48] To streamline wants and desires in the field of consumption and elsewhere was, however, not the only function of truly Fascist advertising: it should also express the national 'spirit', 'our character, our strength, our aspirations, our times', and contribute to the moral unity of the national body. It should pass from being 'an instrument of private greed, without any aesthetic unity' and with sometimes demoralizing consequences in its promotion of individualism and of unregulated private desire, to being 'an instrument of the collective good' that helped to construct the Fascist order and the 'new Fascist man'. To do that, however, Italian advertising needed a common, unifying style.[49]

Similar debates on the stylistic unity of Italian advertising had been going on for a long time. It had been clear already from the start of these debates that the style and execution of Italian advertising had to respect the Italian national character, if nothing else for technical reasons. When journalist Pio Cavalli published his book *La spada d'America* (America's Sword) in 1919, which claimed to present American advertising techniques and suggest how they could be successfully employed in Italy, Emilo Grego, a pioneering 'advertising technician' reviewed it in *L'Impresa moderna* under the heading 'An Italian book on advertising and the ignorance of a journalist'. Even though Cavalli was eager to point out that 'learning from the Americans' only served the legitimate goal of furthering the grandeur of Italy, not of turning her into yet another state in the Union, Grego argued that even the suggestion that American methods could work in Italy testified to a profound ignorance of the marked differences in the 'American and the Latin psychologies'.[50] What makes Grego's reaction even more telling is that the advertising techniques that Cavalli presented as American were in fact French. His chapter on 'advertising theory' was a direct translation of Gérin and Espinadel's influential manual *La publicité suggestive* (see chapter 4). Similar arguments persisted throughout the 1930s, even as American methods were increasingly accepted. In order to work in Italy, they had at any rate to be adapted to the particularities of the Italian national character, Guido Mazzali, one of the founders of *L'Ufficio moderno* claimed in 1932: the 'Anglo-Saxon' advertising style was particularly inefficient in Italy as its grey and dull character was exactly the opposite of the 'individualistic' and 'creative' spirit of Italians.[51]

The discussion of 'style' in the field of advertising theory generally lacked the pragmatic concern of the preceding debate in American advertising trade journals, where the 'modernistic' European poster tradition was criticized for its unlikely efficiency.[52] Here, rather, the search for a 'style' linked up to the general Fascist project of an aesthetic politics, of conceiving social unity as primarily mediated through the aesthetic level. As in the case of Fascist cultural politics more generally, the precise nature of such an 'Italian style', or even the Italian national character that it was supposed to respect, was much less clear.[53] The futurists had made an attempt to proclaim themselves the representatives of the official Fascist style in the early 1920s, but they were quickly marginalized.[54] They remained more influential in the field of advertising. Many of them, like the artist Fortunato Depero who painted a series of posters for Campari, regarded advertising as the medium for modern art *par excellence*. Advertising could potentially bring art out of galleries and museums and into the street: it could spread a new style, a new 'artistic synthesis of modern life' on a mass scale.[55] What, exactly, this entailed was not entirely clear, apart from its vehement opposition to the American representational or 'truthist' (*verista*) style: in this case in the shape of a soap advertisement that featured a '50 metre long "truthist" portrait of a crying child in a bathtub', that Marinetti lambasted in a 1938 article as 'passéist (*passatista*) and picturesque'.[56]

While the futurist did contribute substantially to the modernization of the rich Italian poster-art tradition, it was still not clear what an Italian advertising aesthetic would look like. *L'Ufficio moderno* went as far as to stage a referendum in 1927 asking whether an Italian advertising style was indeed possible and, in that case, what it would look like. Answers ranged from an emphasis on variability, creativity and the 'genius of Italians', to more diplomatic suggestions that Italian advertising be defined as 'everything that is made in Italy, or by Italians'.[57] Most often, attempts to define this Italian style proceed negatively, listing what it was not, usually in terms of nationalist stereotypes: 'Not as heavy handed as the German' or 'not as cold as the English'.[58] Many advertising professionals would, however, denounce the use of a modernist idiom in advertising as too elitist and hence inefficient when aimed at a mass market. Like most of their American colleagues they preferred a realist approach: to show the product and/or its users in a straightforward way. Consequently, the advertising campaigns presented as exemplary of Fascist advertising by *La Pubblicità d'Italia* varied greatly both in terms of style and in terms of how they addressed consumers. The best examples of a self-consciously 'Fascist' approach to advertising are perhaps the campaigns organized by the *ufficio tecnico* of Unione Pubblicitaria Italiana, UPI.

Figure 3.3 Italian style? Marcello Nizzoli's modernist poster for Campari. (Courtesy of the Biblioteca Nazionale, Florence.)

Founded in 1916 from the remains of an older advertising firm created by Austrian entrepreneurs Haasenstein and Vogler, UPI had a long history as a major advertising space broker. In 1922 the agency began to sell the advertising space in *il Popolo d'Italia*, the newspaper founded by Mussolini in 1914 and run by him until the Fascist takeover in 1922, which had since become something of an official propaganda vehicle for the regime. In 1934 UPI became the official agency for foreign propaganda and the agency of choice for the commission for the promotion of Italian products (*comitato per il prodotto italiano*). UPI thus developed into something like the official representative of Fascism within the world of advertising. UPI's campaigns, in particular the propaganda campaigns (*le forze del impero*) celebrating the productive forces of Fascist Italy, and the drive to promote autarchic textiles (like lanital), made heavy use of Fascist as well as 'imperial' imagery. They also used those 'featureless faces' or 'disappearing bodies' – depictions of workers or consumers with no discernable facial traits – that Karen Pinkus has identified as one central element to Fascist advertising.[59] UPI's campaigns were mainly targeted at foreign observers or the already convinced readers of *il Popolo d'Italia* and did not have any wider reach, with the exception of the massive 1935 'Buy Italian Products' campaign, which was severely criticized by other advertising professionals (see chapter 4).

Many other agencies organized 'collective campaigns', but their approach was different. The truth is that contrary to recommendations of a unitary style and appeal, Italian advertisers tended to differentiate their approach according to what they perceived to be the expectations of their audience. This was particularly evident in the campaigns organized by the new American-style advertising agencies that began to emerge in the 1930s. Take, for example, the campaign for Italian beer organized by Enneci, what was left of the American agency Erwin Wasey & Co. that had withdrawn from Italy, or the Italian market in the wake of the Depression. The main message of the campaign stressed the Fascist virtues of this beverage: beer was a modern, national beverage. The campaign advertised 'Italian beer', not individual brands and showed how its use would transcend regional and social differences. Peasants drank it, but so did smart urbanites. It was a modern drink, rational and nourishing. It transcended 'artificial divisions' like class. One central theme was to demonstrate the benefits of beer as a drink to accompany meals, how it goes well with all sorts of foods and contributes to helping the body digest and absorb a variety of other substances. Indeed, as the slogan went, 'Beer drinkers live a hundred years' (*Chi beve birra campa cent'anni*). The common sales pitch was thus to stress the themes of modernity and social unity dear to Fascist discourses on mass consumption. Modern rational Italians drink beer!

This theme was, however, presented in very different ways, depending on the audience addressed. In railway stations (supposedly frequented by a wealthy and cosmopolitan crowd), Enneci used the modernist aesthetic of Dudovich's posters to underline the fashionable and stylish qualities of

Figure 3.4 Italian Style? 'The Forces of Empire', UPI's celebrated iconography of corporativism. (Courtesy of the Biblioteca Nazionale, Florence.)

drinking beer: how beer would help one to stage oneself as an urbane person. In women's magazines the agency used a more realist approach: to show how beer would contribute to fulfilling the role of housewife. In sports newspapers, the same realist imagery stressed how beer would contribute to the shaping of a modern, athletic (!), masculine self. The important thing, according to Guido Mazzali, reviewing the campaigns in *L'Ufficio moderno*, was that the presentation of the argument would become part of the 'natural environment of the prospective reader' and that the advertisement would 'mirror his position and his social function'.[60] Rather than standardizing the message, and using the campaign to promote a stylistic unity, Enneci's beer campaign respected the different stylistic and taste currents – the different *habiti* – that marked the audience. Such a strategy was obviously contrary to the pronounced ends of making advertising into a medium for the standardization and stylistic unification.

Conclusion

Overall, the regime's attempts to make an emerging mass consumption part of its overall cultural politics seem to have had rather fragmented results. 'Fascism' was certainly there as a symbolic resource to be drawn on in advertising. Many manufacturers, from FIAT with its Balilla model, named after the Fascist boy scouts organization, to more esoteric companies, such as the makers of 'imperial' razor blades, or the purveyors of different 'colonial' wares like chocolate or coffee, would often draw on its collective imaginary. It is thus very easy to find examples of Fascist advertising, where ideas of national rebirth or colonial superiority are explicitly invoked. On the other hand, Fascism never managed to give consumer culture in general any kind of overall organization, much less any stylistic unity.

The example of the attempt to foster a Fascist fashion is telling in this respect. Despite the institutionalization of a national organization for fashion (*ente nazionale moda*) in 1932, and despite bombastic pronunciations about the necessity to dress in domestic fashions, for reasons of style and, increasingly after the pronunciation of autarchy in 1935, also economy (if nothing else to counter the wasteful importation of luxury goods), there was no Italian fashion industry to speak of, mainly because of the absence of a consumer market for ready-to-wear fashions. Young style-conscious working-class women made their clothes themselves, and from the middle classes and up one used a personal tailor. This also meant that most Italian fashion continued to be inspired by Parisian fashions or, for the women who sewed their own clothes, by the Hollywood look, as distributed by mass-circulating women's magazines.[61]

Overall it seems that talk about the 'Fascistization' of consumption, and the economy more generally, could, as in the case of the corporativist project, go on in relative independence of actual events. Various actors invoked its rhetoric or pledged alliance to its project primarily in order to further their own particular goals, but rarely saw them as any serious guidelines for real initiative. One reason for such fragmented results was, of course, the overall poverty of Italian consumers. In 1938 (one of the most prosperous years of the *ventennio*), Italy was on par with countries like Albania and Greece in terms of the diffusion of consumer goods such as radios. A still rather fragmented distributional system, at least outside the larger cities, also made it difficult to achieve any overall national coordination of consumer culture. Until the economic miracle, Italy quite simply did not possess the prerequisites for becoming a consumer society where the function of marketing or advertising was comparable to the American case. A limited middle-class market and a fragmented distribution system thus made the utility of trying to use consumer goods in shaping a new, shared consciousness scarce. While this might have been the case for most inhabitants of the peninsula, the urban middle classes, in particular the younger generations, had a different, more modern relationship to consumer goods. It was also there that the regime's efforts had most effect. But in the case of middle-class consumption another factor came into play. While they continued to pledge alliance to its goals and principles in fostering a modern middle-class consumer culture, key actors, such as magazine publishers and the advertising profession itself, took their main inspiration from a different, American conception of consumption and consumer culture.

This chapter has shown, however, that there is not necessarily a link between mass consumption and a privatist consumer culture: a collectivist, nationalist ethic of consumption *is* possible. The privatist direction that consumer culture took during the twentieth century was rather the effect of the perspective developed by the American advertising industry.

4 The American influence

> Whoever arrives in New York and walks up 'Old Broadway' is blinded by the majestic glow of an endless row of neon signs that silently speak of an infinity of products: from gramophones to silk stockings, from show polish to the latest theatre show. If later at night, before he goes to sleep, he decides to browse through an illustrated magazine, he will marvel at the beauty of its illustrations, at the influence that advertising has on its content; at the riches, the abundance, the importance that advertising has in this curious and fascinating country.

Luigi Dalmonte's report from his experiences at the George Ethridge & Co. advertising agency in New York, where he worked between 1919 and 1920, conveyed the same mixture of envy and awe that marked the attitude towards 'America' among Italian advertising professionals in general. Despite frequent recourse to nationalistic rhetoric, the American example was an obvious referent for any serious discussion of advertising, selling and mass consumption. Upon his return to Italy Dalmonte did not hesitate to put what he had learnt into practice. In 1922 he opened Italy's first American-style advertising agency, ACME Dalmonte, which employed the same methods and perspective he had observed at George Ethridge. For him it was obvious that coming from the country where 'even lard' was sold elegantly packaged in coloured tin boxes, American advertising had a lot to teach.[1]

While the sheer novelty of mass advertising explains some of the fascination it produced, in particular with foreign observers, accounts like Dalmonte's were not entirely unfounded. In the 1920s the US was going through its 'consumer revolution', and practices like advertising and marketing developed along with the new nationwide distribution systems for mass-produced goods. According to estimates by business historian Daniel Pope, advertising volume, which had been growing steadily but slowly from the 1880s to the First World War, quadrupled between 1914 and the Great Depression. In roughly the same period (1909–29), advertising's share of GNP rose from 1.9 per cent to 2.9 per cent, and its share of general distribution costs (themselves rising from (current) US$ 6.5 billion in 1909 to US$ 21.1 billion in 1929) increased by 75 per cent (1909–29). Indeed, the

American advertising industry, in Stephen Fox's words, 'would never again have it so plush'.[2]

As part of this general expansion, American advertising went abroad. Between 1927 and 1929 the rising star of the US advertising industry, the J. Walter Thompson (JWT) company, established some 20 offices abroad, in order to market General Motor's cars and Lever brothers' soaps and detergents in France, Spain, Romania, Argentina, Egypt and India. Other major agencies followed.[3] Even though there was some debate about how to present American products successfully in foreign contexts, most American advertising professionals shared a basic faith in the superiority of the American advertising technique. They thought that what had worked in the US would work equally well around the world. Indeed, JWT's advertising philosophy was based on the assumption that 'people all over the world react pretty much the same way'; that people all over the world share a few similar basic emotions and desires that could be appealed to.[4] This meant not only that everyone around the world was a potential consumer, but also that everyone was susceptible to the civilizing impact of American consumer culture. The task of advertising was, then, not only to sell goods, but also to transform the inhabitants of backward societies into modern, rational consumers, behaving, thinking and desiring the same things that Americans did. Judging from the debates in American trade journals and in JWT's own internal bulletins, American advertising professionals working abroad were strongly committed to this civilizing mission of advertising. To transform the Spanish 'Carmen' into a rational, American-style consumer housewife, to teach the French to give up their all-too-individualistic tastes and stop equating leisure time with idle time, to unite young 'beauties from Bangor to Bangkok' in a common quest for a 'movie-star complexion', and people all around the world in the desire for social achievement and domestic comfort, was not only a profitable business, but also something of a service to humanity.[5]

This self-confidence on the part of American advertising professionals came not only from the sheer size of their industry, but also from their firm conviction that their methods were modern, and above all scientific. Rather than a bunch of drinking and debauching 'Hucksters' – as they were later depicted in Frederick Wakeman's novel of 1946 – American advertising professionals now began to see themselves as serious and respectable technicians, in command of the latest techniques of behavioural psychology and managerial science.[6] JWT was particularly marked by this 'scientific' approach to advertising. Its founder and long-time chairman, Stanley Resor, had originally nurtured plans for an academic career. At JWT he created something of a 'university of advertising'. Resor required employees to read through course-like syllabuses and, under his leadership, JWT became the first agency to feature an internal market-research department, an experimental kitchen and later, in 1939, ran its own consumer panel where some 5,000 families would be interviewed every month on their purchases of everything from cars to toothpaste. This 'scientific' approach also entailed a set of formal rules for the process of producing advertisements. In 1919 JWT had set up a 'committee on standardization' in order to attempt to standardize agency procedures along the lines of scientific management. One of its results was a formal scheme, the so-called 'T-square', which creatives were to adapt in thinking about consumer goods and about how to present them in advertisements. Resor also arranged that everything was decided in meetings, and made a point of downplaying the individualistic or 'creative' aura of advertising, or, as he put it in a 1947 interview, 'never to trust the individual opinion'.[7] While JWT would withdraw from the Italian market in 1931 as the mother company began to feel the effects of the depression, the American methods that the company proposed and, indeed, preached would have a significant influence on the debates of the Italian advertising profession in the 1930s. In this chapter I will show how such American methods came to influence Italian debates more generally, and how they began to alter existing conceptions of the proper relation between consumers and consumer goods.[8]

Advertising technicians

Looking at the American example, Dalmonte and his colleagues concluded that advertising in Italy was haphazard, unsystematic and without any semblance of a rational organization: clients defied it (in particular those with a 'peasant mentality' or those 'who have never travelled anywhere'), and advertising agents were seen as no better than common impostors. Above all advertising was all art and no method.[9] With hindsight such claims appear a trifle exaggerated. Advertising was no novelty in inter-war Italy: the last decades of the nineteenth century had had a flourishing tradition of advertising artists who enjoyed considerable public attention. In connection with the development of a middle-class market in the post-war years, this predominantly artistic tradition of poster advertising went through a process of both modernization and institutionalization. The new manuals on modern advertising techniques that began to come out saw advertising as a methodical practice, as part of the new discipline of business administration, rather than as an art form. They stressed that it was a mass medium, to be used with a mass audience in mind. To Carlo Cassola, whose *Advertising from an Economic Perspective* (*La pubblicità dal punto di vista economico*) that was published in 1909 was probably the first such manual to appear, 'mass' meant middle class. The upper classes, Cassola argued, were too intellectually mature to be affected by propaganda, and the lower classes were not only too poor to be interested in consumption but also too 'psychologically inferior' to understand the message of modern advertising. The middle class, on the other hand, were not only interested in consumption as a vehicle for status and identity, but were also quick to change their tastes and in general were open to suggestion and influence. The middle classes, Cassola argued, possessed an intrinsic desire for self-betterment. As Torstein Veblen had argued a decade earlier, their main motivation was to try to imitate the habits of the upper classes.[10] Similarly,

Arturo Lancelotti (see also Chapter 2, p. 20), a journalist who wrote extensively on advertising and propaganda in the inter-war years, and who published another manual-cum-historic-overview in 1912, argued that the middle-class person was motivated by a quest for public fame rather than by any stable values or ideals. More than anything else, he wanted to see his own name in the paper.[11]

Addressing the middle class, however, meant improving one's approach. In a mass market, intuition was no longer enough for good salesmanship, as one article in *L'Impresa moderna* argued in 1914. If pre-industrial markets were embedded in the social fabric of everyday life where success was dependent on the personal characteristics of the salesman, modern salesmanship had to face a market of strangers. Modern commercial activity could hence not be based on the intuition or other personal qualities of the salesman alone, but had to rely on scientifically elaborated and practically proven techniques (including psycho-technic techniques for the correct selection of salesmen). Similar calls for the rationalization of distributive networks and of salesmanship in general would continue all through the 1920s.[12]

Many of the more established names in the poster business would, however, vehemently resist such a 'scientific' conception of advertising. One was Giuseppe Magagnoli, or 'Maga', the founder of the internationally successful poster studio of the same name. His company publication *Il pugno nell'occhio* (*The Punch in the Eye*) launched a series of attacks on 'scientific' advertising. Its 'difficult phraseology' and 'cabalistic formulae' served only to impress an 'audience of imbeciles', or to 'boost the self-image of the speaker'. Good advertising, on the other hand, had nothing to do with psychology or 'science', or even with general laws, but with artistic sensibility. It was about finding creative solutions that made the poster stand out in the turmoil of modern life. A successful *trovata* (gimmick, unexpected juxtaposition) would 'take the audience by surprise' and thereby 'firmly fix the name of the product in their minds'.[13]

But many of the younger poster artists would embrace this need for modernization. Influenced by the international avant-garde they began to devote more attention to the efficiency of visual form. Some, like Luciano Ramo, who had lectured on advertising at the Università popolare di Milano in 1914, argued for a systematic reliance on the objective laws of visual 'suggestion'. He claimed that 'the psychological laws from which directives for efficient and, dare I say, suggestive advertising are unique. They are the same if you aim to persuade someone to buy a bottle of perfume, a sweet, a horse or industrial stocks.'[14] Consequently, modern advertising required that the creativity of the artist be subordinated to the systematic rules of scientific persuasion. Following the theories of a 'scientific aesthetic', elaborated by Victor Basch, professor of Esthétique et science de l'art at the Sorbonne, there was even some talk of an abstract grammar of forms that would achieve its aims by bypassing the moment of intellectual reflection to work directly on the deep drives of the psyche. Basch's theory proposed that:

> visual information was organized and processed through a grammar of abstract forms which correspond to specific psychological states. If such a grammar could indeed be identified, it might then be possible to design images that had been engineered to produce specific and predictable emotional responses.[15]

In 1925 a series of experiments in the psychology of perception were organized by the poster painter Guido Cassi and the Italian authority on psycho-technics Professor Agostino Gemelli, at the Catholic University in Milan. They wanted to find out 'what graphic forms are most efficient in appealing to the sensibility of the audience' using 'psycho-technic machines'. Guido Cassi also proposed the raising of consciousness on the power of images by organizing a poster competition where the judges would be illiterate:

> The true task of the advertising technician is to create an illustration [that can] penetrate the perceptive field of the passer-by, stimulate his passive attention and, by virtue of its very shape, give rise to a thought in his mind that is directly connected to the object to which the ad refers.[16]

More than anything else, however, the rise of a 'scientific' conception of advertising was connected to the emergence of a new professional figure, the 'advertising technician' (*tecnico pubblicitario*). In general, these advertising technicians lacked any artistic training. Some were academics or professionals, like Emilio Grego, who taught many courses on advertising at the Milan Chamber of Commerce and who, with the journalist Arturo Lancelotti, began writing on advertising as early as 1912. Grego had originally been a medical doctor, but switched to advertising after the war as his wounded hands prevented him from continuing to practice. Another example is Giulio Cesare Ricciardi, later to become one of Italy's internationally more famous advertisers. Ricciardi had taken a law degree, but resigned after discovering that he had no passion for the legal profession. 'One day in 1921, when walking past the Chamber of Commerce in Milan, I saw a poster for Emilio Grego's course on advertising and decided to attend.'[17] Many came from journalism and some were just plain adventurers, like Pier Luigi Balzaretti, later head of advertising in the department store Rinascente, and founder, together with Ricciardi, of one of Italy's first advertising agencies, Balza-Ricc. Balzaretti had started out as a travelling salesman in South America, and later worked at the sales department of Macy's in San Francisco.

Apart from the experience of the war, which most of them shared, these advertising technicians nurtured a common view of modern advertising. For the advertising technicians, unlike the poster artists, advertising was not only, or even chiefly, about artistic representation. This was still important, but, as the US example, or for that matter domestic war propaganda, suggested, its true purpose was sociological rather than aesthetic: it was about subjects, about shaping their behaviour, thoughts and opinions.[18] Rather than beautifying existing forms of life as the nineteenth century poster artists had done, advertising should contribute to creating new ones. Advertising could then not only contribute to increasing sales, but also have a civilizing impact. Accordingly, the Italian advertising technicians, like their American colleagues, were convinced that their work served a higher social, and not just economic or artistic, purpose, if not the universal well-being of humankind (as for American advertisers), then the future grandeur of Italy. Indeed, advertising, as Egisto Roggero concluded in his 1920 manual, was 'a powerful weapon in the fight among the nations', able to give Italy the place that she deserved.[19] To achieve this, however, it was necessary that the old system of advertising, where industrialists would personally contact an artist to elaborate the kind of advertising they themselves liked, be replaced. Such an institution would only serve to reproduce the tastes of a bourgeois habitus. Instead, many advertising technicians argued forcefully for the mediating role of an advertising technician who had substituted personal whim for the methodological rigour of 'psycho-mercantile science'.[20]

'To penetrate the brains of a million men'

Despite their conception of modern advertising as founded on behavioural science, the advertising technicians, in contrast to their US colleagues, paid little attention to any empirical investigations of the actual mental make-up of consumers. This was partly because of the relative underdevelopment of Italian advertising and the virtual absence, until the mid-1930s, of any kind of market research. But it was also a result of the theoretical framework they employed, which allowed them to avoid the question of consumer motivations. The key to scientific legitimacy for the Italian advertising technicians, just as for their American colleagues, was psychology. Rather than the American psychological literature, however, they relied mainly on the influential French manual *La publicité suggestive*, written by the two French psychologists Octave-Jacques Gérin and Charles Espinadel in 1911.

Gérin and Espinadel drew on empirical research in applied psychology (at the Salpetière hospital, where Gérin had been active as a researcher) and on the 'crowd psychology' of Gustave Le Bon and Gabriel Tarde. Their manual was treated as a classic, and was often copied – in part or in whole – in Italian publications on advertising theory. Reading it was something of an initiation rite for prospective advertising technicians.[21] Like the crowd psychologists, Gérin and Espinadel were suspicious of human rationality. Rather, they believed that most human actions are conditioned responses to external stimuli. At most, people would attribute their action to free will and rational decisions *ad hoc*, to explain why they had acted as they did. Like Vilfredo Pareto, Gérin and Espinadel saw this attribution as more of a self-deception than a truthful description of what had actually taken place: 'If you ask the consumer what, exactly, made him choose a particular store, it would be impossible for him to answer.'[22] While Gérin and Espinadel's theory of suggestion and J.B. Watson's American advertising psychology, which had set the stage in the US, shared a common mistrust of rationality as a motivating force for action, their subsequent arguments differed substantially. Where Watson would stress the necessity that the individual consumer experienced the product as somehow beneficial from his or her own subjective perspective, Gérin and Espinadel disregarded such individual subjectivity entirely. They believed that people's minds – apart from their more basic features, like the desire for nutrition, self-preservation and possession that resided in the 'atavistic self' (*moi atavique*) – were shaped by the social environment more than by their own individual experiences and biographies. People possessed a basic 'spirit of imitation' through which they tended to assume the characteristics of the mass in which they were momentarily absorbed.[23] This need not be an actual mass of bodies in public space, but could also be an imagined mass of fellow newspaper readers. Someone who, for example, read a scientific magazine, Cavalli argued in the virtual plagiarism of *La publicité suggestive* that made up his chapter on 'advertising theory' in *La spada d'America* (see chapter 3), even if not a scientist, assumed the characteristics thereof, and should hence be addressed as one.[24]

As in Le Bon's vision, media and public space thus turned individuals into a crowd, the characteristics of which they assumed. To quote Agostino Aurelio, an Italian advertising technician writing in 1920:

> All the individuals that happen to find themselves in those establishments [cafés, railway stations] will, as far as advertising is concerned, behave like components of a great mass on which a suggestive force had succeeded in reducing the activities of their individual minds to one single, united process.[25]

Indeed, Gérin and Espinadel claimed that people very seldom think for themselves, but are prone to accept blindly what they are presented with. (They based this claim on interviews with 'millions of people'.)[26] Human perception was guided by *bonne foi*, and critical reflection, when it occurred, resulted not so much from any intrinsic human quality as from being presented with conflicting external influences. This view was generally accepted. Giuseppe Jona had stressed this in his first articles on advertising psychology in 1914, and *La Pubblicità*, the official journal of the syndicate of advertising agencies, founded in 1925, kept repeating it in its recurrent articles on theory: 'Today we know that suggestion is the rule and rational reflection the exception.'[27] Consequently, advertising, if correctly executed, could make people abandon their individuality and take on new needs, desires and habits that had been conditioned from the outside. As pointed out in 1917 in *L'Idea*, the journal of the enthusiastic advertising pioneer Ernesto D'Angelo, advertising was about 'giving birth to your own ideas in other people's heads'.[28] Moreover, as a how-to article claimed ten years later, a repetitive message should enter the consumer's mind, 'like a thief in the night' and 'neutralize his brain'. It could 'make the name of a large manufacturer penetrate the brains of a million men'.[29]

Advertising was thus about presenting people with objects, or representations of objects, that they, by virtue of their *bonne foi*, would immediately desire. Apart from the caution not to advertise objects beyond people's financial means, such as luxury cars to workers, any object could in principle be made to be needed or wanted by anyone: through repetition, the suggestive effects of the advertising message would build up in the consumer's mind to create, in the end, a new want or need that he did not have before. As the journalist Arturo Lancelotti, who wrote one of Italy's first volumes on advertising – a combined history and 'how to' manual in 1912 – imagined the process:

> every morning when he opens the newspaper and every week when he dives into his illustrated magazine, every month when he looks into his monthly review, he sees the same order repeated: *Take a piece home with You tonight!* And one night, when he's in a hurry, without thinking of what he's doing, he enters the nearest shop and exclaims *Give me a piece of Sopersoap!* [*sic*] The order, repeated all around him, has fulfilled its secret task; it has given him the necessary psychological impulse and, goddamn it, you have got yourself a customer.[30]

The faith in the power of suggestion through repetition sometimes reached slightly unrealistic levels: posters, one article in *La Pubblicità* stressed, worked better in the countryside than in the cities, where the visual field was confused by too many contrasting influences. Workers in the fields, on the other hand, 'do not read newspapers' and would thus be directly 'suggestioned' by the isolated impact of the poster (thus ignoring that they probably had never seen the product advertised before, and did not have the money to buy it).[31]

Overall, the theory of suggestion thus enabled the Italian advertising technicians to claim that they could condition new wants, thoughts or habits, so to speak, from above, that they could shape and form consumers almost at will. This was much further than the American advertising professionals would ever go. In their conceptualization, advertising could, at the most, trigger mental processes – stimulate love, fear and rage – that in turn might give rise to a subjectively felt need or want. The route from stimulus to response, however, always passed through a stage of active, subjective reflection. For Italian advertising professionals, on the other hand, simply to present the product in a suggestive way was considered enough to trigger consumer demand. In part this approach was conditioned by a relatively poor and underdeveloped consumer market where any product, by the very fact that it was advertised, was helped by the intrinsic connotations of modernity that this conveyed. Such an assumption was certainly important in the campaign for the launch of FIAT's 'mass model', the 509 Balilla, in 1932. A caravan of cars drove around the Italian peninsula exhibiting the product as something of a fetish for modernity and progress. The same approach also seemed to have worked excellently in Luigi Dalmonte's early campaign for the Santa Vittora liquor: the very fact that the product was advertised in every major newspaper (while competitors' in general were not) meant that 'stocks were exhausted within days'.[32] This approach was, however, also determined by a particular notion of how advertising ought to be done: departing from the product and its characteristics, the task of advertising was to produce a consumer to fit. It aimed to educate the masses in new ways of using goods and, by implication, new ways of living the modern life.

The American influence

The somewhat simplistic assumptions about the psychology of consumers that stood behind the theory of suggestion worked well in legitimizing the advertising profession in the eyes of the regime. As we saw in last chapter, advertising professionals could now appeal to the suggestive power of advertising in putting their efforts at the service of the overall project of nationalizing the masses. During the 1930s such political uses of the theory of suggestion certainly continued, in particular in the more politically conscious medium of the advertising profession *La Pubblicità d'Italia*. In *L'Ufficio moderno* the belief in suggestion was, however, gradually eroded. In part this had to do with the consolidation of the advertising profession. A professional association was founded in 1924, and was recognized by the regime in 1928 as 'The National Fascist Syndicate of Advertising Agencies and Companies' (Sindacato nazionale Fascista agenzie e case di pubblicità). Italian advertising professionals participated in international conferences, and in 1933 Italy hosted the conference of the Continental Advertising Association, a propaganda spectacle of some importance with speeches by Mussolini and visits to the 'Exhibition of the Fascist Revolution' (Mostra della rivoluzione Fascista) that had opened the year before.[33] At the conference, the size of the Italian advertising profession was estimated as 802 'companies, agencies and offices', and its turnover as some 300 million lire, roughly the same size as in 1949.[34]

By the mid-1930s advertising had become a recognized profession. Courses in advertising were regularly taught at the Milan Polytechnic and at a number of professional schools. There was also a steady flow of new books on advertising: practical 'how to' manuals as well as theoretical treatises where advertising was scrutinized from the point of view of psychology or economic theory. There was simply less need for most advertising professionals to be 'politically correct', which could be left to the true believers. More importantly, however, the Italian advertising profession opened up to considerable foreign influence during the 1930s. *L'Ufficio moderno* published a number of articles and book chapters by American marketing and management theorists (as well as by some French authors, notably Paul Nicolas, who pioneered modern marketing in France). Some managers of American multinationals, like Palmolive, would also testify to their approach and experience. Judging from the first bibliography of advertising, *Mille opere sulla pubblicità* (*A Thousand Works on Advertising*), published in 1936, it also seems that the American and the German advertising literature was, by now, well known.[35]

The 1930s also saw the emergence of advertising agencies (with the notable exception of ACME Dalmonte, which had been founded in 1922). The advertising agency, where advertising technicians worked together with artists and designers according to a coordinated overall strategy, was an American invention. (The pre-existing advertising companies or 'houses' – *Case di pubblicità* – like Magagnoli's *Maga*, were more like artists' collectives.) Apart from J.Walter Thompson's short experience in Milan in 1927 and the Milan subsidiary of the New York agency Erwin Wasey & Co. that opened up in 1928 with the accounts of American multinationals – Palmolive, Ford, Frigidaire, Camel and Texaco – all the advertising agencies that opened up in Italy during the 1930s were started by people who had had some kind of working experience in the US. Luigi Dalmonte, who founded Italy's first agency, ACME Dalmonte, had worked for the then famous George Ethridge agency in New York. Pier Luigi Balzaretti (who together with Giulio Cesare Ricciardi founded *Balza-Ricc* in 1931) had been at the advertising office at Macy's in San Francisco, and Nino Caimi, who founded *Enneci* in 1931, had both lived in the US and managed *Erwa*, Erwin Wasey's branch in Milan, where Antonio Domenghini had also worked. Domenghini started the agency IMA (Idea Metodo Arte) in 1933 that took over Erwin Wasey's accounts for Coca-Cola and Gillette.

The advertising agencies formed the basis for the emergence of a 'second generation' of advertsing technicians, who were some 20 years younger than Grego and Lancelotti. Although socialized into the French model through studies of Gérin and Espinadel, their main inspiration was the American example.

In the US, as in Italy, advertising had found its main scientific ally in psychology. In that field as well, the J. Walter Thompson agency had been a chief protagonist. To mark the marriage of advertising to science, J.W. Thompson hired the famous behavioural psychologist John B. Watson in 1920. Experimental psychology had begun to establish itself as a scientific servant to business after having been put to use by the military during the First World War. Watson had earned his prominence through his proven ability to condition the reflexes of mice, guinea pigs and infants. To work on 'Mr and Mrs Consumer', he claimed in his introduction to a manual on the psychology of advertising, was not such a big step.[36] In contrast to Gérin and Espinadel, however, Watson insisted that advertising stimuli would not directly trigger responses but would rather be filtered through the mind of the consumer. Advertising could thus not directly steer consumer behaviour, but it could trigger strong and efficient reactions. The best way to do this, Watson argued, was to appeal to the 'emotional factor'. Indeed, 'it is the emotional factor in our lives that touches off and activates social behaviour'.

The strongest emotions, and hence those most efficiently appealed to in advertising, were furthermore purely personal ones like 'love, fear and rage'.[37]

Under the influence of Watson, JWT developed an advertising philosophy where goods were no longer, as in the hitherto dominant 'hard sell' approach, primarily sold as useful in relation to the practical needs inherent in some given social context. Rather, products were principally presented in relation to an often fearful, anxious and deeply emotional *self*, coping with the problems and threats of modern life. Another influential JWT employee Helen Resor (who was married to the agency's founder, Stanley Resor) developed this emphasis on the self and its fears into a new style of advertising. Her 'soft-sell' advertisements frequently stressed the ways in which products could help their users to achieve a successful 'presentation of self in everyday life', to use Erwin Goffman's term.[38] They underlined how goods could help avoid the social failures connected with presenting an undesirable self, whether this meant the unconscious emission of embarrassing body odours, unattractive skin, bad breath or stained clothing. They also emphasized how success in modern life, whether this meant finding and keeping love, or advancing one's career, was intimately connected to the ways in which one presented one's self, to sporting a film-star complexion, or a neat, clean shave.

As the soft-sell approach became dominant during the second half of the 1920s, American advertising began to use realistic imagery to present goods in everyday life situations.[39] It began to spread what Michael Schudson has successfully termed a 'capitalist realism'. The reality in which the products were inserted, the 'social tableaux', to use Roland Marchand's term, was furthermore centred around the intimate, private concerns of the self. Advertising came to constitute, to quote Marchand once again, 'a re-personalization of American life'.[40] As represented in American advertisements, consumers seemed primarily to be driven by their own, private concerns, fears and desires. American advertising invited them to use products, not only as functional solutions to socially recognized needs, but also, or even primarily, as tools for the solution of their private fears and anxieties, of which the risks connected with the 'presentation of self' were a key concern.

With this focus on the self, American advertising began to promote a specific kind of consumer culture, a specific notion of the relations between people and goods that prevailed, or should prevail, in modern society. American advertising – in the US as well as abroad – presented a general vision of modern life where the concerns of the self were central. There, the private self, its fears and desires, was not only the central principle for judging the utility of goods, but had become the very core concern of the modern existential condition. The lesson to be drawn from the American approach was then to appeal to the consumer's intimate concerns, to his or her 'self'. On a practical level this meant persuasion rather than 'suggestion'. Instead of trying to override or reshape the psychological make-up of the consumer, advertising was to present a message adapted to the consumer's particular life situation, a particular 'product benefit' as the American term went. To use a slightly more cynical Italian rendering, it was necessary to present the consumer with 'an illusion that he will accept because it lets him go on hoping'. Advertisements themselves could thus be both smart and plain, the important thing, an advertisement for the ERVA agency claimed, was that they contained a message that the consumer would accept. To do this, it was important to appeal to the right kinds of desires and aspirations, to show how the product would fit the consumer in everyday life: 'To observe the consumer in his own environment, go get to know the moral environment in which he lives.' In short, advertising had to start speaking about the consumer, rather than about the product: 'Why speak of us and our goods? The reader is most interested in himself.'[41] This new approach to advertising thus entailed a shift of focus from the product and its efficient representation in advertising, to the consumer and his or her wants, whims and desires.

One of the most ardent proponents of the importance to take consumers seriously was Roberto Pomé. Pomé had worked at the advertising department at Rinascente (together with Balzaretti, who, no doubt, shared his experiences from Macy's in San Francisco). In the 1930s he taught courses in advertising at the Milan Polytechnic, which were published in 1936 as *The Modern Conception of Advertising*.[42] By the mid-1930s he made it his task to argue against the older conception of consumers as a homogenous mass that could be freely shaped from above: 'those were many, who until very recently thought that the public of advertising could be compared to an immense herd of sheep that could be moved by crying out just about anything.' Indeed there was, and is a

> calm superficiality among advertising professionals (*pubblicitari*) when they consider the mentality of those at the receiving end of our stimuli. There is too much talk without looking those to whom one is talking in the face; one does not observe their reactions . . . Why not learn how to understand their preoccupations in order to find the arguments that will make them listen, that can distinguish you from many a competitor? Herd of sheep, indeed! The public judges and appreciates with its own proper interests in mind; it has opinions, needs and weaknesses which have to be understood before they are addressed.[43]

Suggestive advertising might give a first impulse, another influential advertising theorist Marco Helin maintained, but then 'the consumer makes his own calculations' and weighs in his appreciations of the costs and the benefits of the product.[44] This reorientation of advertising thought brought yet another important novelty. Like their American colleagues, Italian advertising professionals now began to take seriously the idea that goods had a social, communicative role. People use consumer goods, not only for the benefits these give, but also in order to define and communicate their own ideas about themselves – their own identities. Goods were valued not only for their use-value, but also for their sign-value, to use Baudrillard's distinction.[45] A large part of the 'suggestion' modern consumer goods exercised came, Helin argued, not so much from advertising, but from seeing others using the product. Buying decisions were thus often triggered by the desire to imitate others. It was thus important to stress the function of the product in the social life of consumers, how it could help them to imitate or distinguish themselves from others and acquire their appreciation. It was crucial, in this respect, that the product be endowed with a 'personality'. 'Don't try to sell clothes, but personal appearance', Natale Pluriventi repeated the lesson learned from the US (in this case through the book by Herbert Casson, published as a sequel in *L'Ufficio moderno* in 1935).[46] Adolfo Pellegrini, an experimental psychologist who published widely on advertising in the late 1930s, put it even more radically. He argued that brand names and labels primarily served to enable individual distinction. We use them in order to 'project our light, or our shadow on the world'.[47] Hence, the best strategy, at least for goods that had a direct connection to vanity, like cosmetics, was to provoke a sense of personal inferiority, to show that without the product, the self that the consumer 'gave off' would generally be considered inadequate. (A similar 'shaming approach' had been frequently used by Helen Resor in J.W. Thompson's cosmetics advertisements.)[48] Indeed, for many consumers, Luigi Dalmonte argued, this communicative, or 'ostentatious' function of goods made up their prime benefit: many people would buy things just to imitate someone else, whether a real person or, equally important, it seemed, someone they had seen in the films.[49]

In the 1930s there was thus a growing feeling that consumers were more sensitive to appeals that in some way related to their own interests and life situations, in particular the desire to appear and achieve social recognition. This new conception of advertising also sometimes collided with the emphasis on re-education from above and, above all, the appeal to moral and patriotic motives furthered by the regime and by 'its' agency, UPI. Already in 1931 Guido Mazzali, editor of *L'Ufficio moderno*, wrote a piece that severely criticized the campaign for Italian products launched by UPI for relying too heavily on 'moral' arguments. People are not primarily moved by noble and patriotic motives, by appealing to their public virtues, Mazzali argued, but by their own everyday concerns. Hence a successful campaign must show how Italian products can have a place in the everyday life of real people. It must point to the 'real value and satisfaction that results from their use'.[50] Advertising had to appeal to the consumer's subjective perspective. One had to put the product in the context of his 'small world' and point at the potential private benefits it could give rise to. One had to:

> imagine the reader in his own environment, understand the moral climate in which he lives, and never forget that whatever our character might be, for three-quarters of our day we think about our profession, our family, our interests and our own everyday situation.[51]

This notion of consumers as primarily guided by their own private concerns, their own sense of self, was also stressed by Adolfo Pellegrini. He argued that in advertising, the only thing that matters is the consumer's own lifeworld, what he called the 'I'.

> First there is the I, understood in its empirical sense as my body, my clothes, my family, my home, my radio, my car; the I is what is mine. Then there is the rest, which matters little or nothing. All that does not refer to the I will not be able to touch any sentimental strings in the consumer.[52]

The most influential pioneer of this American approach had been Luigi Dalmonte and his agency ACME.

ACME Dalmonte

After his return form the US and his spell at George Ethridge & Co., Luigi Dalmonte possessed a rare and valuable asset: hands-on experience from the American advertising world. The agency he founded, ACME, was modelled on what he had seen in the US. It was to remain successful all through the 1930s, organizing campaigns for, among others, the department store Rinascente, Cirio, an Italian multinational manufacturer of canned fruits and vegetables, Fernet Branca, Pirelli and the collective campaigns for beer and rice. Like the major American advertising agencies, ACME Dalmonte employed a division of labour that separated the conception of advertising campaigns from the actual artistic production of advertisements. The former was to be managed by an advertising technician who held the overall responsibility for the strategic coordination of media, advertisements and other measures, such as sponsored concerts or other cultural events. According to ACME's American-style advertising philosophy, the coherence of the campaign was the most important thing. Other aspects, such as the artistic qualities of individual ads, were to be subordinated to this overall goal.[53] The campaign should then be planned and executed around one central idea about the product and its potential user. While it was important that this idea remained in tune with the supposed qualities of the Italian national character, or the 'mentality of the race', the most important thing, according to Dalmonte's approach, was that it appealed to the private concerns of the consumer.[54] Thus, in 1933, the new safety razor Autostropp was advertised both as an object that suited a modern Italian mentality, and by means of 'shaming' or at least provoking a sense of inferiority in its potential users. Not to shave every morning was a clear sign of lacking in education and civility.[55] Sometimes a particular idea applied exclusively to a particular class of consumers (in the case of Autostropp it was obvious that 'different classes shave in different ways').

In the campaigns for the department store Rinascente, ACME Dalmonte aimed to expand the market to a wider range of middle-class consumers, in particular those who lived outside the big cities. To attract the provincial middle classes Dalmonte's campaign offered free trips to the nearest Rinascente store (the price of the ticket was to be discounted from purchases). The department store itself was then presented as something of a theme park of cosmopolitan modernity: with a modern restaurant and a bar serving cocktails. The idea was thus to sell shopping at the Rinascente, not only as a form of 'enjoyment and recreation', but also as a possibility actually to take part in the lifestyle of the urban elites. Dalmonte went even one step further, however. A central aspect of the campaign was the Rinascente shoppers' clubs that ACME encouraged provincial middle-class women to set up. Not only did these clubs offer discounts and special instalment schemes, they were also to organize social events and collective excursions to the nearest department store. Dalmonte's idea was to establish the Rinascente shopper's club as an integrated part of small-town social life. Thus, he hoped, membership and leadership of the club would serve to convey social standing, and the Rinascente brand would feed directly into the small-town economy of status and prestige.[56] Dalmonte thus emphasized the communicative value of goods or, in this case, services. To shop at Rinascente would work to communicate something about the shopper, to convey social status.

In addition to stressing this communicative function of goods, ACME Dalmonte began to differentiate the advertising message according to the presumed characteristics of the target group in mind. In addressing urban Rinascente shoppers, Dalmonte used Dudovich's manifestos to stress the urbane and modern air of the department store and to show how it supplies all the objects needed for a modern lifestyle (tennis rackets, beachwear and sports clothes). When addressing politically active women in *Donna Fascista* the message was once again different. Tapping into the popularity of home economics, ACME-Dalmonte now appealed to their qualities as rational shoppers and good administrators of the home. In *Critica Fascista* ACME would place ads that stressed the nationalist virtue of the department stores, how it contributed to the development of the national economy.[57] Sometimes the same idea could be used to address different consumer groups, but it had to be presented differently. Similarly with Cirio, Dalmonte's agency stressed how Cirio's products would save time in the household, breed healthy children, cure intestinal problems, help lose weight, facilitate cooking during holidays or in other ways lighten the burden of the middle-class housewife. An equally important strategy, however, was to stress the communicative function of the product: how housewives could acquire the envious admiration of their neighbours by using Cirio's canned peaches. (In *Critica Fascista*, Dalmonte would stress how the product would somehow remedy 'false female beauty ideals.')[58] The most important thing, Dalmonte stressed, was that the product be firmly placed in the lifeworld of the consumer – that the advertisements showed 'people who used the product' in realistic situations.[59]

In order to successfully inscribe the product within the everyday life of consumers, or at least an idealized rendering thereof, it was essential to get to

Figures 4.1, 4.2 Showing the product and its uses. ACME Dalmonte advertisements for Cirio from the 1930s. (Courtesy of the Biblioteca Nazionale, Florence.)

know consumers. Dalmonte warned that it was very dangerous just to assume complacently that one already knew who one was talking to and what to say.[60] The first step, then, was to get informed, to single out clearly what kinds of needs for the product potential consumers had or could possibly have, and what kinds of instincts to appeal to in order to move them. Only then could an efficient selling idea be elaborated. At Ethridge & Co., Dalmonte had no doubt had a market research department at his disposal to answer such questions. In Italy there was virtually no such thing. Although *L'Ufficio moderno* would run many articles on market research in the late 1930s, this was not a widespread practice in Italian advertising.[61] Adolfo Pellegrini had started empirical research on the reception of advertising at his laboratory in Turin, but this led to very little in terms of published results. Rather, Pellegrini would publish lists of consumer attributes. He claimed, for example, that modern women were more 'realistic' than those of previous generations; they were guided by 'intuition' and 'a practical sense of detail' – as opposed to male 'abstraction, logic and objectivity'. Youth were prone to change, ambitious and attracted by novelty. Above all, they were moved by appearances, while older consumers were more conservative. Rural consumers were suspicious, while urban ones were 'prone to try all that is new'. When not simply reflecting common stereotypes, these lists of categories usually came from the American literature.[62]

Dalmonte's alternative to inadequate market research was personal experience. In practice this meant looking at the media. Usually ACME Dalmonte, as well as other advertising agencies, would differentiate their messages according to the perceived characteristics of different media audiences. Using newspapers, for example, one would reach a male audience, and appeals to rationality, modernity or national character would be effective. Middle-class publications like *Domenica del corriere* were read by frugal housewives who fell for arguments on domestic economy. Such publications were not suited to advertising luxury products. Women's magazines like *Novella*, *Annabella* or *Eva* were read by younger women, and here, as in the film magazines, appeals to beauty and appearance worked well. Fashion magazines, finally, catered to a cultured, upper-class audience where style and distinction were important features.[63] With the establishment of advertising agencies that used a more empirically oriented American approach to advertising, the media system, and in particular the weekly magazines, thus began to become an important interface between advertising professionals and consumers. By looking at the media, advertising professionals could get an idea about consumers and how to appeal to them. Consumers on the other hand would get an education in modern forms of consumerhood, what goods one needed in order to be a modern person, and how to use these properly.

Conclusion

During the second half of the 1930s the Fascist regime began to tighten its grip on society through a series of policies, culminating in mobilization for the war effort. At the same time the advertising profession, or at least a substantial part of it, began to embrace a different approach to advertising and selling, building on an anthropological vision that was very different from that of the regime. Following their US colleagues, Italian advertising professionals acted as if consumers were primarily driven by their private needs and concerns. Relying increasingly on the media system as a guide to consumer mentalities, they began to target different consumer groups in different ways. In so doing they affirmed or even strengthened existing differences, rather than, as had been the regime's approach, trying to unify tastes and habits. They had also begun to think that one main motivation on the part of consumers was the wish to mark and signal such divisions and distinctions. Thus they encouraged the use of consumer goods as a medium for the communication of difference. This 'American' anthropology of consumption was virtually opposed to the assumptions on the nature of people and society that formed the basis of Fascist doctrine, and 'American methods' were still regarded with suspicion outside the circle of already converted advertising technicians. Consequently these would present their arguments coated in politically correct poisoning: seemingly contradictory appeals to the 'unity of the nation' or the 'nature of the race'. Underneath, however, a rather different social philosophy was developing, founded on the individual and his or her immanent everyday desires, rather than on the nation and its goals. As Luigi Dalmonte would write in *L'Ufficio moderno* in June 1943, shortly before the Allies landed in Sicily:

> Centuries go by, different philosophies bloom and then vanish, truths have their hour and then they are true no more, but the search for happiness will always go on . . . Not because happiness is an illusion, but because the ideals that drive this quest cannot stay quiet. The task of industry is to follow these ideals, and the task of advertising is to claim the attention of men, and to show them, in the best possible light, the treasures that industry thus produces. These treasures are within the reach of everybody: from the small bottle of perfume that in the midst of winter recalls the flowers of spring, to the toothbrush and the toothpaste, the precious soap, the boiler that gives you a healthy hot bath, warm and comfortable clothes, transparent silk stockings, solid and practical shoes, the radio gramophone, the vacuum-cleaner, the typewriter.[64]

Dalmonte's almost delirious visions of simple material happiness testifies perhaps to the harsh nature of the war years. All through the Fascist period Italy remained both comparatively poor and relatively underdeveloped with regard to the factors that underpin a modern consumer society: a prosperous middle class, a unified national market and a media system with a capillary-like diffusion. But at the same time, there was a rudimentary development of some of the key institutions that were to guide the growth of mass consumption in the post-war years: an advertising industry that had begun to treat people as consumers according to its own distinct anthropology, and a media system that was both expanding and discovering marketable differences between audiences.

Coda: Fascist comfort?

For the urban middle classes, Fascism and mass consumption developed in parallel. Many of the measures of the regime and its mass organizations were in fact conducive to the development of mass consumerism. The government-sponsored diffusion of radios served to further a market for popular music, *canzonette*, and for jazz music. Expanded middle-class sociality through OND-organized social events, excursions and public rituals provided a place where clothes, make-up and other consumer goods could function as a medium of individual distinction. Government-sponsored sporting events, like the bicycle race Giro d'Italia, which were originally conceived to be part of Fascist political spectacle, soon turned into commercial events. The 1934 Giro, for example, was accompanied by a caravan of promotional cars, advertising anything from spirit to 'coffee, sausages, wedding rings, berets, sports clothing, bananas, alarm watches, mineral water, chocolate, shoe polish, gas stoves, tapioca flour, yeast, cigarette papers' and so on.[65]

To what extent did Fascism and an expanding mass consumerism harbour competing value systems? Was it true, as has sometimes been suggested, that the commercial culture furthered by mass consumption prevented Fascism from penetrating the mentality of the middle classes?[66] Such a hypothesis of conflicting value systems was probably true to some extent in the case of urban youth, for whom advertised and branded consumer goods, together with their media representations, now formed the basis for a new generational culture, complete with its own lingo.[67] In particular for young women, it seems, the values promoted by this cosmopolitan consumer culture were in many respects antithetical to the expectations on them posed by the regime. Mariuccia Salvati cites an inquiry from 1938 among the 16- to 18-year-old women students of the Istituto di orientamento professionale del Governatorato, an elite school for future teachers in Rome, in which it appeared that very few of the respondents nurtured any desire to adopt the forms of womanhood promoted by the regime. The desire to form a family was 'vague or in any case without enthusiasm', very few wanted 'many children', and only 10 per cent expressed any interest in domestic work. Instead, their main interests were make-up and the Cinema. They also valued personal independence and a proper job much more than any 'anti-hedonist self-sacrifice'.[68]

For the middle classes in general, however, things were probably not that neatly separated. Widely consumed domestic replacements for imported or otherwise scarce goods like textiles or petrol, or the 'nationalist' substitution of rice for pasta, and beer for wine, had clear political connotations. The consumption and use of these goods no doubt made up a kind of private political ritual, confirming one's modernity as well as one's alliance with the Fascist project overall. Similarly, the increased availability of modern consumer goods, most prominently such relatively inexpensive items for domestic consumption as canned foods and bouillon cubes, and organized leisure activities like OND's popular trains and summer camps, probably played its part in guaranteeing middle-class consensus for the regime. But if mass consumption worked to generate consensus, this probably worked in ways different from those indicated by the regime. Rather than fulfilling pronouncements of a Fascist, anti-privatist consumer ethic, the very private comfort that such goods could enable became a foundation for support for the regime.

This is particularly clear if we look at advertising campaigns from the 1930s onwards. The most prevalent approach in addressing a mass market in collective campaigns was to appeal to the everyday desires and fears of common people. To show how Italian rice could be transformed into a nourishing and delicious dish, how beer would aid digestion, how milk would keep children strong and healthy, how sugar would give that extra energy and how silk would dress comfortably and elegantly. How, indeed, Italian 'autarchic' goods would contribute to realize middle-class ideals of what Berthold Brecht once called the 'comfortable life', modest and profoundly apolitical, oriented

Figure 4.3 Fascist comfort. Erwa's advertisement for the petrol replacement Littoria shows how modernity can be enjoyed securely.

towards the privatist aspirations of domestic life and away from most preoccupations with national grandeur. The advertising campaign for the Italian petrol replacement Littoria in 1935 relied exclusively on arguments of personal benefit. The campaign for Somalian bananas emphasized how the product would enhance the experience of intimacy between mother and child. If there was anything distinctive to Fascist advertising in the 1930s it was its stress on the link between private comfort and national strength: contrary to official propaganda with its 'campaigns against comfort' and its appeals to 'live dangerously', the prevailing trope can be aptly termed 'Fascist comfort'. Such Fascist comfort recognized no contradiction between the traditional privatist aspirations of the middle class and the organic strength of the nation. Italian fish was both part of 'Italy's treasures' and a convenient way for the housewife of varying the family diet; Italian wines were both a national pride and an excellent substitute for foreign beverages when enacting the same petit bourgeois ritual of afternoon visits.[69]

Fascist consumer culture did not build on a substitution of privatist aspirations for something else as much as on their mobilization. The construction of a middle-class consensus through consumption proceeded through showing, as strategic advice for many advertising campaigns had emphasized, that the development of the national economy was liable to lead to increasing standards of living and make life in general more comfortable. In this respect mass consumption under Fascism probably worked in a way that differed little from Habermas's classic model, developed with post-war liberal democratic societies in mind. It fostered an apolitical orientation to the concerns of private life that was, despite rhetoric to the contrary, one of the foundations for a middle-class consensus.

Part II

The roots of postmodernity

5 The economic miracle

Mass consumption and modernization

In a 1957 advertisement for the detergent OMO, the J. Walter Thompson company pointed at the perilous consequences of not-white-enough laundry. The photo shows two housewives comparing the results of their labour. The ambience is friendly, if competitive, but one of the housewives finds her situation awkward. Her neighbour's washing is distinctly whiter! 'Don't let it happen to you!' is the concluding sales pitch. The advertisement is similar to most featured in the many well-funded detergent campaigns that began to appear in the Italian illustrated press and, in particular, in the women's magazines in the mid-1950s. Most were organized by the big American advertising agency JWT, which was to dominate the Italian advertising scene during the 1950s.[1] JWT, which ran the campaigns for Unilever's competing brands OMO and Sunil, used the same argument all through: both detergents washed whiter. Whiter-than-white laundry was presented as a sign of progress; it was something that had been made possible by a technological development that sought first and foremost to satisfy the needs of ordinary people. The whiter the laundry, the more modern and evolved the housewife. After all, as OMO claimed, 'Today white laundry is no longer enough.'

But there was more to it than this classic theme in 1950s advertising. To compare laundry was also to compare the skills and qualities of the housewife. Not-white-enough laundry was a clear sign of inadequacy in this field and a source of shame; indeed, *Don't let it happen to you!* Ignorance was no excuse. Modern consumer goods were easy enough to use. (And Unilever had their own 'expert in laundry', Emma Rosati, whom housewives could call or write to for advice on the matter.)[2] Rather, not-white-enough-laundry was something of a sign of moral failure. Conversely, getting the laundry whiter allows you to 'improve yourself every day', as Sunil's Foucaultian copy put it. The woman whose laundry is not white enough does not make the most of her resources. She does not produce what is required of her: the best possible representation of the social standing of her family, as staged in the medium of consumer goods. The women who featured in these detergent ads, furthermore, represented a new kind of housewife. Thin, blonde, fashionably dressed, modern, yet modest, they were markedly different from both the ideal of the *massaia* (housewife) promoted by the Fascist regime before the war, and from the teenage-oriented 'Hollywood beauty' who now appeared in the magazines aimed at a younger audience.[3] They looked distinctly American, or at least that was how they appeared to contemporary Italian observers.[4] And understandably so: Unilever's detergent campaigns were run worldwide. They featured the same kinds of arguments and, with some exceptions, the same models in Europe as in the US (as well as in several African and South-East Asian countries).[5] They built on the years of knowledge and experience that had accumulated around the 'American Housewife'. And they tended to reiterate the same kind of motivational pattern that had developed around 'her' (or 'it': the 'American Housewife' is of course a concept, not a human being).

A JWT internal memorandum clearly stated that the almost exclusive area of interest for the housewife was the family. 'Whatever outside interests' she has, apart from her 'role as wife, mother, and home-maker', 'are either extensions of these (such as PTA work), or are strictly secondary to them'. In addition, her main function within the family was to consume. This in order to reproduce the labour power of her husband, but more importantly, to mark off the social standing of the family through her good taste or general skill in handling consumer goods (such as, for example, employing the right detergent). The main labour of the American housewife was symbolic. She arranged the objects that placed the family along the common scale of status; she kept up with the Joneses; she implemented the mysterious 'demonstration effect' that Duesenberry found to be driving the whole US economy. She was an integrated part of her family unit, without which she was nothing.[6]

JWT saw detergents as an opening to the Italian market. This not only in economic terms, but also in a cultural sense. Detergents, cheap, practical and easy to use, could potentially teach Italian women about the benefits of modern American goods. To sell and advertise them was thus a way to overcome the 'resistance' to modern consumer goods that many advertising professionals had found in the Italian market (see chapter 6). It would help to spread the ethic and motivations of American consumer culture. In this way detergent advertising together with other advertising investments from American multinationals were part of the overall Americanization of European institutions of consumption that occurred all around the world in the post-war years.[7] In Italy this American-style consumer culture spread through the dominance that large American agencies exercised over the advertising, and consequently also the media, market. It was to play an important role in guiding Italians through the massive transitions the country went through during the 1950s. As per capita incomes grew, together with internal migration flows, consumer culture became a new referent for notions of modernity for the majority of Italians. Indeed, consumer culture now became the first nationally common reference system, its symbols familiar and recognizable from Milan to the Basilicata. If, however, the country went though a process of 'Americanization of the Everyday', to use Stephen Gundle's term, this proceeded rather differently from what was the case in the more prosperous countries of northern Europe.[8] Italy still remained comparatively poor, in particular in the south, and if modern consumer goods were now visibe to all, they were hardly affordable to all. Thus the first main effect of the spread of consumer culture was what sociologists Guido Baglioni and Francesco Alberoni called 'anticipatory socialization' (borrowing the term from Merton). This chapter will describe the new American-style consumer culture with its distinct ethic of consumption, as it was fleshed out mainly in

Figure 5.1 Laundry can never get white enough. J. Walter Thompson's transnational campaign as adapted to the Italian market (featured in *Gioia*, 27 November 1958). (Courtesy of the Biblioteca Nazionale, Florence.)

the women's magazines, together with its larger social effects. It will show how consumer culture became a hegemonic referent for discourses on modernization in general, something the mass parties also had to come to terms with.

The American consumer ethic

During the 1950s Italy was rebuilding (in a literal sense: housing was scarce after the war and, together with exports, the building industry was a main engine of growth). Annual increase in GDP averaged around 6 per cent all through the decade, to accelerate further during the 'economic miracle' of 1958–62. This meant that GDP just about doubled between 1951 and 1963 (and GDP per capita grew by 86 per cent). While little of this actually trickled down in the form of higher wages, it was still an impressive result. Even more impressive, however, was the growth of the advertising industry. Its turnover grew by 150 per cent between 1949 and 1958 (and advertising continued to sustain a 60 per cent increase between 1958 and 1969). As part of total consumer expenditure, advertising costs more than doubled, reaching circa 0.7 per cent in 1962.[9]

Much of this expansion can be interpreted as Italian advertising catching up from its comparatively underdeveloped state in the inter-war years. With this catching up there was also a significant restructuring of the industry. While the Italian tradition of advertising art was by no means dead (and would live on throughout the 1980s, as the example of Armando Testa shows) the stage was now set by large international agencies like JWT and later Lintas, CPV and McCann-Erickson. They all employed the 'American method' as pioneered and preached by JWT. That agency self-consciously saw itself as something of a 'university of advertising' during the 1950s. With its responsibility for advertising the various initiatives of the Marshall Aid, there was also an implicit imperative that JWT act as something of an advertising ambassador, spreading the American philosophy of advertising and marketing in countries undergoing reconstruction.[10]

The American approach to advertising built on two fundamental pillars: realistic advertisements that showed the product and its intended users in real-life situations (or at least what was represented as real life in the idealized rhetoric of advertising), and the use of the illustrated weekly press as its main medium, rather than advertising posters, if nothing else, for pedagogical reasons. According to advertising professionals, the weekly Press and, in particular, the women's magazines would serve as a kind of schooling in modernity. There women would observe and read about modern consumer goods. Moreover, the women's magazines would illustrate not only how to use such objects, but also how to relate to them in a proper way, how to *be* a modern housewife. Pedagogically they would present modern consumer goods as part of a new gendered ideal.[11] As Adriano Pasqualini, a frequent contributor to *L'Ufficio moderno*, wrote apropos women's magazines in 1957:

> and in the American-style advertisements we find the housewife, beautiful and good-hearted *(brava e bella)*, who dominates the scene in the weekly magazines. And all the housewives (*massaie*) young and old, recognize themselves in her and absorb the advertising message. Often she becomes their friend and advisor: someone who has eliminated their long hours of daily fatigue: someone whom they have to thank for their refrigerators, their domestic appliances and for all the canned and packaged products that help them to save time and money.[12]

Consequently, much of the increased advertising revenue went to the weekly press. (Printed advertising in general was estimated to attract some 70 per cent of all advertising revenue in 1951.)[13] This resulted in a significant expansion of the weekly press in general, and of the women's magazines in particular. To the 10 or so titles that had emerged in the 1930s, 22 more were added between 1944 and 1963.[14] The amount of advertising in the women's magazines also increased drastically. *Grazia*, for example, which had accommodated some 15 quarter-page or larger ads per issue in 1948, averaged around 30 ads per issue in 1954. *Annabella* saw a similar development, from slightly fewer than 10 ads per issue (as in *Lei* in the pre-war period), 3 or 4 during the war, to around 30 in the mid-1950s. As the number of ads increased, so did the number of pages, and the magazines became glossier. There was also an increase in editorial advertising and an even greater attention to the everyday aspects of consumption, particularly through advice columns that dealt with the proper use of domestic appliances, cooking schools and etiquette columns. The women's magazines now made up what advertising professional Guido Benelli defined in 1951 as an 'organic unit' of advertising and editorial material, 'to the point that it is practically impossible to point out where the two diverge and develop independently'.[15]

This expansion also led to tighter institutional couplings between advertising and the publishing industry. Publishers now became increasingly interested in quantifying and commodifying their readership, transforming it into audiences that could be successfully sold to advertisers. A first step in this direction was to yield to the demands for increased control of circulation and readership. These demands began to be put forth by advertising clients, recently united in the Association of Advertising Buyers (Utenti pubblicitari associati, UPA, founded in 1949), who wanted clear guidelines as to the value of different kinds of advertising space.[16] To meet such demands, publishing companies began to employ the American techniques for audience research that had now become available, mostly through newly founded opinion-polling companies, like Doxa.[17] With such 'data' at hand, they would proceed to advertise the size and socio-economic composition of their readership. The result was, however, not that publishers came to present a more adequate picture of actual readership. Rather, they tended to use such data to present their magazines as representative of the kinds of readers they thought advertisers would like to pay for.

The first result of this was that audiences were standardized. As advertised, they tended to fall into two categories that mirrored the notions of market segmentation held by the advertising agencies. The minor segment was that of young women. Some magazines, like the 'glamour' publications *Bolero* and *Confidenze*, or the romantic 'comics' (*fumetti*) like *Grand Hotel*, would thus present their audiences as made up of teenage girls and suggest that these publications were a good way to reach the youth market.[18] Given the growing market for household consumer goods, and the common-sense assumption that women controlled the buying decisions for such goods (or, for everything except 'tobacco and drinks in bars') most publishing companies would use their new data to argue that their publications were in fact read by housewives.[19] Thus Mondadori's *Grazia*, which had been directed at a rather diffuse target of both teenage girls and more solid middle-class housewives in the 1930s, was now repositioned as a magazine exclusively tailored to housewives. In their advertising, Mondadori claimed that readership surveys had clearly shown that the publication was read mainly by 'women who care for the home' and who manage domestic budgets. While the result of the survey presented *Grazia's* readership as composed of roughly equal proportions of married and unmarried women (56.37 per cent and 43.63 per cent respectively), only the former category was presented as representative of the readership as a whole. Mondadori's ambition in doing audience research was thus not so much to give an objective rendering of the actual readership, as to provide solid evidence that *Grazia* was, in fact, a publication read by middle-class housewives, and hence an 'excellent medium for goods directed at domestic consumption'.[20]

Publications like *Grazia* also began to change their editorial content. They increased their focus on consumption and modern consumer goods; the number of 'aditorials', or paid-for articles and editorials material, increased and these magazines became more 'American' in their visual make-up as well as in their focus. Their articles covered American middle-class life; their advice for home building and decoration began replicating American design and architecture and, most importantly, the female ideal they proposed began to mirror that of the American housewife. *Grazia*'s reader now emerged as a woman whose prime interest in life was consumption and social mobility or, more precisely, who would use consumer goods primarily to stage the social standing of her family unit.

This new way of framing the uses of consumer goods differed strongly from that which had been dominant in the 1930s. Then, most women's magazines emphasized the comfort that consumer goods could bring, how they would serve to make private, domestic life more enjoyable. The ostentatious functions of goods, their capacity to communicate status to engage in competition with one's neighbour, on the other hand, were generally downplayed (although they would sometimes be stressed in advertisements), if nothing else by the regime's emphasis on the disruptive effects of such bourgeois 'individualistic' consumer practices. Even the American-style magazines directed at younger women who flirted with Flapper-style practices of flamboyant self-presentation paralleled this with a strongly moralistic 'ethic of renunciation', which stressed how such individualistic forms of self-presentation should be restricted to the level of fantasy and not be put into practice.[21]

In the 1950s, however, women's magazines like *Grazia* and *Annabella* and cooking magazines like *Cucina italiana* put the link between status and consumption at the very heart of their discourse. This was paralleled by a significant weakening of the public function that the housewife had acquired during Fascism. While the Fascist *massaia* had been encouraged to put her 'labour of love' in the service of the nation as a whole, the concerns of the American-style housewife were strictly confined to the domestic sphere. Her concern for the well-being and advancement of her family was not linked to any engagement with the fate of some larger social unit. The family was not so much a 'moral fortress of the nation' as a privatized unit of consumption and reproduction, driven predominately by the overall goal of social mobility.

This gave rise to a different kind of rationalization of the domestic labour of the housewife. She was frequently referred to as 'a professional', indeed, as a member of 'the perhaps most difficult profession'.[22] Her task was to produce the love that keeps the family together. In the women's magazines, like *Grazia*, directed at middle-class housewives, the pre-war romantic ideal of love as the sudden realization of a metaphysical unity, as the unfolding of a pre-given destiny, was now replaced by a more pragmatic approach[23] (although romantic love remained the main theme of publications directed at younger or working-class women). Rather, love represented the emotional side of the family economy. It would grow out of a common existence, characterized by a common quest (to get along) and the exchange of utilities. As a lonely-hearts column in *Grazia* comforted a desolated girl in 1951, 'Even if you don't love your fiancé now, you will surely begin to do so when you take your place at his side.'[24] Indeed, love came out of hard, purposeful household work, guided by an ethic that stressed the postponement of gratification. Time was money, laziness was comparable to 'burning a bunch of 1,000 lire bills' and the lazy woman who 'puts off until tomorrow what she can do today', or even 'keeps her pyjamas on all day long', 'lacks a spirit of competition' and was not fit to manage the upwardly mobile family of the 1950s. Rather, such behaviour made her a 'parasite' that ideally should be got rid of.[25] In view of the availability of new time-saving consumer goods, and housewives' increasing isolation in the home, resisting temptations to idleness and instead engaging in ceaseless activity was even more crucial, not only in order to achieve love and recognition from the husband, but also to make him 'work better' As *Cucina italiana* advised young wives in 1955:

> In the morning (if you don't have a maid) dress appropriately as you hurry up with your household tasks. Don't walk around in your nightgown until noon. And don't lie around in bed until late, but get up early.

> You have no idea how much can be accomplished in the first hours of the morning. So make it a habit to get up at least half an hour before your husband and make him find you in perfect order, fresh and proper. As he goes to the bathroom, prepare his breakfast. If he has the bad habit of just drinking a quick cup of coffee, make him get used to a proper meal (it won't be difficult if you put your mind to it). That way he'll be in good spirits until lunch and he'll work much better.[26]

The love produced by the housewife through her caring work served the immediate purpose of enhancing her husband's productivity. By elaborating on themes like household work within a markedly utilitarian logic the women's magazines presented an ideal version of everyday life deeply marked by commodified economic exchange. Her labour of love served to enhance his productivity and, consequently, maximize the common financial space available for family consumption. With this privatization of the role of the housewife, consumption and consumer goods acquired an unprecedented presence on the pages of the women's magazines, and the ways in which they would transform family life were often stressed: either in terms of their potential for rationalization and variation – like the simplified cooking routines and varied diets that new objects, like household machinery, frozen foods and dry soups brought with them – or in terms of the radically new experiences they would enable. Assisted by modern consumer goods, one could now develop a hobby, plan and decorate a (although modest) second house – something that, according to *Grazia*, would shortly be within the reach of the ordinary family – or, equipped with a car, or at least a scooter, some cheap camping gear and a collection of pre-prepared and canned foods that simplified cooking, embark on a weekend hike into the countryside, or even a longer seaside holiday.[27]

The most desirable thing about such modern consumer goods, often represented as 'American', was not so much their capacity for increasing the consumer's comfort, as was stressed in the 1930s, nor even the hedonist enjoyment that they could enable, but their ability to mark and communicate the sensation that life was becoming fuller, that an expanding range of articles had brought new pleasures and experiences within the range of the average person. This expansion of the range of choice also meant that the home was now a permanent exhibition of the family's latest achievements. As it would inevitably reflect the status of the family, its importance lay not only in its comforts but also in its looks. The task of the housewife was therefore to use her taste and good judgement to make the most of limited resources. As an article on home decoration from *Grazia* of 1948 underlined, the home would inevitably reveal the moral character of the housewife:

> Did you ever ask yourself if and how your house mirrors your taste, your goals, your personality, in one word, yourself? The house is not only there to meet needs that come from our physical existence, but it should also be an expression of our own intimate world. In the house, past and future,

> tastes and aspirations, character and feeling, should fuse together in a harmonic whole that expresses our own will.

Complacent consumption, just buying a ready-assembled set of furniture without adding something of one's own, was not an act of non-communication but stands out as a symbol of sinful negligence:

> It seems incredible but there are a lot of people who don't think of their homes at all. They buy a ready-made furniture set in Cantù and just put it in their living room. But this also testifies to a certain character. You can rest assured that the inhabitants of that house dress just to keep warm, that they eat anything just to fill their stomachs and that they never think of rearranging their furniture.

A well-managed domestic surface, on the other hand, testifies to moral character: 'here, instead, we find a home that has character. The housewife probably wears a nice apron with frills, she always has clean hands and is a good cook. The plants flower and grow.'[28]

Consumer goods, like detergents, cosmetics and beauty products, which effected the visible self-presentation of the woman and her family unit, were also marketed as objects that served not so much to stage the individual identity of the woman consumer as to stage her moral capacity as part of a functional system – as a housewife – as well as the social standing of that subsystem itself. They were not so much tools for her own individual self-presentation, but were to be used in the interest of the family enterprise. Her taste and skill in selecting and combining them were to be put at its service. Consumerist self-expression no longer occupied a marginal place within a largely traditional family model, but had become the very basis of the modern, American-style nuclear family for which consumer goods had become the main medium for the communication of social standing. To a certain extent the dangerous female individuality that consumer goods were feared to enable in the 1930s had by now been neutralized, not by its repression, but by the virtually complete integration of the woman consumer into the family unit. Not even when moving in public space, as many cosmetics ads would stress, was the woman consumer an individual. Rather, her main concern was respectability: not to stand out and expose herself, but to conform and protect herself. The family was in turn presented not as the moral or emotional foundation of the national collectivity, but rather as an isolated economic unit, geared to social achievement and its staging by means of consumer goods. (Ironically, the 'amoral familism' that American anthropologist Edward Banfield lamented as a symptom of southern Italian underdevelopment at about the same time was precisely what stood at heart of the American-style consumer culture featured in the weekly press.)[29] The family was a private unit of enjoyment and achievement that had been virtually delinked from public concerns.

Figure 5.2 FIAT refrigeration. The meaning of a new kitchen (featured in *Cucina italiana*, August 1956.) (Courtesy of the Biblioteca Nazionale, Florence.)

As the closer links developed between the advertising industry and the weekly press, a new classificatory grid for organizing mass consumption thus emerged. In the case of the largest, middle-class segment, closer links with the advertising industry had made publishers stress an American-style connection between consumption and social mobility. In the women's magazines goods were no longer, as in the 1930s used primarily for purposes of comfort or enjoyment. Rather, they functioned as symbols to mark the social achievement of an isolated nuclear family. Their main use value was their capacity to communicate and signify.

Consumption and social change

What, then, were the overall effects of the new communicative ethic of consumption that the women's magazines now spread? These magazines themselves, for one thing, were fairly widely read. Their overall readership matched that of newspapers. Gioacchino Forte, in his 1966 study of women's magazines *I persuasori rosa* (*The Pink Persuaders*), even estimated a combined circulation of 7 million, which exceeds by far the contemporary combined circulation of newspapers: 5.3 million in 1962. The circulation of women's magazines was also more evenly spread between the north and the south than that of newspapers (where differences were substantial). And even though readership was predominantly female, cursory evidence shows that among particular groups, like southern migrants in the northern cities, men read womens magazines as well.[30] Overall, sociological investigations of migrants and rural communities, investigations of the conditions of the working classes published in the Communist party journal *Rinascita*, and investigative journalism in general mention a widespread readership of women's magazines.[31] Widely acclaimed books like journalist Gabriella Parca's *Le italiane si confessano* (*Italian Women Confess*) from 1959 also directed attention to the phenomenon. Parca pointed at the function women's magazines fulfilled in providing new and modern moral guidelines. It was to these magazines that Italian women turned in order to find directions on how to live the modern life.[32]

This function of the women's magazines as a kind of school in modernity was also underlined by the first qualitative audience research carried out in the early 1960s. According to a series of interviews conducted by the research company Misura among the women readers of *Gioia* in 1963, it appeared that they saw *Gioia* as a medium that 'taught (*insegna*) them to become women'. They would be most interested in editorial material and advertisements that 'teach (*insegnano*) how to dress and behave'. Given that most of *Gioia*'s readers were married women in their mid-twenties to thirties, and hence, by all applicable standards, already women, what the publication taught was not so much how to become women in general, but how to behave as modern women. According to Misura's research report (also used as a marketing tool in relation to potential advertisers), the 'completely female world' *Gioia* represented was marked by a more modern, more emancipated and more balanced 'moral vision' and a more progressive view of family life. *Gioia* proposed a 'modern moralism, without exaggerations'; it offered 'a moral vision for the emancipated modern world'.[33] The view of the medium as a vehicle of modernization and of separation, or at least a distancing from a pre-existing tradition, was also stressed by Misura's 1962 study of the readers of the popular Catholic weekly *Famiglia cristiana*. This journal, Misura's report argued, would offer 'a way of expressing, within the limits of catholic orthodoxy, a clear emancipation from parents and family'. Again this process of modernization was chiefly mediated by consumer goods that, while marked by a 'certain modernity and capriciousness', still did not threaten the 'very sensitive moralistic defence mechanisms' of the readers.[34] In short, women's magazines were perceived to supply a blueprint for how to live as a modern woman, differently from what traditional models of femininity prescribed, and to point at consumer goods as both the most important and the most socially acceptable medium for enacting such a modernization. In this way the women's magazines were part of the general 'mediazation' of Italian public culture that took place during the 1950s, a process that, in historian Guido Crainz's words, now made markets and media into 'powerful actors in the construction of identities'.[35]

The prospects for enacting the kind of modernization-through-consumption that the women's magazines proposed did, however, vary greatly. For some groups modern consumer goods became a source of a new identity to be lived out on an everyday basis. Alessandro Pizzorno's study of upwardly mobile workers and artisans in a small town in the prosperous hinterland of Milan shows that the penetration of new consumer goods and new ways of relating to them caused a profound transformation of everyday social relations. As soon as they could afford to, the inhabitants of the community under study would build a house of their own. (Many got over their heads in debt to do so. Pizzorno mentions one family that had renounced feeding their children meat in order to undertake the investment).[36] In traditional peasant culture, Pizzorno argues, to build a house was an acceptable way to channel prosperity, while more conspicuous forms of consumption like cars or fancy clothes were not. But the new houses introduced a series of changes in the everyday lives of the inhabitants of the community. Modelled and decorated according to the American houses presented by the women's magazines, they contained a series of new amenities such as a television room, a living room and an 'American kitchen'. These rooms were furnished in the latest modern style, but in many instances were never actually used. The new house, Pizzorno argues, was not built to be lived in as much as to be shown off. It was first and foremost a sign of prestige. Furthermore, the new houses were located outside the traditional residential areas. Moving there thus meant isolating the family from the traditional (if often litigious) communal life of the neigbourhood. Instead, social interaction became more formalized, channelled through visits and invitations, and increasingly geared to showing off the house, the furniture and the general accumulation of modern consumer goods. After a first general invitation to the old neighbours to inspect the new house, 'no one enters the house again, except on special occasions', as Pizzorno rather drastically put it.[37] In the case of the community under study it seemed clear that the penetration of modern consumer goods had been accompanied by a substitution of a more isolated nuclear family form for the traditional neighbourly networks.

Another case where it was clear that modern consumer goods were giving rise to tangible transformations was the case of youth. In the big cities and in the more prosperous pockets of the northern countryside, consumer goods now made young people behave and dress in new and different ways. New consumer goods like scooters, records, jukeboxes, leather jackets and blue jeans effectively served as the basis for a new youth culture with a set of motivations and aspirations that differed radically from those of their parents.[38] Some, although by no means all, young people embraced this new youth culture and enacted its new identities. In the countryside scooters seemed to be particularly conducive to altering the social fabric. They would enable young people to travel to dances and social events in other villages or even out in the fields where social relations could develop in a less controlled and supervised way. This led to the formation of an unsupervised sociality among young people, which gave rise to a distinct youth culture that, as Pizzorno showed in his study, differed substantially from the traditional ways of parents and that caused a widening gap between the generations.[39]

These new youthful patterns of consumption were generally received as a threatening challenge to the established values of society. The emergence of leather-clad working-class youth in Milan, for example, sparked a sustained moral panic about 'Teddy boys' that lasted between 1957 and 1962. (The term 'Teddy boys' was inadequate, however. Italian working-class youth dressed like Marlon Brando and his consorts in *The Wild One*, and not in Edwardian ('Teddy') fashions. The choice of the term was rather triggered by the preceding British moral panic.) Crimes committed by Italian Teddy boys were read as instances of a new generalized criminal orientation among young people. This new youthful criminality, or *teppismo*, was mainly directed at petty theft and public brawling. It appeared to be different from previous forms of criminality: it was not motivated by poverty (*miseria*) but rather by wealth (*benessere*), or rather by the diabolic attraction that new consumer goods and new practices of consumption would exercise on young people. In a Doxa opinion poll from the early 1960s on attitudes to the 'increasing juvenile delinquency', the most probable causes selected were too much freedom, too lax parental authority, the bad influence of movies, 'bad readings' (*cattive letture*, meaning, probably, the comic strips that were expanding rapidly in the 1950s), and excessive leisure time. Overall attitudes towards the younger generation in general were negative: they lacked respect and a work ethic; they were lazy and hedonist; they did not have the necessary spirit of sacrifice and responsibility. Of the respondents to one poll, 60 per cent argued that the state had to intervene. Judging from public opinion at the time, what the state should do ranged from imposing more severe censorship of films through mildly paternalistic proposals for the formation of youth organizations that could reintegrate and re-educate, to demands for public corporal punishments, medieval style.[40]

To many observers, journalists, sociologists and intellectuals it thus appeared that mass consumption was causing a profound reorganization of the social fabric, substituting status competition for community ties, subcultures for paternal authority and individualization of social solidarity. While this was true for some groups, the overall situation was more complex. Actual research shows that most young people were well integrated. They had more or less internalized the privatist, status-oriented kind of consumer ethic featured in the women's magazines. Guido Baglioni's survey of northern Italian youth from 1962 showed that most of them had 'rather modest aspirations'. Generally they did not challenge the constituted order; indeed, they were profoundly uninterested in politics – most wanted a good job and a family. They craved consumer goods, such as clothes and, most importantly a car, for the social status these objects would convey, not for their potentially challenging or 'counter-cultural' sign values. A couple of years later, Baglioni's fellow sociologist Achille Ardigò would call them the 'Generation of the 3 Ms': *Mestiere, Moglie e Macchina* – or 'a job, a wife and a car'.[41] While modern consumer goods and the modern status-oriented consumer culture that came with them probably made its mark on some groups – upwardly mobile pockets in the north and young people with money to spend – the overall picture was more varied. In the picture of the 'miracle' that emerged from academic and journalistic representations, however, youth came to symbolize the radical transformations induced by a rapidly expanding consumer culture.

Anticipatory socialization

The economic situation in the early 1950s was fairly desperate overall. A parliamentary inquiry from 1951 revealed endemic unemployment, malnutrition and a lack of housing. Overall standards of living were worse than in the by no means prosperous 1930s, and most working-class families lived on close to subsistence levels.[42] Although things progressed over the decade, only 31 per cent of the respondents to a Doxa survey of 1955 declared that they thought their standard of living had improved since 1938 (26 per cent thought that they were worse off).[43] While the war was certainly to blame for the misery of the 1940s, the fact that the situation lingered on through much of the following decade was contingent on a series of political choices. Under minister of finance Luigi Einaudi, the Christian Democrats pursued a deflationary fiscal policy and used the funds resulting from the Marshall Aid to stabilize the currency (much to the annoyance of the Americans who, fearing that unemployment and generalized social unrest might increase the popularity of the Communists, pushed for increases in public spending). The sacking of older, experienced and politically militant workers, combined with widespread unemployment, kept wages down and further enabled Italian big capital to engage in price competition on export markets. Even when more substantial infrastructural investment was injected during the first years of the 1950s, to meet the pressing needs for transport infrastructure and housing, little of the spoils of the sustained economic growth of that decade reached the pockets of ordinary Italians. While exports had increased by 139 per cent between 1951 and 1958, and investments by 78 per cent, private consumption only grew by one-third with respect to the precarious situation of 1951.[44] Not until the last years of the 'economic miracle', the real take-off in growth that occurred between 1957 and 1962, did the average yearly 6.5 per cent increase in GDP begin to trickle down in the form of improved standards of living. By 1962 the previously readily available supply of cheap labour had been used up, so business had to make wage increases (8 per cent) that exceeded productivity gains. As a result, the following years saw the growth of a demand for consumer goods, in particular consumer durables like fridges, scooters, cars, washing machines and television sets, that helped to form an internal market for the hitherto largely export-driven manufacturing industry. The number of cars circulating increased from 342,000 in 1956 to 4.67 million in 1964, and scooters from 700,000 to 4.3 million (while public transport, as well as public services in general, remained underdeveloped). As Table 5.1 shows, however, it took until 1965 before half the population were in possession of at least two articles of the 'standard package' of mass consumption.

Even then, the 50 per cent of the population that did possess this standard package were largely concentrated in the north. Wage differentials, as well as differentials in standards of living and the quality of life (unemployment, crime, availability of private and public goods) between the north and the

Table 5.1 Distribution of the 'standard package'

	1953	*1960*	*1965*
Television	–	20	49
Washing machine	4	5	23
Refrigerator	14	17	55
Car	1 (4)[a]	4 (14)[a]	10 (35)[a]

Source: Figures are derived from the statistical index to Ginsborg, P., *A History of Contemporary Italy*, London: Penguin, 1990.

Notes

a The figure within parentheses shows the percentage of individuals to own a car. I have recalculated these figures based on an average family size of 4 in the 50s and 3.5 in the 60s. The result is to a certain extent a statistical construct, given that family size was related to socio-economic standing, and hence families more likely to have a car were probably also more likely to be smaller. Anyhow, the figure within parentheses, can serve as an indication of a general trend.

south remained large all through the post-war period. (In 1951 the difference in GDP per capita was 140 per cent; in 1984, it was 91 per cent.) Even in the case of the north, accounts of a rapid penetration of new consumer goods have to be qualified, as possession of the 'standard package' of mass consumption remained largely concentrated in the middle classes. According to the respondents to a 1964 Doxa survey, the median monthly income stated to be enough to 'live comfortably without luxury but also without lacking any necessity' was 93,000 lire. The definition of what such a 'comfortable life' might consist of was purely subjective but if we provisionally accept the suggestive power attributed to advertising and the media (on the part of both advertising professionals and social critics – see below), we can take it as an indicator – highly unreliable to be sure – of what the lifestyle proposed by the women's magazines would cost to realize. Assuming the single-income family model set out by the women's magazines and comparing actual incomes with this aspirational figure, we can see how the highest paid workers, skilled workers in the Milan mechanical industry, almost made it (with a contractual monthly salary of 80,985 lire in 1964), while unskilled workers (*manovali*) certainly did not (62,775 lire). Among white-collar workers in the same mechanical industry the two upper categories (managers and assistant managers) were well above the norm (133,890 lire and 100,359 lire), while clerks and secretaries were not (an *Impiegato di 3A categoria* in the Milan mechanical industry earned 74,650 lire in 1964, *5A categoria*, 62,222 lire).[45] The economic miracle did not, with the possible exception of a few well-paying, modern and high-status factories, like the Ivrea works in Piedmont, produce the 'affluent workers', of northern Europe.[46]

That the 'standard package' of mass consumption was materially absent from the everyday life of most Italians, particularly those in the south, did, however, not mean that it was not 'there' on a symbolic level. In rural areas, it seemed, consumer goods and their uses formed the basis for a new spectacular myth of modernity, which managed to give new form to the millenarian hopes of peasant culture previously projected on America – the distant goal of dreams of migration and escape.[47] Now America came to them, in the shape of detergents, chewing gum, Coca-Cola, rock music and, most importantly perhaps, through television. This new medium had a radical impact, in particular outside the big cities. After transmissions had begun in 1954 the television set, placed in a bar or recreational circle, became a new centre for village life. Both Italo Calvino, who reported from the Po plain in 1954, and Mauro Calamandrei, writing from the Tuscan village of Scarperia in the same year, reported scenes where 'peasants walked several miles even in pouring rain, carrying their own chairs' to watch television. As in the women's magazines, television was generally received as an educational medium.[48] Lydia DeRita, in her study of television viewing among the inhabitants of one of the new, popular housing projects in rural Puglia, found that most of the viewers found the programmes to be primarily 'instructive'. The intentionally instructive material that made up most programmes was, however, consciously avoided, in favour of lighter entertainment – like the highly popular quiz show *Lascia o radoppia* (modelled on the American '64,000 dollar question') and the collection of advertising films known as *il Carosello*. According to most of DeRita's respondents, the educational value of these programmes was that they allowed one to 'see new things', to 'get to know the world' and to 'learn about life'.[49]

Apart from diffusing Italian as a national language (one of the main achievements of television, according to linguist Tullio de Mauro),[50] these programmes also drew the outlines of an Italian version of modernity where, as DeRita coments, the northern cities had replaced America as the main spatial reference. Here, as well, consumer goods were central. There were programmes like *il Carosello*, a sequence of three-minute dramatizations of consumer goods (itself a product of DC attempts to regulate television advertising: see below); *Campanile sera*, where families from small towns competed for domestic appliances and fully equipped 'American kitchens'; or *Lascia o radoppia*, where, guided by the suave Italo-American hybrid Mike Boungiorno, the most abundant riches became available to the quaintest and seemingly most useless of talents, and consumer goods represented the wonders of an affluent and civilized modern life in principle accessible to anyone.[51] For DeRita's respondents it was clear television showed a life that was not only different but also better. One older farmer interviewed by De Rita even spoke of himself and his family as animals (*bestie*) in relation to the gentlemen (*signori*) who appeared surrounded by modern consumer goods on *il Carosello*. The way to attain such a 'better life', most seemed to think, was through purely individualistic efforts, to get ahead, and to move up to the north if necessary. (DeRita also noted a widespread incomprehension of, and even aversion to, politics among the people interviewed.)

Driven by what they saw on television, in advertisements and in the women's magazines young women would significantly alter their life expectations, refusing to marry peasant men, thus putting additional pressure on the men to migrate. Instead, Alberoni and Baglioni argued, they had begun to identify with a new 'nation' (*patria*) of 'domestic appliances, fashion clothes and lipstick'.[52] As soon as they acquired the material resources to do so, young women would use such goods to enact a femininity that broke radically with the standards of peasant culture. In some cases such an open assault on traditional norms could cause a profound transformation of community life. In Ragusa, Sicily, for example, the money trickling down through employment in the newly built oil refinery caused a spread of 'sinful and corrupt entertainment'; in Stefanaconi, Calabria, young women had become more prone to take on increased amorous initiatives, sometimes even visiting their fiancé's house. This, most people interviewed argued, had led to a general moral decline.[53]

While the actual spread of modern consumer goods remained marginal by European standards, and in particular in the south, the symbolic importance of modern consumer culture was far greater. Mediated by television and by the weekly press, modern consumer goods and the 'American' models of life to which they were connected served as the basis for a new, nationally common culture of modernity. As historian Pier Paolo D'Attorre has argued, 'Americanism' and 'Consumerism' blended together in the Italy of the 1950s, to form, for the first time, a vision of modern life that was widely diffused and embraced by all inhabitants of the peninsula.

Consumption and modernity: the political discourse

Whether one judges from the actual spread of consumer goods, or from the place that consumer practices occupied in the everyday life of Italians, it would be hard to label the Italy of the 1950s, or even of the ensuing 'economic miracle', a 'consumer society'. Nevertheless, in media self-representation of the Italy of the 'miracle', reflecting an increasing sociological weight of mass consumption, new kinds of consumer goods and practices became increasingly important. This also meant that mass consumption and the new kinds of identities and practices it brought about came to feature as an important cause for a whole series of social problems. As can be expected, this later role for consumer goods was particularly prevalent in the version of the 'miracle' told by observers of the left. After all, the promotion of mass consumption and of the privatist ideology of achievement that it entailed formed one important part of the DC promotion of consensus. Overall, however, attitudes to mass consumption on the part of the Communist Party, the PCI, remained ambivalent. On the one hand, it was clear that the ways in which mass consumption was actually institutionalized constituted nothing less than an outright imposition of an American model of life, which played right into the hands of the Christian Democrats. Modern consumer goods came with an ethic of privatized status competition that was downright inimical to the formation of a true class consciousness. The whole aim of Communist cultural politics was to create an alternative civil society able to compete both with the Catholic world and its organizations, and with the allure of American-style mass consumption. As the motto went under Togliatti, 'One party section for every bell tower.'[54]

On the other hand, there was nothing wrong with modern consumer goods *per se*. Intellectuals and party cadres generally recognized the progressive potential of modern consumer goods, in particular domestic appliances. These would reduce the workload of women in particular and generally allow a higher level of 'civility' (*civiltà*). The obvious counter-example here was the popular prosperity supposedly enjoyed in the Soviet Union. There domestic comfort, neat clothes of good quality and a certain amount of luxuries were considered indispensable: 'The average Soviet citizen now considers indispensable things like paid vacations and free medical care, but also a radio, a television set, going to the theatre or to the movies.'[55] In the Soviet Union, unlike in the US, modern consumer goods were not used as tools for inter-family status competition, but valued solely for their use-values, their ability to make life simpler, more comfortable and more civilized. The PCI did attempt to promote such a utilitarian consumer culture. Among other examples, Sandro Bellasai cites the case of the Communist administration in Prato that put up a number of collectively operated washing machines. Such a Communist utilitarianism, however, by no means excluded fun and frivolity. There were Party organized dances, annual 'Feste dell'Unità', and the Communist Party women's magazine *Vie nuove* organized its own beauty contest, popularly known as 'Miss Vie Nuove'. The important thing was that this was utilitarian fun. It did not imply anything else. At Party dances people enjoyed themselves precisely because they were there to enjoy themselves, not to flirt. The winners of the Miss Vie Nuove contests went back to work the day after. They had no dreams of Hollywood stardom, fame or riches.[56] In their critique of mass consumption, Communist intellectuals, then, tended to focus not so much on the goods themselves but on the ways of using and relating to them that the new consumer culture proposed.

In their widely acclaimed work on the migrant communities in Milan, the so-called *Coree*, the Communist militants Francesco Alassia and Dino Montaldi observed how community life had been virtually stifled by an avid competition for consumer goods. Migrant women, who 'had known each other since they were kids, and often made the trip to the north together', now 'competed in using lipstick to show their neighbours that their family did not live in poverty'.[57] The consequence, here as among the 'affluent workers' studied by Pizzorno, was a virtual stifling of social interactions. Migrants in the *Coree* were unable to reach any form of collective agreement. Moreover, they lacked any consciousness of what their real needs might be:

> The migrants who work in factories have never before eaten as well as now. Before, they walked; now they have a motor scooter and their wives have bikes. They have many things, a well-furnished house with many conveniences. But never before have they felt as deprived as they do now, as frustrated by their own desires. [The old way in which objects used to make sense] has been lost in a consumer economy where needs are created artificially to guarantee sales.[58]

Mass consumption tended to alienate them, from others as well as from themselves.

Giorgio Bocca, a socialist journalist, made similar observations in his books about the 'miracle'. He reported that in Milan, were average income had increased substantially between 1955 and 1963, the consumption of milk and meat had actually *declined*. 'In the Milan of continuous expansion', he concludes, 'the richer you get, the less you eat.'[59] Bocca also saw how young workers in Milan would sacrifice basic necessities in order to set up a household of their own as soon as possible. After doing so, he observed, affective relationships were weakened and social interaction became increasingly scarce, 'even among brothers'. This lack of sociality appeared to be replaced by an increasing presence of objects, consumer goods. Spouses were increasingly alienated from each other and communicated through the pure economic exchange of money and goods. New forms of family life centred around television and the acquisition of consumer goods. The family was reduced, as Bocca expressed it, to 'him and her among shining household machinery'. He worked and 'she got her satisfaction from buying things'.[60]

Similar observations were common among most leftist journalists and intellectuals. This critical narrative of consumption-as-alienation had a wide impact through the rise of socially interested journalism that accompanied the transformation of Italian society during the 'miracle'. Weekly newsreels like *Oggi*, *l'Europeo* and, most notably, *L'Espresso* painted a rather bleak picture of the Italian modernization process, focusing on crime, poverty, prostitution, the squalor of migrant communities, but also on the overall passivity that seemed to result from the DC sponsored 'consumerization' of everyday life. As *L'Espresso* depicted the situation in 1959:

> Italy has gone back to being a country where nothing happens, where happiness is within the reach of everyone, even for those who don't know how they are going to get their hands on their daily bread. They have the comfort of the sun, and if they have a radio, or if, close by the hut where they dwell there is a bar with a television set, they can fill their ears with popular songs and their eyes with the weekly fairy tale of this Italy, happy and content after ten years with the Christian Democrats.[61]

The reception of mass consumption on the part of the Catholics was generally more positive, but not unreservedly so. On the one hand, the DC had aligned itself with America and drawn on its promise of popular affluence through consumption ever since the 1948 election. There the horrendous consequences of a Communist victory were described depicted with traditional stereotypes like an overall dissolution of the family, 'Cossacks in St Peter's square', but also as the decisive end to contemporary promises of consumerist opulence, as 'nothing but Togliatti's speeches to go with your pasta'.[62] On the other hand, many currents within the party, like the influential faction leader Giuseppe Dossetti, initially resisted this turn to America.[63] Within the party and within the Catholic world in general many embraced a picture of Italy as a *civiltà contadina* (peasant civilization), essentially alien to the materialism that came with American modernity. While the political centrality of this position tended to dwindle as the DC consolidated its power and moved in the direction of day-to-day *realpolitik*, it was by no means dead as an ideological position. Many Catholic intellectuals, like sociologist Sabino Acquaviva would produce descriptions of consumerist materialism very similar to those produced on the left (and to those that had come out of the Frankfurt School some ten years earlier).[64]

One good example of this profound ambivalence was the DC management of the state television RAI during the first years of its operations. Under

Filiberto Guala (later to withdraw as a Trappist monk) it was enforced that no erotic scenes, nor anything that 'did not make it explicitly clear that extra-marital relations were deeply sinful', or that could spread 'hatred among the social classes' was shown. Guala was not only a prudish monk-in-the-making however, he also successfully managed and promoted a highly popular medium. His administration also gave rise to the *Carosello* format for television advertising, by means of which consumer goods acquired a particular prominence (even if the intention was rather to the contrary, to control and contain advertising). As in the case of Guala, Catholic policies towards mass consumption in general recognized its popularity but would try to contain its more undesirable effects. The Catholic weekly *Famiglia cristiana*, for example, became a mass-circulating, advertising-financed glossy magazine under the management of Giuseppe Zilli, an experienced journalist who took over in 1954. The magazine would now contain editorial material roughly similar to that of the purely commercial women's magazines (and that went well with the advertising), like articles on the American family, the American kitchen, comparisons of different types of household machinery, and articles on the use and care of cars, floors and modern furniture. Articles and advice columns would give advice as to how to counteract the threatening materialism that came with such goods and how to safeguard the virtues of the family and the uncorrupted innocence of children. The latter subject was particularly prevalent. *Famiglia cristiana* would give instructions on how to reward children with material gifts, but warn against using goods as replacements for human relations or against spoiling children, making them feel entitled to new consumer goods. In particular it would warn against using the child as a tool for the family's self-presentation, as a status object:

> No mother should ever think terrible thoughts like this: my little boy (or my little girl) will outshine all the others with his or her new dress. That is an offence to God for whom the innocent souls of all boys and girls are equally beautiful and radiant.[65]

During the course of the 1950s, DC attitudes towards consumption would change gradually. For one thing, the rapid modernization of the countryside made it difficult to think of Italy as essentially a *civiltà contadina*. Sociologists observed how people left rural areas or, at any rate, identified and imitated an urban way of life deeply marked by consumer culture. (Among some Catholic sociologists this provoked fears of an ongoing *dechristianization*).[66] Thus the ascent of Amintore Fanfani (who campaigned in 1958 under the slogan 'Progress without surprises') to Party leadership signified, according to historian Paolo Pombeni, that the Party was getting accustomed to a future marked by characteristics of industrial modernity.[67] Within Italian intellectual debates more generally, American social theory like that of Lipset, Bell and Parsons or, for that matter, more critical voices like those of Riesman and Mills had an increasing impact. They envisioned a future where values or ideologies would lose their importance to the administrated culture of mass consumerism and the media.

Within Italian debates these visions inspired the emergence of the concept of 'Neocapitalism', which was central to the renewed political analysis of the left in the late 1950s. As an article in the influential journal *Passato e presente* concluded, a Neocapitalist future would entail a disintegration of older forms of class consciousness. Through the pressures exercised by mass production and mass consumption, class would disintegrate into a bundle of lifestyles loosely contained within the 'middle strata' and mainly based on consumer choice. This, they argued, would put an end to political militancy as hitherto conceived: 'you don't become an activist by trying to keep up with the Joneses'.[68]

These arguments also influenced the Catholics. The most prominent example of such a reorientation of Catholic social thought and, more importantly, DC political strategy, was presented in a speech by sociologist Achile Ardigò at the congress on social transformation held by the DC in San Pellegrino in 1962. Quoting again American thinkers like Mills, Lipset, Darhendorf, Rostow and Galbraith, Ardigò depicted a profound transformation of the predominantly rural Italy – the 'peasant civilization' in relation to which the Party's earlier social vision had developed. He foresaw an expansion of the middle class, an increasing entrance of women into the workforce, a growth of secondary social groups, like bureaucracies and large-scale industrial organizations, a further growth in the power and influence of the media and an increasing power of technological elites. This would be accompanied by a declining importance of religion and tradition and an expansion of mass consumption as the main source of popular motivations. In a coming 'age of abundance' increasing material resources and increasing leisure would favour the general diffusion of a 'car-culture' that would form the main source of both social integration and ideological cohesion. The cornerstone of Catholic social thought, the family, would go through particularly important transformations. As family members would become increasingly absorbed by the roles assigned to them by large-scale social organizations, the family itself would fragment. Contacts between the generations would be reduced and the family would no longer function as the prime unit of socialization.

While far from embracing these tendencies wholeheartedly, Ardigò did argue for their reality and inevitability. To equate, for example, mass consumption with alienation, as the Communists did, would mean to presuppose that people had other things to do with their free time than to consume, a proposition without any empirical foundation whatsoever. On the contrary, these were 'models of consumption that the working masses, in particular those with a materialistic orientation, seem very happy to accept'.[69] Indeed, in so far as these tendencies were proven real, they had to be accepted. To do differently would mean to aim at a totalitarian control of the modernization process, something that Ardigò considered intrinsically dangerous. The best way to govern a social body that had acquired a certain autonomy – that was guided by the logics and 'iron-cages' of bureaucracy and large-scale organizations, by the logic of systems as Habermas would later put it – was post-ideological. The political system should not try to impute its own ideological vision on the social but rather limit its role to checking and balancing development. It would intervene locally and concretely to avoid excesses, guarantee basic forms of freedom and security, and safeguard pluralism. As a party without a proper ideology, Ardigò argued, the DC was particularly suited to play such a role.[70] The real novelty with Ardigò's speech was not so much that it proposed a new political programme, but rather that it suggested a new concept of governance in general. In a post-ideological society it was best to leave the social to itself, to let motivations be formed by mass consumption and the media, and to limit governance to the administration of development. This was indeed a far step from the vision of a politics as the safeguarding of a traditional, Catholic peasant morality, which had guided the Party in the early years.

Conclusion

During the 1950s, and in particular during the years of the economic miracle, Italy saw a radical increase in the sociological importance of mass consumption. While the country remained poor by European standards, a modern consumer culture diffused by the media managed to establish itself as an overall referent for discourses on modernization. Even the mass parties (or at least the DC) had to accept the prospect of entering a post-ideological age, where social order would be guaranteed by the apolitical motivations of consumer culture. This consumer culture was far from monolithic and unchanging, however. Developments within the advertising profession meant that the strategy of just copying and imposing an American model, thought to possess global relevance, were gradually abandoned. Instead advertising would begin to engage seriously with and attempt to guide and resolve the actual contradictions of the Italian modernization process. As the following two chapters will show, the advertising profession now became an important agent in mediating the social transformations that took place during the 1960s and 1970s.

6 The new ethic of consumption I

The new housewife

'There is a great cook in you. . . . And Barilla will bring her out' (*C'è una gran cuoca in voi. . . . e Barilla la rivela*). The 1964 campaign for pasta Barilla differed markedly from the 'detergent wars' that had set the stage for advertising in the women's magazines during the preceding decade. Unlike the fearful housewife of the 1950s – ever weary of the comparative merits of her housework – the woman in Barilla's 1960s campaign looks us straight in the eye, confident in her own value and abilities. Her family remains peripheral to the situation, if not entirely absent. What counts is her *self*: her individual effort and contribution. The new Barilla-woman did not even look like a housewife. Casually dressed, of indefinite age, neither young or old, she is depicted alone with the product: no kitchen, no husband, no kids. (In the accompanying television spot, Mina, a rising star of the new wave of Italian pop music with a slightly transgressive look, brought this delinking of the woman consumer from her family context one step further. She referred to the product as 'something for your kids and your *man*', not 'your husband'. Quite a step in Italy of 1965!)[1] Thanks to the product, the woman consumer had become an individual for whom pasta was primarily a way of channelling her own creativity and desire for self-expression; a way of marking off her presence in the world, and only secondarily something that fulfilled the needs of kids and 'man'. It would be an exaggeration to claim that Barilla's advertising now appealed to a woman who had emancipated herself from traditional demands. Her place was still in the family, and her cooking was still done with others in mind. The main use-value of the product, however, was not that it allowed her to live up to the expectations contained in a given social role, but that, within the contours of that role, it gave her a space for creativity, self-expression and agency. In Barilla's campaign, the woman consumer had become 'subjectivated', to use Alain Touraine's term.[2]

The emergence of this new female consumer identity in advertising was in part a reflection of a changing social reality. During the 1960s the situation of women had begun to change, as a result of migration, increasing exposure to the media and, not least, consumer goods. As many sociologists had observed, these tended to alter the power balance within the family and gave a more

Figure 6.1 'There is a great chef in you and Barilla brings her out! You'll put in your efforts, and Barilla makes the pasta.' Barilla addresses the woman consumer as an individual. (Courtesy of Archivio Storico Barilla, Parma.)

independent role to women. This became increasingly visible as new forms of consumer practices emerged, as, notably, those connected to the revolution in fashion that occurred in second half of the decade (see chapter 7).[3] These transformations also acquired a certain unprecedented visibility. The media, and not least the women's magazines, began to scrutinize the situation of women and would frequently expose the dysfunctional nature of the nuclear family or widespread instances of discrimination and sexual harassment. These media initiatives contributed to putting women's issues on the public agenda, something that accelerated with the growth of the Italian feminist movement towards the second half of the decade. But the 'New Housewife' that figured in advertising was not only the result of a changing social reality; it was also the outcome of a new approach to advertising. During the 1960s the advertising industry acquired the tools to engage more directly with the world of consumers. These new methods, however, also contained a particular ideological bias. Viewed through the interface that they provided, the changing situation of women began to look like a progressive step in the direction of a dawning individualized, post-materialistic society. This chapter will show how the advertising industry changed its view of women and their consumer desires during the decade.

The marketing approach

The New Woman that featured in Barilla's advertising was a result of the company switching to one of the big international advertising agencies, the British CPV (that had now taken over from J. Walter Thompson as the intellectual centre of the Milan advertising world)[4]. Previously Barilla had handled its own advertising by directly employing the artist and designer Erberto Carboni. Although Carboni's advertisements were increasingly inspired by the new American realist style, he remained firmly anchored in the Italian modernist poster tradition, with roots going back to the inter-war years (when Carboni worked for Motta and Agip, the state petrol company, among others). Similar moves away from a conception of advertising as 'corporate art' – denounced, as we remember from chapter 3, by the advertising professionals from the very start – were common during the 1960s. Until the 1960s the many domestic companies like Star, Motta, Ferrero, Campari, Zanussi, FIAT and Cinzano had relied on their own advertising and sales departments and employed their own artists.[5] Now this approach was replaced or accompanied by the services of a big multinational advertising agency. And the supply of such services increased, with McCann-Erickson, BBDO, Ogilvy & Mather, Young & Rubicam, and Ted Bates opening up shop in Milan in the early 1960s. At the same time, Italian graphic and industrial design (with some exceptions) began to leave the rationalist heritage of the inter-war years (revitalized in the 'democratic design' movement of the first post-war years), for an American-inspired aesthetic of styling and streamlining.[6] As the preceding chapters have shown, an American approach to mass consumption had been around since the 1930s, Now, however, it had its first real breakthrough.

With the dominance of the American advertising agencies came a new conception of how mass consumption should be organized, known as the 'marketing approach'. As an academic disicpline, marketing had developed in the US in the 1910s as the growing interest in the mechanisms of commercial distribution on the part of academics in the new business schools met with the advertising psychology of Walter Dill Scott and later James B. Watson. In contrast, both to the German school of institutional economics that had prevailed in American business schools, and to the rationalization debates that ranged in Italy in the 1930s, marketing concerned itself seriously with the subjective reality of the consumer. Indeed, it was from the world of consumers that needs and wants were thought to arise, and not from any attempts at forceful propaganda or 'suggestion'. From the point of view of marketing, the key to successful business practice was not to try to create new needs and wants from above. Rather, one should seek to adapt to a demand that already lay immanent in the social life of consumers (see chapter 3). As a management philosophy, marketing then meant to let production as well as overall management be guided by this immanent demand. To arrive at this, however, it was necessary to study the product from the point of view of potential consumers – not only its physical or technical properties, but also the psychological and sociological context of its use.

This was pedagogically explained by David James, head of the JWT agency in Milan, in an article in *Panorama della pubblicità* from 1952. He emphasized how prior to launching an advertising campaign and, ideally, prior to developing the product itself, it was necessary to understand how potential consumers would use and benefit from it. This product benefit was to be at the focus of selling efforts. Marketing was about selling 'holes not drills', 'beauty, not make-up', 'cakes, not stoves', and so on.[7] As chapter 4 has shown, similar ideas had influenced the debates of the Italian advertising profession since the 1930s. Now, however, they were much more influential, not least through the support they received from powerful agencies like the National Committee for Productivity (Comitato nazionale produttività), financed by the Marshall Aid. Through study trips, seminars and articles in the journal *Produttività*, marketing and American business practice in general was propagated as the key to democracy and prosperity.[8] In aligning themselves to their new American benefactors many Italian advertising professionals had paid lip-service to the marketing approach since the immediate post-war years.[9] During the 1960s, however, this approach became much more useful, for practical as well as for ideological reasons. On a practical level, the empirical or even sociological approach of marketing seemed to offer a way to render mass-produced consumer goods acceptable. Contrary to most expectations, the diffusion of such modern amenities as domestic appliances and canned foods was slow. Housewives in particular were suspicious and preferred traditional forms of distribution to both branded goods and supermarkets.[10] The marketing approach promised a way to overcome this resistance by placing the product in the life-world of the consumer and making sure that it satisfied an existing need. By adapting advertising and packaging to the expectations of consumers, it would be possible to create a reliable brand image able to create trust and overcome the anonymity of the modern mass market. As the American experience had shown, this was particularly important in modern commercial institutions, like supermarkets, that involved virtually no personal contact at all.[11] Only by creating such trust in modern consumer goods would it be possible to set in motion the anthropological revolution necessary to transform Italians into a people of consumers, to make the existing 'philosophy of saving' give in to a 'philosophy of spending and of immediate satisfaction'.[12]

On an ideological level the marketing approach served as a new source of professional legitimation. Advertising professionals were well aware of the growing presence of advertising, of the new social importance that mass consumption had assumed, and of the critique directed at its human and social consequences, like standardization, alienation and the creation of 'false needs'.[13] The marketing approach then allowed them to argue that mass consumption was nothing but a rational response to already existing needs. Indeed, it was a basic institution in any open and democratic society. Writing in *Produttività*, Silvano Spinetti, founder of the brand-new Italian Institute for Public Relations, argued that marketing (and public relations) were central to a new, democratic kind of capitalism. This American 'New Capitalism' was no longer oriented primarily to private profit, but guided by the common interest. Citing the American ambassador David Zellerbach in his speech to the Milan Chamber of Commerce from the previous year, Spinetti affirmed that 'the main characteristic of this new kind of capitalism is its sense of social responsibility . . . it gains the support of workers and of the public in general by actively serving its interests'. Consequently, in 'New Capitalism' there was no need for any overall political control – neither to keep the captains of industry in check, nor to make sure that corporations moved within the limits of the public interest. Rather, this would be achieved by the corporations themselves. It was in their interests to stay in tune with popular attitudes and demands through techniques like public relations, market research and opinion polling. Indeed, the power of consumers was understood to be the key element to this democratic self-regulation. Quoting Zellerbach once again, Spinelli affirmed that 'New Capitalism aims to consider the consumer as a kind of voter whose electoral support is essential to the survival of companies.'[14] Seen from this perspective, advertising was not only about selling, or even primarily about mediating between consumers and corporations; it allowed the former to play the important role of an ultimate electorate. Rather than hidden persuaders, as denounced in Vance Packard's influential book (translated into Italian in 1958),[15] advertising professionals were the key guardians of democracy, and the marketing approach, some argued, could very well be extended to other social fields as well, like, for example, politics.[16] In order to make this happen, however, it was necessary to get to know consumers. Marketing required market research.

Motivation reseach

Even if the idea of conducting empirical market research surfaced in the discussions of advertising professionals in the 1930s, the real breakthrough came in the post-war years. The first research company, Doxa, was founded in 1947 by statistician Pierpaolo Luzzatto-Fegis with the financial support of American corporations like IBM, Palmolive and Gillette. It was soon followed by SIRM (Società Italiana Ricerche di Mercato) and CISER (Centro Italiano Studi e Ricerche), both based in Rome. In 1955 the market research companies organized in AISM (Associazione Italiana Studi di Mercato) and began publishing their own journal (*Studi di Mercato*). Through this initiative and the knowledge diffusion operated by other trade journals, methods became increasingly sophisticated. The proponents of market research now argued for its necessity in an emerging mass market where consumers could no longer be known by means of rules of thumb, where 'the consumer lives in a different world than we do and has to be studied and investigated'; and where the advertising professional, in turn had to evolve from 'Bohemian to rational technician'.[17] While many companies would commission market research to survey actual product use, the main source of growth for the business remained the media. With the growth of the advertising market, publishers needed reliable statistics in order to market their readers as a sellable audience of consumers. Advertising agencies, on the other hand, became increasingly aware of the possibility of targeting different consumer groups through the use of different media.[18]

As chapter 5 has shown, audience research would initially be limited to circulation statistics, and possibly some additional information on the socio-economic composition of readers. During the 1950s, however, publishers began to offer information of the purchasing habits of readers. *Reader's Digest*, which self-consciously saw itself as an ambassador of all things American – values as well as marketing techniques – commissioned a highly publicized study of the readers of its Italian edition *Selezione* in 1954. This 'Portrait of the *Selezione* family' encompassed purchasing data on 'everything from refrigerators to shoe polish'.[19] This initiative was followed by many others. The weekly newsmagazine *Epoca* launched a similar survey of its readers in 1956, as did *Grazia* the year after, and the 'lowbrow' women's magazine *Bolero Film* traced the use of canned foodstuffs among its readers for the benefit of the food company Cirio.[20] Towards the early 1960s similar surveys of puchasing patterns had become standard practice and magazine publishers would routinely sell their audiences as representatives of distinct commodity bundles. So far, however, market research only offered quantitative data. It only told advertising professionals *what* a particular segment of consumers usually purchased, not *why*. Given the marketing impetus to penetrate the world of the consumer, this was clearly inadequate, and demands were raised for deeper, qualitative data. In order to market, rather than just sell, advertising professionals needed to know not only who the consumers were, what they bought and how much they earned, but also what they actually thought and desired. This kind of information was supplied by a new brand of qualitative market research: motivation research (MR).

MR was pioneered by Austrian psychologist Ernest Dichter (together with a few contemporaries like Luis Chesikin and Pierre Martineau, but Dichter stands out as the 'father' of the new technique). In this new approach, Dichter broke with the prevailing paradigm of market research as well as consumer psychology in general. Rather than attempting to construct lists of elementary human 'drives and fears' as in the then dominant behaviourist tradition, Dichter relied on the Freudian psychoanalytic tradition to locate the true stimuli for consumer decisions in the hidden reality of the individual unconscious. Letting his interviewees talk at length about their relations to soap or cars, Dichter discovered that this could not be adequately phrased in terms of a language of function alone. Rather, such relations were both much more complex than imagined and highly individualized. He then emphasized the necessity of investigating, in each separate case, the subjectively perceived meaning of the product that consumers entertained – the 'product image', as he termed it (drawing on Gestalt psychology).

MR thus performed something of a Copernican turn within market research. From the product conceived as a functional part of a social context in which needs and desires were given a priori – the detergent that cleans, the bouillon cube that nourishes, the skin cream that makes you look like a film star – to the individual meanings attributed to it by consumers. To put it in Dichter's own terms, motivation research unveiled the true lived experience of 'the mass produced product as a carefully crafted individualized product'.[21] Such deep meaning-systems were, however, not easy to get at, as people had a tendency to 'rationalize' their consumer decisions. When asked directly, people's answers were tainted by the prevailing 'fetish of rationality' that, according to Dichter, prevented them from becoming aware of their frequently irrational real motives. The task of motivation research was then precisely to penetrate this shell of rationality in order to formulate hypotheses about the underlying continent of 'real motives' that were the true cause not only of people's consumer decisions, but of their behaviour in general. To do so, MR relied on in-depth interviews, group interviews, dramatization, projective tests and even secret filming of interviewees as they answered questions or interacted with consumer goods. In the 1950s MR was an influential trend in the US advertising world. Under the threat of over-production, increasing 'consumer satiation' and a feared reduction of product differences resulting from standardization, advertising professionals welcomed a technique that opened up a new field – the unconscious – as a source of product diversity. Dr Dichter and his Institute for Motivational Research in Croton-on-Hudson (NY) researched just about everything and published an influential (and extremely expensive) monthly bulletin, *Motivations*. In 1957 Dichter charged $500 a day for consultations.

In Italy MR was first introduced by the multinational advertising agencies. Soon, however, Italian research companies began to appear. The first and most influential was Misura, financed by textile industrialist Bassetti, and run by soon-to-be-famous sociologist Francesco Alberoni, who came to found something of his own school during the 1960s. In 1959 Misura employed 300 interviewers, 20 of whom were experts in motivation research. During the 1960s it was accompanied by a number of small companies and individual freelancers.[22] After his frequent travels and lectures in Italy, first in 1956, visiting the old Italian agency IMA (Idea Metodo Arte), Dichter opened a branch of his own Institute for Motivation Research in Rome in 1962 (one in a chain of foreign franchises encompassing Croton-on-Hudson, Zurich, London, Barcelona, Buenos Aires, São Paolo, Caracas, Istanbul, Tel Aviv, Sydney and Johannesburg). The institute in Rome was, however, a short-lived affair – it closed down after a public fiasco with the Christian Democrat election campaign in 1963.[23]

Even if there are no reliable figures as to the spread and impact of MR, one of the pioneers of Italian motivation research, Gianpaolo Fabris, claimed that by the mid-1960s Italy had become a European leader in this field.[24] In the mid-to late 1960s studies of consumer motivations were employed across the board: underwear, detergents, spirits, tobacco, cars, washing machines, pasta, petrol, airlines and even university enrolments.[25] The success of MR in Italy probably had something to do with the generally uneven spread of mass consumption. While journalism, sociological investigations and public opinion in general had created a growing awareness that parts of Italy were entering a new age of affluence, this movement always remained partial. Modern consumer goods and modern consumer culture with its ethic of status competition were openly embraced by some groups, notably younger consumers who would generally prefer modern consumer goods like canned or pre-cooked foods, and be sensible to the sign-value of brands. Appealing to the sign-value of the product would work well with certain kinds of goods, like cars, for which 'social motivations' seemed to matter much more than more pragmatic concerns of utility.[26] For the traditionally most important target group, the housewives, however, things were much more complex. Not only did housewives generally, and to the astonishment of advertising professionals, prefer non-branded to branded goods, but some of them 'resisted' modern consumer goods. The motivation studies performed by Francesco Alberoni's research company Misura in the early 1960s indicated that modern products were often perceived as tasteless, fake, artificial and even poisonous. Both margarine and bouillon cubes were understood to be foul tasting, without nutritious value and made of just about anything.[27] Such 'resistance' concerned not only food, where the public attention to the frequent food frauds in the early 1960s gave it some form of justification, but a whole series of modern consumer goods.[28] Washing machines, for example, were perceived to be sadistic and destructive. Together with modern detergents they would rip clothes apart and damage textiles.[29]

The first profitable niche that opened up for the new MR companies was thus to explain such seemingly irrational attitudes on the part of housewives. Rather than attributing such resistance to rational judgement, founded perhaps on experience, the motivation researchers agreed that it originated in housewives projecting their own insecurities on modern consumer goods. A series of investigations in newsmagazines like *Espresso* and *Panorama* had revealed a domestic environment that was changing rapidly and where migration, social mobility, the mediazation of experience and the arrival of new consumer goods tended to undermine the traditional role of the housewife. In this situation of turmoil, Misura's researchers argued, housewives rejected modern consumer goods in order to preserve their own identity and sense of place. As Gabriele Calvi concluded in a Misura study of attitudes towards mass-produced foods in 1961:

> The woman discovers that the use of mass-produced foods in a domestic setting takes away a large part of her duties and deprives her of one of her most proved weapons in securing her government over the hearts of her family. . . . The woman consequently finds herself in a defensive position, in which natural foods become an ideal to protect, and mass-produced foods a threat that has to be fought off.[30]

The solution originally recommended was thus to try to domesticate modern consumer goods in the traditional world of the housewife, to downplay their threatening connotations and to try to argue that they were, in fact, compatible with her traditional role. In the case of plastics, for example, Misura's researchers recommended that the new, anonymous, and therefore threatening material be rendered more familiar by associating it with values and symbols that were well known to housewives. One possible way of rendering this new material less anonymous was to show where it was produced, and by whom, to depict and describe the factory or even the artisan quality of its workers: to show that plastic, for example, was something made by human beings, and not the fruit of an anonymous technology. Another way was to try to transform plastic materials into a meaningful medium for status competition. By differentiating between high-class and low-class plastics and thus make it possible to use plastics as a sign of social prestige, it would be easier for status-seeking housewives to conceive of a place for plastics in their everyday life. Eventually they would assume the same 'connotations of love' that were connected to traditional objects.[31]

The most frequent solution, however, was simply to negate the threat posed by modern consumer goods. This was usually done by emphasizing how the product would serve to strengthen the position of the housewife within the family, rather than threatening to undermine it. In the advertising agency Lintas's campaign for Gradina margarine from the early 1960s, a motivation study on attitudes towards margarine had made the agency change the emphasis of advertisements. Rather than stressing the virtues of the product, Lintas now reassured housewives that apart from forming part of a healthy and nutritious diet, margarine would work to procure the attention from family members that housewives craved. In the new advertisements, which featured across the women's magazines in the early 1960s, the husband expresses his appreciation (addressing the housewife/reader), 'Yes, you were right; one eats well with Gradina', and, as the smaller text points out, this is a 'complement that you have deserved'. The small copy proceeds to explain how to use this new ingredient (that 'it need not be combined with oil', for example, but works as a substitute), and stresses that it is made of completely natural ingredients. The most important point, however, is that it does not compete with you as a housewife, or threaten to replace you, but it will render you personal recognition. You can use it as a tool that will actually strengthen your position in the family. With Gradina, husband and kids will love you even though it's not butter. Under the influence of motivation research, advertising, as Francesco Alberoni argued in his magnum opus *Consumi e società* of 1964, went through a maniacal phase. It tried to deny and suppress the inherent contradiction that, according to Alberoni, prevailed between modern consumer goods and traditional consumers: between a traditional housewife and factory-produced margarine.[32]

The new woman

Such a reassuring, or to use Alberoni's term, 'maniacal' strategy, resulted from a conception of motivation research as a kind of therapeutic practice, which would work to domesticate recalcitrant consumers into a given model of consumption and everyday life more generally. Such a conception of MR was, however, slightly at odds with Dichter's own view of the matter, at least as it evolved towards the early 1960s. Dichter now began to emphasize the emancipatory possibilities of MR and of mass consumption in general. His defence of MR against charges of manipulation and Big Brotherism (most influentially voiced some years earlier by Vance Packard) was to claim that its role was rather to bring already existing but hitherto repressed desires into the open. In recognizing and bringing into the open people's real motives, often repressed by the 'iron cage of rationality' or the puritanism that governed their public behaviour, MR could help to realize an accepting 'hedonistic morality'. This would sanction the pursuit of desire and enable consumption to realize its potential as the main purveyor of happiness and creativity in modern society. Motivation research was thus an excellent example of a 'democratic practical application of the social sciences'. As Dichter put it on another occasion:

> If we want to form reliable programmes for future development we must

> radically alter our moral concepts. Not only will we need a whole range of goods and products to fill up our free time, but we also need a moral absolution that will free us from those feelings of guilt that have been so profoundly rooted in us.[33]

MR thus offered a way of liberating the individual from the bonds and expectations of society, rather than adapting him or her to them. In his 1964 introduction to an Italian translation of Pierre Martineau's *Motivation in Advertising*, Gian-Paolo Fabris, who was to become one of the most important names within Italian market research, argued for the possibility of such a 'liberatory' use of motivation research. The technique invited a new way of treating consumers as individuals, or, as 'pyschological realities in their own right', rather than as social categories. This turn was crucial, Fabris argued, because, 'at the present stage of social evolution, the main value of any product is psychological'. Before, it had perhaps been enough just to advertise to give products connotations of modernity that would make them intrinsically desirable. Now, however, such standardized models were breaking up, and consumer tastes were becoming increasingly diversified. Consequently, advertising and marketing had to abandon standardized mass approaches and concentrate on the individual, psychological reality of demand.[34]

This break-up of a standardized model was particularly evident in the case of women: in public debates, in particular in upmarket women's magazines like *Grazia* and *Annabella*, there was a widespread questioning of the model of the housewife, and an emerging feminist consciousness, if only of the bourgeois, Betty Friedan, variety. Like the article series 'The Modern Woman on Trial' (*Processo alla donna moderna*), written by Brunella Gasparini in *Annabella*, these investigations generally concluded that not only had the situation of women changed drastically, but women had also begun to refute their old gender role.[35] More importantly, perhaps, consumer goods themselves seemed to be inviting new kinds of uses and new kinds of attachments among their female users. At least in the case of American women, consumption seemed to be the main arena for the affirmation of individuality rather than for attempts to conform and live up to a role. By making consumer choices and using consumer goods, it seemed, women could realize themselves, receive recognition for their skills and fantasy, in short, agency, from the other members of their families. From available reports, it seemed clear that in the US the consumption and use of goods was experienced as an empowering activity. It was intimately connected to the affirmation of women's individual personality rather than to tradition or the wish of the husband, and it allowed them to affirm that personality by making choices.[36]

In Italy a similar modern, empowered female subjectivity could be traced in certain environments, like the few, but fascinating, supermarkets that appeared towards the end of the 1950s. Supermarkets were perceived as intrinsically modern institutions. The construction of a supermarket was part and parcel of modernizing investments in industrial infrastructure, like ENI's housing and office complex in San Donato outside Milan, Metanopolis, or the petrochemical works at Gela in Sicily.[37] The first experiment with supermarkets in Milan in 1950 was accompanied by something of a moral panic as the sheer abundance and availability of goods was thought to induce criminality.[38] The supermarket was, however, also a space were it seemed that individual choice could be exercised more freely than before, where the consumer herself could choose and emerge as an empowered subject, rather than being the mere object of suggestion or 'traditional habits'. If built in the right way, to permit the consumer to 'wander' and 'give her the impression that she makes her own choices', the supermarket could provide an 'escape from the domestic walls' that also entailed a certain amount of individual empowerment.[39] In the supermarket the woman consumer could select exotic ingredients for menus and meals that arose from her own imagination, rather than from traditional recipes.[40] The supermarket constituted a new kind of public space where the housewife could realize herself in an unprecedented manner, even to the point of provoking, as Francesco Alberoni argued (referring to an unpublished piece of research by Misura), delirious feelings of omnipotence, and compulsory buys.[41] In view of this changing situation, advertising should elaborate a new model of consumption that could work to legitimize – in the eyes of women themselves as well as in those of society in general – a set of new needs and desires, linked to self-realization rather than to role-attainment. This was not only considered a successful marketing strategy, but also something of a moral duty.

In his introductory speech to the 1968 conference on 'the woman and the market', organized by the Genoa Chamber of Commerce, Fabris offered such a strategy. He described how research had showed the emergence of a 'new housewife' replacing the older model. The 'traditional housewife' – conservative and deeply connected to the home with which, when not disturbed by an intruding modernity, she had a basically harmonious relationship – had been replaced by a woman who often had worked, but when she had married or was forced to by the post-1964 recession, she had returned to the home. As such, according to Fabris, she lived a frustrating contradiction between the power and individual autonomy offered by working and earning her own income, and the more rigid structural situation of a housewife. She resolved this tension by ceaselessly seeking to manifest her own, if only symbolic, autonomy. The most important aspect of the 'new housewife' was then her continuous search for means of self-affirmation, for – and this was a crucial point – substitutes for the autonomy she had once enjoyed, or perceived that others enjoyed. Cooking was one such substitute. According to Fabris, most women saw it as an enjoyable opportunity to experiment with fantasy and creativity (in contrast to cleaning, which symbolized duty and confinement to the home). The most important area for self-expression, however, was shopping:

> [Shopping] represents an existential sphere to which the housewife can easily retreat in order to escape the boredom of an everyday existence that

> gives her but few satisfactions. To shop, to wander around the shops means not only to feel, once again, like a full member of the community, but also gives a sensation of being informed, of being 'with it'. Shopping, in this respect, fulfils a function similar to that of mass media, albeit in a more intense way. *To consume offers the new housewife an illusory way to fulfil the void that characterizes her existence, to fill it with meaning.* [my italics][42]

The 'new housewife' consumed, not primarily to fulfil the needs of her family, but primarily to 'fill the void that characterized her existence'. The significance she gave to shopping was psychological rather than utilitarian. It was not so much a matter of meeting needs in a rational way, as of simulating a freedom and autonomy that she now perceived as not only possible but also rightly hers. Shopping and cooking were her main ways of expressing herself and affirming her identity, her main *raison d'être*. Family, duty and tradition were but secondary to this. To fill the gap in an illusory and purely symbolic way was, of course, an impossible task. The stimulating function of consumption thus rendered the new housewife insatiable. Unlike her conservative and fearful predecessor, the 'new housewife' was something of a compulsive shopper: 'If her husband did not stop her', she would 'throw herself at cans and frozen foods headlong'.[43]

Women were still understood to be frustrated, but their frustration was different, indeed opposed to that of the traditional *massaia*. They did not so much feel their safety threatened by an invading modernity, as they perceived their drive for autonomy and self-affirmation constrained by restrictive environmental conditions. (A research report on canned foods from 1968 even claimed that it was precisely the absence of creative potential, of the possibility to 'express themselves in the kitchen', that made modern women reject such products. This was precisely the opposite of what market research had claimed ten years earlier.)[44] On the one hand, modern ideals and modern life, in particular modern consumer culture – the wider range of choices on the market, the beginning of the generalization of a vaguely counter-cultural youth fashion – offered the opportunity to be an emancipated woman in control of her own life, with her own money and power to make proper choices. On the other hand, the objective situation of most women as housewives, sometimes combining that role with work, presented in most cases serious obstacles to the pursuit of such autonomy. Consumer goods should thus work as a substitute, as a repressive desublimation of desire, as Herbert Marcuse put it; a substitute that could channel the desires for self-affirmation in a way that would endanger neither the established order, nor the psychic health of women.[45]

In the second half of the 1960s this new model of consumption, a 'New Woman' who used goods as tools for self-realization, even in traditional settings like the kitchen, was institutionalized in a series of advertising campaigns for cosmetics, lingerie, fashion, but also more mundane goods like Barilla's pasta. The most important actors in making the new woman real were, however, the women's magazines. In particular the upscale trio – *Annabella*, *Grazia* and *Gioia*, 'target A' as they were now being called – changed their editorial make-up to supply an environment to fit New Housewives. They gave more space to beauty products, cosmetics (a market that was expanding during the mid-1960s) and exotic cooking, and continued the realist investigations into the problems facing women who tried to work outside the home, or to affirm their independence otherwise. It was the new women's magazine launched by *Corriere della sera* in 1962, *Amica*, however, that set the stage for a new image of the woman consumer. Indeed, *Amica* was primarily launched as a response to the demand on the part of advertisers for a medium that could reach 'modern women'.[46] Seeking primarily to differentiate *Amica* from the equally upmarket, but more traditional and conservative *Grazia*, *Corriere della sera* thus positioned its new publication as directed at modern, emancipated women (rather than housewives), 'who no longer believed in fairy tales':

> The modern woman no longer believes in fairy-tales or in other useless evasions. The reader of *Amica* is an active woman who lives with open eyes, attentive to the important events of our times. She needs to be informed in a quick and fulfilling way, as she has little time to lose. She has many responsibilities. She works, she takes care of the house, she brings up her children and she does most of the shopping. Every day she makes new choices.[47]

This image of a New Woman reader was also reflected in the editorial content of *Amica*, where a fairly radical questioning of existing gender roles took place. The magazine harboured open discussions on issues like sexuality, fidelity and the adequacy of the traditional family as an institution (leading up to *Amica*'s embracement, together with other 'target A' magazines, of the pro-divorce side in the referendum of 1974).[48] *Amica*'s general attitude towards the institution of the family was very different from that contained within the classical model of the housewife. As one of the many articles on women who work concluded in 1964:

> If you reflect on it, the family is not everything for the individual, and society is no longer just a meeting place for families, but rather a meeting place for individuals. Today's individual gets her qualifications through her work, and seeks to affirm her personality in her own way.[49]

Much of the advertising catered to a similar emancipated female subjectivity. Cosmetics advertisements (following the discovery that women used cosmetics not only to look but primarily to feel beautiful) presented the product as a way of experiencing one's own body, rather than, primarily, presenting it in a favourable light to the evaluating (male) gaze of strangers. Similarly with sexuality: the woman as a sexual subject and not just an object

Figure 6.2 'Camay makes his head turn', *Gioia* 7/3, 1962. Empowering consumption. New materials and new design give a new kind of freedom, mobility and self-assurance. (Courtesy of the Biblioteca Nazionale, Florence.)

Figure 6.3 On Bravo you are your own boss! The scooter as a tool for practical empowerment, early 1970s. (Courtesy of Fondazione Piaggio, Pontedera.)

became a frequent theme in selling anything from contraceptives to sweets and the words 'freedom' or 'to be free' proliferated in advertising copy.[50]

In the early 1970s this 'commodity feminism', to use Robert Goldman's term, suggested by *Amica* was taken up by a number of campaigns, like Piaggio's advertisements for their new Bravo scooter that would enable women to move around freely, and 'be their own bosses'.[51] Even if *Amica*'s stance was at the vanguard end, a number of women's magazines began to deviate from the traditional housewife model, or at least present it differently: as a chosen identity rather than an imposed role. In part this was due to the increasing availability of qualitative market research that allowed an increasing differentiation of audiences. But it was also triggered by the concern on the part of publishers to represent their readers as subjects, moved by their own personal interests and choices, as New Women. Thus *Rakam*, a hitherto rather traditional magazine for housewives, now sold itself as a medium for women who had a particular interest in household work; *Madre*, a magazine for mothers, similarly sold motherhood as a chosen lifestyle. In 1970 Mondadori would differentiate the characteristics of their publications according to the chosen preferences of an ideal reader.

Conclusion

The emergence of the 'New Woman' in advertising discourse reflected a change in the real situation of many of Italian middle-class women. But that these transformations were translated into a new normative ideal of femininity was contingent on the affirmation of a new way of looking at and thinking around consumers on the part of the advertising profession. Indeed, advertising professionals had begun to rethink their conceptualizations of women and of consumers in general even before Italian feminism put women's issues on the public agenda. Rather than a conservative force that in the end gave in to the pressure of new social movements, the advertising profession reconceptualized not only consumer culture but the ideology of gender in general. This role of advertising rested on a new social vision that had crystallized during the decade. As argued by new gurus like Dichter, Katona and Maslow, the spread of consumer goods was thought to lead to a more open, creative and individualized society. As the consumer psychologist Antonio Miotto put it in a 1968 article that reassumed many of these new ideas:

> We are not quite prepared to arrive at McLuhan's position that the man of tomorrow (and hence the consumer of tomorrow) will live the life of an artist who manages to give a vital cultural content to the growing parentheses of leisure time. But we do agree with him when he affirms that the man of today, and of tomorrow, cannot renounce the imposing need to progressively widen his experiences and to participate in an ever more intense manner in the ongoing collective dynamism. In today's and tomorrow's society we might have chaos, but not conformism.[52]

Part of the new *raison d'être* of the business, then, was to sell consumer goods as objects that could enable and inspire new ways of living the modern life. The furthering of mass consumption was seen not only as a profitable business, but also as a step to furthering the individualization process and the emancipation from repressive or restrictive older, traditional models, in

Figure 6.4 Beginning lifestyle segmentation. Piaggio uses a hippy to address the teen market in 1969. (Courtesy of the Biblioteca Nazionale, Florence.)

particular for women. Francesco Alberoni, who during the 1960s had become one of the chief intellectual exponents of this new vision (and who had expanded his market research activities to engage quite extensively in corporate consultancy) reassumed this vision in his work *Consumi e società* of 1964, an early sociological treatise of consumption. He drew on his experience from studying for Bassetti young women's relations to nightgowns, underwear, towels and bed linen. When mass produced and purchased rather than made by the woman herself as part of her *corredo* – the supply of linen, underwear and such that she brought with her into marriage – as was the tradition, such objects were directly antithetical to the traditional order, in particular in the south.

> To possess and use a modern [mass produced] nightgown carries a connotation of rebellion against the old austerity of the *corredo*. It means to introduce motives that were previously rigorously excluded, to affirm, symbolically and implicitly one's own freedom to choose any man that one desires and to be desirable even after marriage. It carries the possibility of a fantastic, playful and sensual affective life that was unimaginable before. To buy such a nightgown not only radically weakens the very institution of dowry, but introduces the opportunity for choice in a context where the strength of that institution has been derived from its traditional immutability. It carries a challenge to the traditional meaning of marriage, the traditional relation to the husband and to the children. It means to imagine a different kind of family, with different roles and new kinds of freedoms.[53]

During the 1960s advertising thus began to develop a proper project of modernity, with a proper view of the modern subject *qua* consumer. While this built on perspectives that had already been articulated during the 1930s, it now became much more coherent. More importantly, the advertising profession acquired the methods necessary to promote its realization. It made its own interpretation of events and acted according to that interpretation, promoting consumer goods as tools for individualization and the emancipation from restrictive social norms. During the 1970s, as the next chapter will show, this (relative) autonomy of advertising would be even more pronounced and the profession itself even more influential in shaping the modernization process.

7 The new ethic of consumption II

Crisis and reconstruction

In 1976 Barilla launched a new line of products: the Mulino Bianco biscuits. This strategy of diversification was to a large extent a response to the price regulations imposed on basic necessities – among them pasta – in the wake of the oil crisis in 1973. (While the regulations themselves softened soon enough under the pressure of industrial interests, Barilla's American owners, W.R. Grace, got cold feet at anything that reeked of political pricing.) The move proved a great success. By 1978, two years after the launch, Mulino Bianco had captured 8.5 per cent of the Italian biscuit market, and it kept growing. Given that many other Italian food manufacturers had tried to enter that market in the early 1970s and failed, the success of Mulino Bianco was extraordinary. To a large extent it certainly depended on the high quality of the product itself. Barilla had decided to use only real milk and real eggs from the very start (not the otherwise common powdered version). What really set Barilla's biscuits apart from the competition, however, was the product image they offered. At a time when industrial society was felt to be under threat from an impending energy crisis, and was under continuous critique from the emerging new social movements, Mulino Bianco proposed a return to an imagined pre-industrial past. Authentic, genuine foods, honest work on the land, and 'values that never change', like the family, community and nature. This pre-industrial image was masterfully fleshed out in advertisements which featured copy that began with 'Do you remember when', rural landscapes with rolling hills, girls milking cows, rustic breakfasts in the open, and the ever-present, iconic White Mill (Mulino Bianco), initially modelled on English nineteenth-century drawings. (In 1985 the White Mill acquired a 'real' referent in a series of spots shot at an old mill located in the idyllic Tuscan landscape of Chiusdino, outside Siena.) The television spots starred real peasants (they were the only ones able to give off a proper air of authenticity); the biscuits themselves were designed to look and feel non-industrial, with irregular shapes and *naif* design; they were given archaic names and packed in paper bags.[1]

According to Francesco Alberoni, who worked as a consultant on the Mulino Bianco project, the success of the biscuits rested largely on this particular sign-value. Mulino Bianco incorporated the kinds of values that average Italians now craved. Under the weight of a seemingly terminal economic crisis, the anomie that came with the end of the post-war trust in continuing growth and prosperity, and increasingly violent politics, Italians nurtured a latent desire to abandon the values of industrial modernity, Alberoni thought. (The launch of Mulino Bianco coincided with the build-up of terrorist violence that culminated in the Moro kidnapping in 1978, the so-called 'years of lead', or *anni di piombo*.) They wanted to go back to a more genuine world where things had remained the same, where the family was still a haven of domestic intimacy. Mulino Bianco, Alberoni argues, gave Italians something new to believe in. It anticipated, he claims, the turn towards the private sphere (what is known as the *riflusso* or 'backlash') that marked the end of the decade.[2]

Mulino Bianco was also a novelty in the field of marketing practice, however. Barilla's strategy was not primarily directed at selling biscuits, but at selling a value complex. The biscuits were marketed as a fetishistic incarnation of a particular attitude to modernity and to life in general. (Indeed at the beginning of the product development process it was decided that just selling excellent quality biscuits was not enough. Barilla would not move on with the project unless such a particular sign-value could be developed.) With Mulino Bianco, Barilla entered the era of branding and 'lifestyle marketing' that was to dominate the 1980s. The product was connected to a particular way of life that was elaborated more or less *ex novo*. Even if the relevance of the meaning complex to be attached to the product was continously tested through market research, it did not derive from any actually existing form of life, nor from any established tradition within consumer culture (as in the case of the 'American housewife'). Mulino Bianco was entirely 'made up' by the mediating labour of marketing and advertising. This work of mediation had hitherto worked with what we can call a realist outlook, aiming to fit the product to the needs and desires of what was thought to be an actually existing consumer subject (observed, however distortedly, through some form of market research). Now, however, marketing and advertising began to work with a greater degree of freedom. The task was rather to produce new sign-values for goods, by recombining elements from disparate cultural contexts, which, even though they might not be related to any actually existing consumer lifeworld, might be thought to have a potential appeal. With objects like Mulino Bianco the identity of goods had thus been set free from the constraints of structure and tradition, and were allowed to develop the relatively autonomous realm of simulacra.[3]

The Mulino Bianco project can thus be read as a response not only to an increasingly risky pasta market, but also to a crumbling social model. If, as Alessandro Pizzorno has argued in a famous article, consensus for the Christian Democrat-headed modernization process during the preceding decade was secured by guaranteeing middle-class prospects of prosperity, the late 1960s marked the beginning of a crisis in that arrangement.[4] First, the DC model was challenged at the political level. The youth cultures that had been

Figure 7.1 'Do you remember when the mills were white.' Mulino Bianco as nostalgia for an authentic imagined past. (Courtesy of Archivio Storico Barilla, Parma.)

building up momentum all through the 1960s now became increasingly political, as expressed in university occupations and frequent clashes with the police. The students were joined by the workers, who set off the long wave of strikes and protests known as the 'hot autumn' (*l'autunno caldo*) in 1969.[5] This gave rise to a plethora of groups and movements that made up the active and vociferous civil society of the left. Second, the oil crisis of 1973 precipitated a profound economic crisis that seriously challenged the viability of existing economic institutions. Even to the people who adhered to the older social model it became increasingly evident that some form of restructuring was necessary. The main political attempt to, so to speak, 'redraw the social contract' during the 1970s, the 'historical compromise' between the DC and the PCI (see chapter 8), was largely a failure, and after a period of intense conflict the impact of politics in general began to fade. Advertising, on the other hand, was highly successful in translating the value revolution that came out of 1968 into a new kind of lifestyle consumerism that would come to have a general appeal during the following decade. There the emancipating and critical thrust of 1968 was translated into an ethic of consumerist self-affirmation; the critique of industrial society that had grown during the 1970s found its expression in new simulacra of authenticity like Mulino Bianco, and its political discourse in the communication of brands and labels. This chapter will trace how the critical discourse of the 1960s was transformed into the consumer culture of the 1980s. The first decisive factor was the growth of the counter-culture.

The discovery of youth

In the post-war years new visible and provocative consumer habits contributed to putting youth on the public agenda.[6] Generally their new patterns of consumption were considered deviant, or even pathological. Invariably consumption featured as the cause of the alienation and cynicism often attributed to members of the younger generation. By their very innocence, young people were easy victims to the persuasive images of advertising and mass culture, it was thought. Giorgio Bocca painted a particularly bleak picture of the connection between consumption, alienation and criminality thought to prevail in youth culture during the years of the 'miracle':

> In the province of the economic miracle [the rural north], nobody is hungry any more and hunger has lost its imprint on childish mentalities. [Instead of stealing apples or fruit] our dear youngsters steal cars. Adolescent gangs roam the roads from Padua and Verona to Bolzano, passing from one car to another. One youngster managed to steal ten cars to cover the distance from Padua to Riva del Garda and back. Alongside the young men, there is always a girl, a friend and accomplice. Together, with the money stolen from some petrol station, the little couple go to the movies. There, in the dark, chewing sweets, they partake in the

dreamworlds that have been tailored to everybody's tastes: ever shinier cars, ever sweeter advertisements, stars that are ever easier to imitate. There is no element of rebellion in these acts, but rather good old conformism. These adolescents want what everyone else wants, what the shop windows tempt them with, day after day.[7]

The attitude on the part of the advertising profession was hardly any more optimistic. While they did keep an eye on the booming US youth market, Italian youth were at the most regarded as future adult consumers, but their actual consumer practices were generally considered too diverse to be of any practical interest. As one article in Piaggio's company magazine put it in 1957 (Piaggio was one of the few major companies to take an interest in the youth market), 'Today it is common to speak very badly about young people.' The author proceeded to defend Piaggio's involvement with the younger generation by pointing out that 'it is absolutely not true that they are degenerates just because they behave in ways that are different from ours'.[8] At the most, the advertising press recommended investment in advertising for young people in order to shape their future, adult preferences at an early stage; to re-educate and normalize their consumer patterns; to 'place the seeds of tomorrow's market today'.[9]

In the 1960s there was a new institutionalization of the Italian youth market. Teenage magazines, like *Ciao* (1961), *Big* (1963), *Ciao Amici* and *Giovani* (1966), offered a medium to reach a distinctly young, or teen audience.[10] This spurred a growing number of investigations of young people's consumer habits. How often did they use juke-boxes? How many owned a radio or a record player? How often did they go to the bar or go out dancing? To what extent did the fact that a record featured in the top-ten list influence its sales? What triggered the buying decisions of youth in relation to records in general? And so on.[11] Following an influential European Society for Marketing (ESOMAR) conference in Brussels in 1962, advertising professionals began to emphasize the importance of understanding the diverse lifeworld of youth. At the conference on 'Youth and the market' organized in Genoa in 1967 it was argued that youth formed a society of their own, with its own values and standards.[12] Apart from the occasional lecture or seminar – like the one on 'Beat Culture' sponsored by the Turin salesmen's association in 1967 – not much was done to understand this youthful society.[13] While considered an interesting niche, the Italian youth market remained too small or too isolated to trigger any substantial investments. (Or, as in the case of the international market in records and music, it was beyond the control of national advertising.) As a Doxa study had shown in 1966, the youth market was mainly restricted to products like 'ice-cream and sweets, coffee, beer, soft drinks, sandwiches and snacks, magazines, public transport, movies and other forms of entertainment and cigarettes'.[14] With some exceptions, like Piaggio's successful campaigns for their Vespa scooters, this was not enough to feed any overreaching concerns on the part of advertising professionals.[15] This passivity would vanish during the second half of the 1960s, not so much because of the growing size of the youth market, as because of the appeal of the different consumer practices it launched. The most important of these was fashion.

In the early 1960s London became the international centre for a new kind of youthful fashion. What the Beatles did to pop music, Mary Quant and the many other new designers who sold their wares in the small boutiques around the King's Road did to fashion. New materials, new cuts and new daring designs and patterns came with a new set of attitudes not only to fashion, but to life in general. 'Swinging London' became a concept that stood for a new youthful civil society where the boutique was a central institution. In California, similarly, the hippies blended the Bohemian tradition of the 1950s Beatniks with oriental influences into expressions in clothing, hair styles and new forms of public behaviour. During the early 1960s these influences filtered into Italy, where they mixed into what was known as 'Beat' fashion. Initially these new trends developed around the second-hand clothes markets of Milan and through personal imports on the part of the many young people who began to travel to London, but soon Beat fashion too was institutionalized.

In 1963, the first proper boutique, Cose, opened in via della Spiga. It sold clothes by Nuccia Fattori – inspired by London designers – as well as imports: Emanuelle Khan, Paco Rabanne, Zandra Rhodes, Karl Lagerfeldtzs Chloé, and other names from the new international fashion movement. In 1966 Cose was accompanied by a new shop, Altre Cose, which stayed open at night above Milan disco and nightspot Big Bang. The following year saw the arrival of both Fiorucci and the Equipe 84 chain, started by the agent of the famous Beat pop group with the same name. Other famous spaces like Gulp in Milan and Piper moda in Rome followed (the latter connected to a famous nightclub of the same name). By the mid-1960s Beat fashion, and the Beat style in general, represented by singers like Mina or Patty Pravo, became all the rage. This new fashion, or 'antifashion' as it was called, contained not only a new aesthetic or style, but also a whole new attitude to shopping and consumption in general.[16] The shops were not only conceived as points of sale, but also as spaces for social interaction, where design and music were crucial elements. Altre Cose, for example, was entirely built from steel and plexiglas and exposed its wares in transparent cylinders lowered from the roof. The less expensive new warehouse shops that mushroomed in big cities during the 1960s put a similar weight on music and interior design. Also, relations between salespeople and customers were different. The new shops did not feel so much like commercial spaces as spaces for a new kind of youthful sociality. As sociologist Gerardo Ragone observed in relation to Fiorucci's new shop in Rome that opened in 1976 (but with basically the same kind of concept as his original 1967 shop in Milan), it featured halogen lights, steel and plexiglas shelves, pounding rock music and young personnel without the traditionally subservient attitude of regular sales assistants. One entered the premises, not necessarily to buy something, but to interact, to 'walk around freely and try out clothes', to talk and socialize.

> There is a certain communitarian climate that tends to homogenize, socially and culturally, who buys and who sells. This commercial universe is deeply marked by a particular ideology, to hide, to negate as far as possible the economic and productive conditions on which it rests. Indeed, one feels rather like in a refuge, an almost magical place where the act of selling merchandise is only an excuse for meetings, little breaks, exchanges of sociability.[17]

'Antifashion' built on the participation of consumers, where street style and design were put in constant communication, and the process of innovation was moved from the studio to the immanent creativity of not-yet-institutionalized social relations. Before the polticization of youth culture in the second half of the 1960s it was this aspect of agency, of taking charge of one's own look and self-presentation, that constituted the main oppositional element of Beat culture. As Jerry Rubin emphasized in his counter-cultural manifesto *Do It!* (transalted into Italian in 1971): long hair makes you an actor. And that, he argued, was revolutionary in a society made up of passive consumers.[18] (Pier Paolo Pasolini made similar observations on long-haired youth: 'they became more and more numerous, like the first Christians, but they remained mysteriously silent. Their long hair is their true language and there is little more of importance to add. Their speech coincides with their being.')[19]

This concept of consumption as contestation and agency was key to the fortune of perhaps the most successful designer to come out of the *anti-moda*, Fiorucci. Fiorucci, influenced by hippie fashion, opened his first shop in Milan in 1967. (And Italian hippies would sell in his shop their wares brought back from India, Nepal and Afghanistan.) It featured a vast variety of garments, all available relatively cheaply, and customers were encouraged to recombine them creatively in a sort of ongoing masquerade. Fiorucci's clothes served to create 'a generalized, yet personal image that expressed the wish to stay young and not to be sucked up by that great devil, "the system"'.[20] This institutionalized creativity was crucial to the Fiorucci philosophy. Fashion, he argued should be about free and creative self-expression, not about imposed standards or canons. As *Amica* described it in 1974:

> The age of imposed fashion is over, Fiorucci says. 'Why does someone have to wear beige if he doesn't like beige. No, let everyone dress as they want.' That's why you'll never find one single trend in Fiorucci's stores; you find hundreds. Negozio Fiorucci: A Bazaar where you'll feel younger. 'Tonight I'll be a Geisha and bring you some tea.' 'Why not try a green watermelon bath tonight.'[21]

The reliance on such a general social creativity was also central to Fiorucci's way of working. His design study was non-hierarchical, based on loosely connected project teams with many people working there only temporarily, continually coming and going. Designers were encouraged to travel, and a lot of money was spent on books and magazines. The whole management style (which in many respects anticipated contemporary ideas of 'project management') was geared to keep in touch with a highly fluid street style, and programmed to produce a new collection every six months.[22] In 1974 Fiorucci was acquired by the retail chain Standa and his shops spread across Italy. With the backing of Standa, Fiorucci went international and launched a successful campaign on the American market, where his clothes were intrinsically connected to the mid-1970s disco wave. In many respects the fate of Fiorucci was indicative of that of antifashion in general. After some initial resistance the giants of the Italian textile industry decided to go along. The result was a series of new collections, like Max Mara's Pop collection from 1965 that contributed to revolutionizing the *prêt a porter* segment available to middle-class consumers. (From 1960 to 1970 the annual sales of *prêt a porter* garments increased from 390,000 to 2 million.)[23]

As antifashion gave new life to the Italian fashion industry, youthful attachments to consumption and, so it seemed, to life in general, appeared to be spreading to people who were no longer young in a biological sense. New kinds of music, like that of the *cantautori*, achieved an unprecedented popularity. The habit of wearing jeans as an everyday garment spread to different classes, as did the adoption of colourful shirts and ties and more relaxed manners of interaction even in office environments. Women's magazines saw a substantial rejuvenation of their editorial content. *Amica*, for example, opened a section for teenagers, *il giornale dei giovanissmi*, and a youthful appearance began to replace the ideal of a more grown-up elegance as a general model for the presentation of self. 'Never', an article in the trade journal *Marketing e pubblicità* claimed, 'will middle-aged women be as young as they are now. They dress and behave like young people.'[24]

The rise of this youthful influence was also channelled through a transformation of the advertising industry itself. Now the large multinational companies of the 1960s were paralleled by a number of smaller agencies, often opened by young professionals who had had their schooling in one of the large firms, but who now saw the need for a more independent and creative approach to advertising. (The emergence of small agencies was also connected to a transformation of the advertising market. With the revival of small producers of consumer goods, notably in the fashion sector, a new market for smaller advertising investments opened outside the control of the larger multinational agencies.)[25] There was something of an Italian 'creative revolution' in advertising. New advertising campaigns made more or less direct use of the visual language of youth culture, as in the case of Leader's campaigns for the Vespa and, perhaps most famously, Agenzia Italia's downright blasphemous sales pitch for Jesus Jeans.[26] To be young and to be against, was, it seemed all the rage in advertising, or as Gianpaolo Ceserani, an advertising professional and frequent writer on advertising, put it in 1975, advertising seemed to be 'submerged in a wave of youth'. Since a youthful image now seemed to be a must, the first task of any campaign was to rejuvenate products and company images.[27]

Youthful habits of consumption were no longer marginal or deviant, but the very source of new fads and trends that, it seemed, had a general appeal. Indeed, it appeared that young people were a vanguard of a general reformation of consumer tastes, where the Italian middle classes moved away form the standardized packages of mass consumption to embrace instead values like self-expression, creativity and 'quality of life'.[28] In the eyes of the advertising industry this new model was most clearly expressed in the new 'antifashion' which was generally interpreted as tangible expression of more general latent trends.[29] Consequently, advertising and marketing professionals began to devote a lot of attention to fashion. In 1967 the marketing trade journal *I Prodotti di marca* (*Branded Goods*) dedicated a whole issue to the fashion industry, arguing that the new relations between people and goods that it furthered were on their way to dominate consumer culture as a whole. As marketing theorist Claudio Stroppa claimed in his article on the economic potential of fashion, 'Fashion has become one of the great powers of our times. It determines the character and direction of consumer demand, because to be out of touch with fashion is like being out of touch with the world.'[30] The initiative was accompanied by a series of enquiries into the dynamics of fashion, frequently cast in a psychoanalytic framework, like the influential research report *La donna e la moda* (*Women and Fashion*) prepared for the American advertising agency Foote, Cone & Belding by psychologist Antonio Miotto in 1969. In the same year, the textile company Gritti financed a volume *La psicologia del vestire* (*The Psychology of Clothing*) with contributions from market researchers and sociologists Francesco Alberoni and Marino Livolsi, but also figures like Umberto Eco and art critique Gillo Dorfles. (Men's fashions was a relatively new field that had developed with the growth of the *prêt a porter* market.)[31] In these studies, antifashion was read as indicative of a new ethic of consumption. As *La psicologia del vestire* concluded, clothes are not just utilitarian objects; they also serve to 'express our selves, realize our selves and our hidden desires, to exalt our personality and our culture'.[32]

As interpreted by the advertising profession, young people's consumer practices were understood to be motivated by an implicit alternative social vision, where things like self-realization and creativity mattered more than the crude accumulation of material possessions. In addition, their habits, values and outlooks, in short, their identity, was not given, it seemed, by their position in relation to social structure, but rather derived from their own consumer practice. Indeed, as had been clear ever since the conference on youth in Genoa in 1967, it was chiefly their ways of using consumer goods that served to set them apart from adult society. Young people were also shrewd interpreters of media and advertising. This made them accustomed to a kind of reflexivity in relation to consumer culture that older consumers, who still took advertising seriously, generally lacked. With everyday habits and even a generational *patois* in which consumer goods and advertising slogans formed an integrated part, youthful consumer practices indicated how people who had grown up and been socialized into a fully developed consumer society would think and act.[33] In short, the theories about a coming post-materialist or post-conformist age seemed to have a concrete reference in the consumption styles of youth. Young people seemed to have progressed beyond the desire for novelty or the mere satisfaction of 'material' needs, to articulate a new value structure.

To the advertising profession, three things were to be learnt from youthful consumer patterns. First of all, the way in which young people related to consumer goods appeared to be markedly different from that of the older generation. Adults, most marketing professionals agreed, would generally appreciate consumer goods for their ability to signify adherence to or, as would be increasingly prominent during the 1960s, distance from a particular social model. They would either function as citizenship goods that testified to one's status as a modern, accomplished person, or, in the case of the new housewife, as tools for articulating one's independence or emancipation from accepted models of consumption and identity. Adult consumption remained in some way determined (negatively or positively) by a conformist mass culture. Young people, on the other hand, did not use consumer goods to distance themselves from or to imitate dominant models, it seemed. They used them to articulate and express their own identities. The meaning of consumer goods was effectively delinked from dominant models and even from socio-structural determination in general, to refer back to an autonomous practice of collective 'bricolage'. In youth culture, consumption was about individual self – expression, not social belonging. Youth culture thus pointed at a conception of consumer goods as a kind of 'free-floating language', where distinct elements could be creatively recombined by the individual consumer. Second, this creative use of consumer goods appeared to be an all-absorbing practice. Differently from other social groups, youth had virtually no other identity, and, to advertising professionals, few other interests than their consumption. This would involve their whole personality. In youth culture, consumption invested the whole life of the individual. This indicated that consumer goods could be given meanings that went far beyond their actual uses; that they could be made to signify a particular way of life or, as the term would become, 'lifestyle'. Third, in youth culture, consumption was a cooperative rather than a competitive activity. Youthful consumption did not follow the Veblian model of imitation of one's superiors. Rather, youthful consumer culture was non-hierarchical, and directed primarily at the creation and reproduction of a communitarian sociality based on consumer goods. In contrast to the individualism and social isolation that appeared to result from the spread of mass consumption in the 1950s, young people's consumption was social: it built on the participation in certain communal environments of consumption. This consumer sociality, furthermore, appeared to have a certain autonomy – it remained unaffected by both advertising and more subtle attempts at control, and its fads and fashions seemed to be the outcome of this collective consumer effervescence itself. This indicated that a future consumer culture had to be based on and encourage the participation of consumers themselves.[34]

Crisis and reconstruction

As the youth culture turned political and the university occupations began, the challenge that it posed – when viewed through the lens of recent marketing thought – began to be taken seriously by the Italian marketing profession. At the conference of the Italian centre for management studies (CISA) in 1968, established models that emphasized planning and attempts to manage demand had been criticized for not taking the marketing message seriously enough, and, consequently, not listening closely enough to what was actually happening.[35] While such critiques were first put forth by a younger generation of cadres who had entered the profession in the late 1960s, some of the older names also joined in. In the congress of the Institute for Public Relations in 1971, Roberto Tremelloni, an old advocate of planning and rationalization who had been connected to the Italian world of advertising from the start (see chapter 3), expressed his fears that too strong an emphasis on planning risked going against what seemed to be the present trend. Instead, a development towards a more diversified and 'creative' society required that individual tastes be given more space to grow and prosper. Hence, Tremelloni argued, it was necessary to listen to the movements and tendencies that pointed towards a new 'consumer sovereignty'. As the rising new American marketing guru Philip Kotler had suggested in a recent article, it was crucial to open up the practice of marketing to the new diversity of the social. Unless marketers learned to be more open and flexible, they would not be able to keep up with what seemed to be accelerating change in consumer tastes.[36] Such concerns were not only of a pragmatic, technical nature however. Many also feared that an overemphasis on technocratic planning and economic growth would produce a neglect of democratic participation and social solidarity that would increase 'the discomfort that man feels today and the growing tensions that he experiences in society'.[37]

This self-criticism was not shared by all. In the debate that followed Tremelloni's address, many emphasized the utility of planning and a 'scientific approach' to marketing. Despite its negative effects in terms of standardization or even alienation, planning and rational overall management had been shown to be able to 'diminish the possibility of errors due to human and personal factors' and, more importantly perhaps, 'stimulate private consumption', making sure that marketing worked to boost economic development. To meet a future, more complex and diversified society, these voices concluded, research and scientific method would surely become more, not less, important.[38]

Such arguments for the defence of older models of consumption and marketing were, however, effectively undermined by the oil crisis. Even though it did not lead to any marked decline in consumer spending and advertising budgets, except in the very short run, it provoked fears and reasonable expectations that a prolonged period of austerity and sacrifice would follow. It seemed, indeed, that the economic crisis expected to follow would block, perhaps permanently, a return to pre-1973 standards of living. The oil crisis also confirmed previous speculations on the limited range of capitalist development, the most influential being the MIT report on the limits to growth, translated into Italian in 1972.[39] As the critique of 'the wasteful society' now seemed to find its confirmation in reality, even the proponents of an Italian version of 'Theory X capitalism' lost their most basic argument: that planning and bureaucratic administration, no matter how stifling and inhumane, would, in the end, contribute to an economic development that would eventually trickle down and make life easier for most people.

With the loss of this basic *raison d'être*, the marketing and advertising profession fell into something of a legitimacy crisis. Many felt that, as the title of the congress of the Italian association for market research (AISM) in 1976, 'Marketing and the search for consensus' indicated, marketing and corporate capital in general, had lost its legitimacy.[40] Advertising and marketing professionals confessed not only to having created false needs and having sacrificed utility for futility, neglecting their 'contribution to society' for the maximization of profits, but also to having based their practice on a flawed ideology of perpetual growth.[41] In a survey of business leader opinions from 1975, the overwhelming majority put the responsibility for the present discontent first and foremost on their own shoulders. Advertising appeared to be particularly worthy of blame, as 50 per cent of the sample showed that 'it presented products in an exaggerated and unrealistic way and served mostly to fuel consumer suspicion'.[42] In the face of this new situation, several voices for the regulation of marketing and advertising emerged. Some argued for the institutionalization of national planning authorities that would work with social and not purely economic interests in mind. Others, more frequently, proposed some stricter kind of self-discipline.[43]

This legitimacy crisis opened the marketing profession to the critique advanced by the social movements on the left. These movements themselves were, however, viewed with some suspicion, and more radical voices were, so to speak, psychologized away. In particular, radical measures like the 'autoreduction campaigns', which began to be adopted by trade unions and in a number of local neighbourhood struggles, were considered to be symptoms of irrational reactions and 'anarchic rebellion', rather than rational proposals.[44] Such 'exaggerated' manifestations originated in a generalized insecurity and an 'emotionally charged search for scapegoats', not in rational discourse.[45] In the words of successful motivation psychologist Gabriele Calvi, the more radical manifestations of anti-capitalist social protest were but the spearhead of a general tendency towards infantile regression:

> Today's most prevalent psychological phenomena are . . . panic, deprivation, hoardings, the rediscovery of archaic forms of needs-satisfaction, the flowering of evasive practices (like sports, travel, exotic holidays, restaurants, films) and, more pathologically, increasing attacks on private property. This is an adaptive reaction that is not motivated by any intention to possess or consume, but is rather immature, egoistic, dangerous. It can foster reactivate infantile and irrational patterns of behaviour, perhaps akin to the desperate and furious attempts of a child who does not want to let go of a toy that he thinks rightly his.[46]

Precisely because of the irrational and neurotic character of their contestation, the more radical social movements, according to Calvi, did not harbour the capacity to produce anything new. They were purely reactive and lacked realistic new models to propose. They would hence soon exhaust themselves, leaving consumers as anomic and confused as before.

Nevertheless, the large-scale trend that the social movements represented was real enough. Reports from the US had shown that middle-class consumers were less interested in pure material accumulation, and more open to developing their spiritual sides through 'personalization, self-expression, creativity and a return to nature'. Research indicated that such a scenario was a likely possibility for Italy as well.[47] In addition to the heavy criticism that it faced, marketing thus seemed to be confronting a new, different structure of needs. In recent years, according to the introductory address to the 1975 conference, 'Refunding Marketing' (*Rifondazione del marketing*), 'the very model of consumption, and probably the model of life in our community generally, would change radically'. Society was moving towards a 'post-consumerist age', where people would 'make love, and not buy petrol'.[48] A radical reconstruction of marketing practice was thus desperately needed, in order to save the legitimacy of the profession, but also in order to counter the general anomie that people like Calvi saw as indicative of the Italian crisis of the 1970s.

New marketing

As marketing professionals were debating the future and legitimacy of their trade, important changes were underway in Italian society. While the memory and, for that matter, the self-representation of the 1970s was marked by the predominance of the political, from the lively alternative groups and social movements that initiated the decade, to the gloomy years of terrorism that ended it, this was not the whole picture. The 1970s were also the time of the affirmation of consumer culture in Italy. With but a few downturns in the wake of the oil crisis, both GNP per capita and family consumption kept rising steadily, and an increasing share was spent on leisure and recreation. As a result, the diffusion of consumer goods like cars and television sets rose steadily, and new kinds of goods like pre-cooked meals, deep-frozen foods, fast-food restaurants and sports and leisure gear now entered the Italian market on a wide scale. Even more importantly, a generation of people who had entered the decade as politically active now came to turn increasingly to consumption for their self-definition and identity. The result was an emerging middle-class consumer culture that was rather different from the hierarchical mass consumerism of the preceding decade. Middle-class consumers now began to have more varied tastes; they valued the quality and ethical standing of goods and, increasingly, their expressive and communicative function. (The 1970s also saw the emergence of consumerist movements and of 'progressive', i.e. socially engaged, advertising – *pubblicità progresso*.) Most importantly, the qualitative composition of demand seemed to result from the interaction and communication that took place within the social itself. This could no longer be reduced to the principle of status competition that had been central before. Consequently, it seemed it would no longer work to try to impose a single model on everyone.[49] Instead, as Gerardo Ragone put it, the main problem for the advertising industry was 'no longer to try to persuade, but to try to keep up with the social evolution under way'.[50] In order to do this, advertising began to leave its psychological theories behind to concentrate more on the social life of goods, on the way in which consumer goods were used in interaction and communication.

One direction that such an approach could take was suggested by a recent development in US marketing thought. Under what was known as 'New Marketing' Philip Kotler, the US marketing guru *par excellence* during the 1970s, offered a way to navigate the complexities of post-materialistic consumer society. Launched by Philip Kotler in a seminal article in 1969, which had an immediate impact in Italy, new marketing stood for a substantial widening of the marketing concept.[51] Taking Dichter's philosophy of 'emancipating hedonism' seriously, the task of New Marketing was to realize not-yet-manifest desires, and to produce consumer goods that could work as tools for living out such new wants. In contrast to Dichter's vision, however, there was no necessary anthropological vision behind New Marketing; new products did not necessarily have to cater to a pleasure-seeking user. Indeed, there were virtually no limits for the kinds of needs they could cater to. This, as Kotler would argue in a following article, opened up the practice of marketing to virtually any social field. Its task was to furnish 'new sensible social values' in general, as Kotler's Italian interlocutor, Giuseppe Morello, argued in 1972.[52] Marketing could become a modern and sophisticated applied behavioural science that was capable of taking on and guiding social transformation. The new element, however, was that people were to be made participants in this creation of new needs and values. New Marketing thus aimed to utilize the new socialized creativity in ways similar to those of antifashion. In order to accomplish this, marketing had to abandon fixed models of consumer tastes and preferences and instead confront the reality of the social. Marketers had to develop a general sensitivity. Like advertising creatives and fashion designers, they had to be able to interpret a latent demand and make it manifest in offering consumer goods. They had to open to a certain creativity and 'lateral thinking, to develop their capacity to connect'; its purpose would be to identify 'new forms of life', 'new ways of living in society', and give them a material foundation in consumer goods. [53]

New Marketing seemed an even more viable strategy given the new image of society that emerged from a new market research technique, psychographics, or lifestyle research, which had had a relatively long history in the US. The technique had developed during the post-war years through the close interaction of sociology and market research mediated by firms like Burleigh Gardner's Social Research Inc. By the late 1960s the technique had become well established as the advertising agency Leo Burnett & Co. performed the first national psychographic survey, using so-called AIO variables (Attitudes Interests Orientations) to create consumer typologies differentiated by socio-economic standing as well as by values and attitudes, not only to consumption but to a plurality of topics. The technique spread during the 1970s, leading to the publication of perhaps the most famous psychographic study, Andrew Mitchell's *Nine American Lifestyles* in 1983. In Italy psychographics had been debated since the late 1960s, but was not put into practice until the mid-1970s.[54] There had certainly been some applications of psychographic variables and cluster analysis before, for example in Doxa's study of youth, sponsored by Shell in 1970 and a Leo Burnett & Co. survey, conducted as part of a general mapping of the European market in 1974, though they never led to any published results.[55] The first general psychographic monitoring of Italy was launched in the autumn of 1976 (and published in 1977) by former Misura researcher Gabriele Calvi and his research institute Eurisko. Eurisko conducted a survey of 3,000 individuals using modified AIO variables divided into 30 value scales and 13 so-called 'behavioural areas' (*aree comportamentali*). The results were divided into nine different clusters, representing nine general lifestyles (and in a parallel analysis, five 'food styles', *stili alimentari*).[56] Eurisko soon faced competition from Gianpaolo Fabris's GPF Associati. They launched their first Monitor survey in 1977 using a sample of 2,500 individuals. The results were then transformed into eight principal clusters represented as a typology of eight lifestyles, the 'eight Italies' (later to become ten).[57]

The growth of psychographic research was driven by a notion that society was becoming far too complex to be captured by traditional methods where structural variables like class, gender or geographic position were determined a priori. In the psychographic approach, on the other hand, no variable was assumed to be determined a priori, but the lifestyles resulted from an inductive clustering of the data generated. The result was that individuals appeared to be moving in a multidimensional social space where traditional structural variables were much less important than before. In the results of

Figure 7.2 Capturing the emotional side of consumption. A computer can know her age and how much she earns . . . but not what makes her cry or laugh or buy. Young & Rubicam advertising themselves as an agency in 1970 with a more holistic perspective. (Courtesy of the Biblioteca Nazionale Florence.)

psychographic surveys, individuals appeared to have been effectively delinked from structural determination – their social collocation was a result of their own choices: what values to embrace, what behaviours to engage in. In addition, a large part of the variables used regarded attitudes to consumption. (After all, this was market research.) In Calvi's survey, for example, only one of the 13 behavioural areas, 'the education of children', was not directly concerned with consumer choices. The image of society that psychographics produced thus not only conceived of social position as a consequence of individual choice but also represented consumption as the overwhelmingly most significant area for such choices. In the psychographic surveys produced by Eurisko and GPF Associati, Italians appeared as consumers.

The result of the impact of lifestyle research and the philosophy of New Marketing was a growing attention to semiotics within the discussions of advertising professionals. Semiotics offered a new way of thinking about the relations between people. It would permit the overall marketing of consumer goods as tools for a set-free and delinked process of identity construction. Conceiving of the consumer as a free-floating and self-reflexive *bricoleur*, marketing and advertising could serve to create a language that would facilitate such a creative self-expression, where goods would work as sign-values that were open to be recombined in diverse and individualized ways. Rather than trying to condition the wants of consumers, a semiotic approach would try to appropriate the various expressions that came out of their socialized creativity. Rather than trying to manipulate people's behaviour and desires, marketing was now about 'giving meaning to things, charging objects with new significations', to 'manipulate, not necessarily people, but ideas, communicative codes, symbols, fashions, social languages'. The role of advertising was to furnish a new language for social communication.[58] Indeed, as the definition of the consumer as a subjectified communicator began to proliferate, market researchers increasingly abandoned their positivistic references to an underlying subject. Rather than, as Calvi had done in his study of 1977, presenting lifestyle clusters as referring to actually existing, subjectively embodied values and practices, 'the specific behavioural aspects of a segment of the population',[59] Fabris and Mortara in their presentation of the eight Italys in 1986, chose to present their segments as ideal-typical patterns of consumption and behaviour that had no reference in actually existing, embodied, consumers. As Morello stressed in 1982, consumers were conceived to be free to move between such consumer styles or, indeed, adopt several different ones depending on actual situations without there being any resulting internal contradictions.[60]

A postmodern consumer culture

While Barilla's Mulino Bianco line was the first example of the implementation of this new model, it would become the dominant marketing paradigm during the 1980s. Barilla's marketing consultants would continue with this

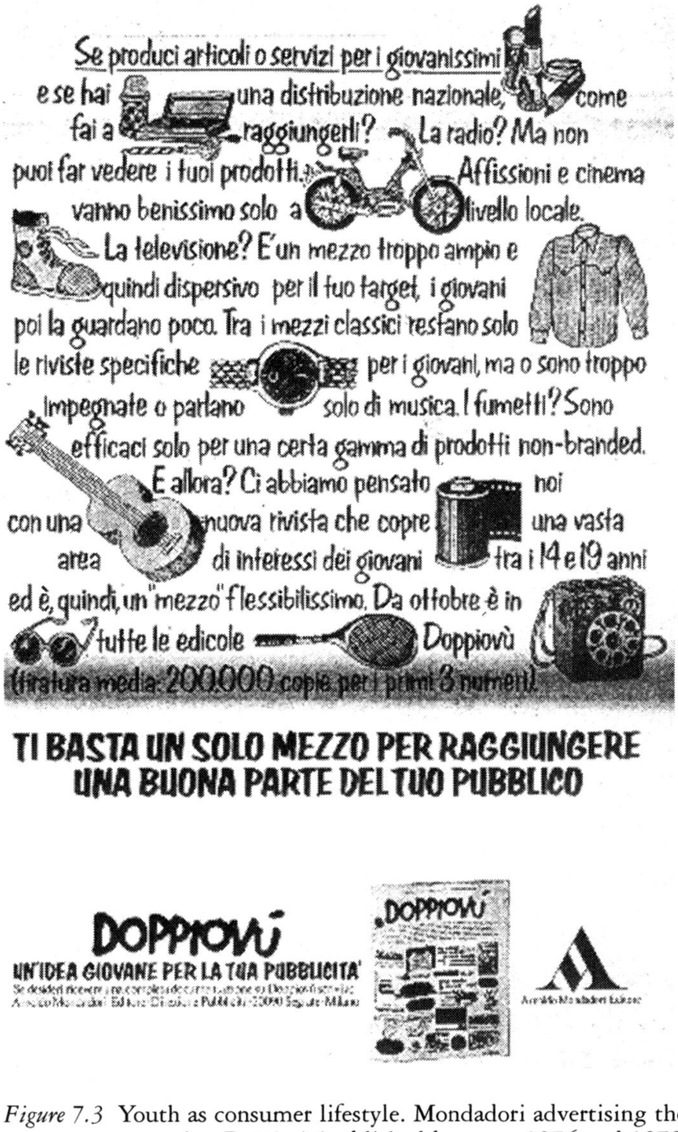

Figure 7.3 Youth as consumer lifestyle. Mondadori advertising their new youth magazine *Doppiovù* (published between 1976 and 1978) as representative of a lifeworld made up of ideas as well as objects. (Courtesy of the Biblioteca Nazionale, Florence.)

approach and, in a market study carried out in 1983, recommend that pasta be sold as a kind of building block through which free-floating 'deritualized', 'post-traditional food-styles' could be individualistically constructed.[61] During the 1980s Zanussi began breaking down the market for domestic appliances into a plurality of segments and created models distinguished by their daring design and creative colouring, and FIAT, launching its new model Uno, which replaced the old 127, put heavy emphasis on design and variability. Indeed, it is estimated that, bearing in mind the possibility of changing colours and adding or dropping optionals, FIAT Uno now came in some 1,500 possible varieties.[62] In the late 1970s Piaggio began to market their scooters as a foundation for a particular (now adult) lifestyle.

As in the 1950s, the weekly press was an important factor in spreading this new model of consumption. *Amica*, for example, relaunched by Paolo Pietroni (who had been editing *Amica* during the publication's 'feminist' period, 1974–75) as a slightly more expensive and stylish weekly, dedicated most of its material to fashion and appearance. The ideal readership of *Amica* was made up by women whose identity and very social existence were primarily founded on their use of consumer goods:

> women for whom dressing up is a playful masquerade that is pursued with intelligence, beauty and a sense of fun, a pursuit that aims to express their own personality, and not to please others, or even to meet others' expectations. They engage in this masquerade because they know that doing so is a necessary condition for being able to live pleasurably and intelligently. They use it to create personal relations, for purposes of seduction, provocation and self-presentation in general.[63]

Amica set an example for the expanding, but increasingly tight, editorial market. Paolo Pietroni launched *Max*, a 'women's magazine for men with high aesthetic aspirations' (to be exported to France, Greece and Germany during the early 1990s), which pioneered a similar approach to men. In general, the tendency to segment the weekly press according to consumer 'lifestyles' (underway since the mid-1960s) now accelerated. The youth segment saw the birth of a series of new titles: *Cioè*, *Cioè Girl*, *Supermatt*, *Debby* and *Cleó*. Mothers, another apparently profitable category, were supplied with adequate lifestyles in *Io e il mio bambino* (1984) and *Donna e mamma* (1989), and marketed to advertisers as the potential recipients of distinct commodity bundles. Rusconi launched two weekly magazines promoting a lifestyle characterized by concerns for 'fitness', *Vital* (1984) and *Vitality* (1987) – catering to the expanding gym and sports industry. The most important incarnations of this new marketing approach were perhaps the fashion designers, who by now had come to dominate both the Italian celebrity scene and the image of Italy abroad (Giorgio Armani made the cover page of *Time* magazine in 1982). This professional figure was relatively new. It had developed with the efforts on the part of the Italian textile industry to appropriate the logic of the antifashion movement. The new fashion designers, or *stilisti*, worked differently from an older generation of *haute couture* designers. Their task was not so much to impose a new style, so to speak, from above, but to interpret the micro-movements of a diffuse consumerist effervescence and translate these into a distinct lifestyle centred on the particular label. Armani, for example, would draw on a vast repertoire of pop culture, Hollywood films, street style, nostalgic retrospective and *haut couture* to create his distinct concept, sold in the form of clothes, but also perfumes, soaps, accessories and gadgets, and elaborated in Armani's own in-store publication, *Emporio Armani Magazine*.[64]

The transformation of marketing and advertising was not the only factor behind the rise of such a set-free, postmodern consumer culture during the 1980s. The growth of small-scale flexible production in the many successful Italian industrial districts contributed to an increased product diversity and made possible the strategies of rapid turnover that New Marketing suggested. Benetton, for example, through its reliance on such flexible networks (where much of the flexibility was due to the unregulated status of domestic sweatshop labour) and through its sophisticated computerized distribution system, was able to produce some 1,000 different products in every collection, a figure unheard of previously.[65] Similarly, transformations of the distributive sector were crucial. Departing from very modest levels in the early 1960s, the share of the market for fast-moving goods held by supermarkets had been doubling, on average, every six to seven years, to occupy levels close to the European average in the mid-1980s.[66] The expansion of supermarkets and above all the spread of new boutiques (even outsside of the major cities) and of American-style shopping centres – often the targets for Sunday excursions – made shopping an increasingly popular pastime and a new arena for social interaction.[67] It also made brand identity a more crucial element than before. In addition, the rise of advertising expenditure and of private television was crucial to the spread of consumer culture in general during the decade. (The next chapter will look closer at this.)

The transformation of advertising and marketing, however, produced a new vision that would give coherence to these developments. It suggested a new consumer culture, with a distinct model for the relations between people and goods, and a particular set of assumptions as to what people desired to get out of their consumer practices. While this new model had been inspired by developments in American marketing thought, it was also driven by the challenge posed by the domestic counter-culture. Advertising and marketing professionals discovered a new way of relating to consumer goods in the youth culture of the 1960s. The legitimacy crisis that followed the oil crisis in the early 1970s made them increasingly prone to look there for new inspiration. With new marketing techniques and new market research methods, this new model began to acquire a general appeal. What the counter-culture had suggested, and marketing practice developed, was that goods could be sold and used as a free-floating language that permitted a creative bricolage on the part of the consumer. The meaning of consumer goods no longer needed to respect any actually existing worlds, but could be set free from such restraints. Like Mulino Bianco, consumer goods could be delinked from lived social reality, the society of people, to make up a society of goods, a world of simulacra on which the lived reality of everyday life could be modelled. Designers like Trussardi and Armani thus took pride in selling not only clothes but an entire lifestyle, not only appearances but the 'real' thing, 'not only *prêt a porter*, but also of *prêt a vivre*'. As Francesco Alberoni argued, the new model of consumption had developed as part of a revolt against mass society. During the 1980s it had become the very basis for 'a restored social order'.[68]

8 The triumph of consumer culture

'love means . . . dressing alike'
(*Il Paninaro*, January 1987)

At first, the *paninari*, who were to become the most visible protagonists of 1980s' youth culture, used to gather on what was once the historic terrain of neo-Fascist youth gangs, piazza San Babila in Milan. Now, however, their attention was directed at the newly opened Italian imitation of McDonald's hamburger restaurants, 'Burghy', rather than at signs of *cinesi* daring to trespass.[1] (The name *paninaro*, 'sandwich-er', from *panino*, sandwich, came from their close association with the fast-food outlets of either the American or the domestic, *paninoteca*, type that began to appear across the country.) Although, in many respects, the heirs of the neo-Fascist subculture of the 1970s, politics proper had little or no relevance for the *paninari*. Rather, their main interests were the timeless concerns of the careless: fun, parties, petty romances and, above all, style, surrounding themselves with the 'right' mix of objects. By the mid-1980s the *paninaro* style had spread from a few circles of well-to-do *figli di papa* (brats) in Milan to become nationally dominant among young people and, later on, the only youth style Italy ever exported.[2] The apparent lack of interest in politics on the part of the *paninari*, as well as on the part of 1980s' youth overall, was generally taken as a sign that the long wave of radicalism that had gone from the student occupations in 1967 through the desperate movements of 1977 had finally receded, and that everything had gone back to normal. The loud but small radical minority, which had established a connection between youth and radical politics that lasted for more than a decade, had now lost its monopoly on the symbolic representation of the younger generation. After the years of terrorism, state repression and the subsequent *riflusso* (retreat to the private, 'backlash'), the aspirations of the silent majority of young people, the 3 Ms *Macchina*, *Moglie/Marito e Mestiere* (a car, a wife/husband, and a job) – discovered as far back as 1966 by sociologist Achille Ardigò and largely replicated in youth studies ever since – had now finally acquired a voice.[3]

The *paninari* can certainly be read as a symptom of such a return of the repressed, silent majority, a shift of focus away from politics and protest towards integration and acceptance. A closer look, however, suggests that this is not the whole truth. Despite frequent accusations of superficiality, the *paninari* did not ignore the existential side of life. Growing up and developing an identity was not – as it was, according to Ardigò, for the generation of the 3 Ms of the 1960s – a simple matter of taking on one of the existing roles of adult society. Rather, the main organ of the *paninaro* 'movement', *il Paninaro*, placed a lot of importance on the problematic of identity. Similarly, both novels by the poetess of the 'movement' Lettizia Mottica – *Sposerò Simon LeBon* (1985) and *All'infinito mondo paninaro* (1988) – were deeply concerned with issues of being, behaving, relating and feeling. For the *paninari*, identity work was as pressing a matter as ever before. Now, however, the problematic of identity was staged, acted out, and (sometimes) resolved on the arena of consumption, rather than, as had often been the case in the previous decade, that of politics. Questions of being and identity were almost exclusively framed through the medium of consumer goods, whether these were compared and ordered according to the extent to which they were 'too right', 'acceptable', or 'out' (Valentino jeans were 'too right', Coveri were acceptable, but Pop 84, an old icon of the 1960s, were definitely 'out'), or listed as part of introductory self-presentation in letters from readers ('Hi, my name is Micina. I'm an 18-year-old girl. I live with my mother. I have three pairs of jeans (Valentino, Armani and Americanino), Best Company sweaters, Timberland shoes and soon a pair of Durango as well, an El Charro belt and a pair of Armani gloves . . .').[4] Not only was the identity work of the *paninari* chiefly acted out on the arena of consumption, but their conceptions of identity and selfhood were also, it seemed, virtually limited to that domain.

Unlike the case of the 'metropolitan indians' of the late 1970s – a subculture that showed close similarities with the punks – the consumer practices of the *paninari* were not expressions of some, however vague and unarticulated, but still political, stance that encompassed wider concerns.[5] Rather, to be a *paninaro meant nothing more* than possessing the, frequently very expensive, objects that made up the uniform: a Moncler overcoat, Armani jeans and Timberland shoes. (As one *paninaro* poignantly put it, the Timberland shoe 'is *not* a symbol for me'.)[6] There was simply nothing there to symbolize. Objects meant nothing and everything. It follows that the relationship to objects on the part of the *paninari* had little of the irony and symbolic creativity of the punks. Rather, it was dead serious in its fetishism: the *paninari* followed advertising as youth before them had followed pop or film stars (on Berlusconi's newly opened youth channel, *Italia Uno*, and on all-night projections of advertising clips, the so-called *notti dei publivori* in Milan cinemas). Even their opponents, the remaining *cinesi*, quickly realized the crucial importance of objects for the *paninari*. They would prey on the lonely *paninaro* and strip him of his *paninaro* attributes, his Moncler jacket and Timberland shoes. Even if generally apolitical, there was an oppositional element to the *paninari*. They perceived their own identity work and consumer practices as something antithetical to the world of teachers and parents. In *il Paninaro*, the role of the latter was limited to their function as gatekeepers to the world of consumer goods, and readers would brag about their successes (or lament their failures) in making parents buy things for them ('Dear editor, I have finally managed to make my parents buy me a pair of Timberland . . .'). The former were often ridiculed as representatives of an antediluvian, provincial mentality, as expressed in their often parodied archaic Italian and incomprehensible concern with shady figures of a distant past like Carducci or Dante. Rather than formulating their opposition to adult society by means of an alternative political ideology, the *paninari* did so by means of consumption: they embraced consumer culture as an expression of a new social order, a 'New Times' to use a famous British label, where advertising, brands, commercial television, fast food and fashion labels stood against the outdated realities of religion and politics, something that only parents or teachers would take an interest in.[7] They identified with the new self-image of Italy as the dynamic home of fashion, design and stylish consumer culture, rather than political conflict and violence. The *paninari*, then, represented a full realization of that anthropological revolution that Pier Paolo Pasolini had identified already in the 1970s. For them, as for the young Fascists that Pasolini wrote about, Fascism or anti-Fascism, or, for that matter religion and politics in general, had no deeper meaning beyond that of signs to be taken on or discarded at will: they were sign-values with no a priori ties to any lived reality.[8]

Arguably, the *paninari* were an extreme example, an expression of a Milan that had become the true centre of the new Italy, with its high society and nightlife dominated by fashion designers and their entourage, its yuppies, its stock market and Craxi's climber politicians (*rampanti*) running the political machine. But their attitudes towards consumer goods were no isolated phenomenon. A series of surveys and sociological investigations now showed that consumption, rather than class, politics or religion had become the most important source of self-identity for Italians in general. Indeed, a Censis study from 1987 claimed that consumption had now become the most important arena for the articulation of 'subjectivity', a pursuit that, at least according to common-sense historiography, had been previously located in the political arena. As the survey continued to argue, 'self-exploration, the most important aspect of subjectivity (*soggetività*) . . . seems today to be acted out, almost entirely, through the use of objects'. Clothes, foodstuffs or 'media images' now primarily served as a medium for the 'experimentation with different versions of the self'.[9] While this pursuit remained constrained by the limitations imposed by different endowments of resources and opportunities, ultimately it was determined by the individual pursuit of meaning. During the 1980s, these surveys presented the Italian middle classes as chiefly concerned with the private rather than the public sphere: with appearance, personal authenticity and individual distinction. The concept of subjectivity contained in the new marketing approach that had developed during the 1970s, the view of consumer goods as an open-ended language and of the subject as a *bricoleur*, of subjective identity modelled on the sign-values of consumer goods, rather than the other way around, had now acquired a salience that went far beyond the field of consumption proper. This logic now invested the whole social field. To quote media theorist Mario Pilati:

> While the symbolic functions [of consumer goods] used to be subordinated to the dominant position held by other institutions of acculturation (like religion, the school system, the political parties, tradition) consumer goods have now . . . assumed a primary role in supplying behavioural models and subjective structures of feeling that fit a turbulent social landscape.[10]

In addition, such an identity elaborated by means of the language of consumer goods was understood to be not only apolitical, but antithetical to the very logic of the political. To sociologist Gerardo Ragone 1980s' consumer culture has been completely delinked from the concerns and interests that result from social structure. Consumption was no longer even a matter of marketing social status but 'pure play, spectacle, enjoyment, pleasure'.[11] To Francesco Alberoni, Italy of the 1980s had finally left 'the era of Catholicism, the Counter-Reformation, Marxism-Leninism . . .: the twentieth century, the century of grand ideologies of insane monotheisms', to enter the epoch of private pursuits, comfort, pleasure and, above all, style.[12]

A new hegemony

How seriously can we take such sweeping claims like Alberoni's? The new model of advertising with its emphasis on branding and product identity was by now well established also for less glamorous, everyday necessities. In part this was driven by the transformation of the distributive sector. Supermarkets, which had hitherto occupied a fairly marginal place, now increased their share of the Italian market for fast-moving goods from about 33 per cent in the mid-1970s to 41 per cent in 1985 (which was still a fair step from the European average of 70 per cent). Where previously the local grocer had been the main intermediary between producers and consumers, this place was now taken by supermarkets and, predominantly, television advertising.[13] Consequently the importance of creating a successful brand image grew; the relevance of advertising and marketing in the corporate decision process increased, as did the weight of the creative function within advertising itself. The influence of this new exaltation of the brand, of the commodity as a spectacular simulacrum, built up with the increase in advertising budgets, chiefly connected to the rising importance of private television. As Table 8.1 shows, the advertising industry went through a massive expansion during the 1980s. Its share of private consumption expenditure virtually doubled, from 0.51 per cent of GDP in 1980 to 1 per cent in 1988. Even if the advertising budgets of the weekly press grew significantly, most of this expansion was linked to private television. Television's share of total advertising investments increased steadily during the 1980s, whereas that of newspapers and weeklies declined (although total investments in all three media rose constantly). After the abolition of the state monopoly in 1977, local stations financed by local advertising were put together into networks by the publishing houses Mondadori and Rusconi, which administered the programming and sold advertising time for the local stations. In the 1980s Silvio Berlusconi became the dominant actor in the advertising market, partly on account of his good relations with the Craxi establishment. Berlusconi's Publitalia significantly lowered the price of advertising and introduced a series of bargaining practices that stimulated even middle-sized firms to use advertising, thus expanding the market to some 500 firms that had previously never advertised. Where the state television, RAI, had been restrictive and forced advertisers to accept a strictly contained format until 1977, Berlusconi's channels put advertising slots not only in between programmes but also interrupted ongoing transmissions, and sold advertising time aggressively, sometimes bypassing the intermediary role of the advertising agencies. As a consequence of this aggressive marketing strategy, the turnover of Publitalia grew from 12 billion lire in 1980 to 200 billion in 1982. It continued to expand and soon passed the RAI concessionary Sipra as the most important advertising broker. In 1985 their respective shares of the advertising market were 60 per cent for Publitalia and 30 per cent for Sipra.

With Berlusconi's Canale 5, and the other two private channels he bought from his competitors, Rusconi's Itaia 1 and Mondadori's Rete Quattro, the supply of advertising-financed television time increased radically. Private television was now instrumental in spreading a commercial media culture where advertisements mixed with the products of the global, US-dominated entertainment industry, either through direct imports or through imitations. The result was that a commercial media culture that was built around

Table 8.1 Advertising expenditure 1970–90

Year	*Newspapers (% of total advertising investments)*	*Weeklies (% of total advertising investments)*	*Television (% of total advertising investments)*	*Advertising investments as % of GDP*	*Advertising investments as % of total private consumption*
1970	30.0	35.0	12.4 RAI	0.40	0.66
1975	30.3	31.3	15.4 RAI	0.29	0.45
1980	27.0	31.7	12.0 RAI 11.7 Private	0.32	0.51
1985	22.2	20.1	48.7 (total)	0.49	0.78
1990	24.4	19.0	47.9 (total)	0.62	1.00

Source: Pilati 1994.

advertising and its creation of brand images now acquired an unprecedented position in public culture. On television, furthermore, a new visible elite of entrepreneurs, yuppie speculators, stock-market traders and advertising, fashion and media personalities took the centre stage where they set the trends. Ordinary Italians appeared in advertising spots as consumers whose lifestyles and personalities were intimately connected to the brand they used. Private television thus brought about an important shift from production, the worker and the factory, to consumption, the entrepreneur and the market as the central reference system for the everyday staging of social reality. As the women's magazines had served as a means of anticipatory socialization into mass consumption in the 1950s, private television now served as an important means of acculturation to a postmodern, brand-based consumer society.[14] The rising importance of consumer culture during the 1980s was also driven by a growing affluence, and by new possibilities to consume. From having taken a deep dive during the second half of the 1970s, Italian GDP now grew at an annual rate of, on average, 3–4 per cent (in 1983–87).

This mini-boom was in part caused by the general resurgence of global demand that resulted mainly from increased US deficit spending on the part of the Reagan administration. In part it resulted from the weakening of the labour movement and the restructuring of the productive process through the automation of factories and the subcontracting of certain activities to small-scale family firms of the emerging industrial districts. These restructurings had made the Italian economy more 'flexible' and competitive, and had allowed new and more intense forms of accumulation, in particular in the export-oriented industrial districts of the north and centre, which in many respects were the engine of this new 'second economic miracle'. The middle classes were also pampered by the economic policies of the Craxi governments, which to an increasing extent used the state budget to buy consensus and support. Most of this increased middle-class affluence translated into private consumption and the ratio of private consumption to GDP more than doubled between 1979 and 1992.[15]

This new prosperity was by no means accessible to everyone. The inequalities between the north and the south remained, as did substantial levels of unemployment and comparatively high wage differentials (the new industrial districts also produced new forms of hyper-exploitation through their reliance on unorganized labour and domestic sweatshop production at the margins of legality). Working-class families with only one income, pensioners without support from children, immigrants and the numerous unemployed (particularly in the south) were certainly excluded from these consumerist pursuits. Even if such inequalities persisted and the new culture of consumption was accessible only to a part of the population, this part now, at variance with the years of the economic miracle, made up the majority. The goods of the 'standard package' that, in 1965, were present in roughly 50 per cent of all Italian households, were now virtually omnipresent. In 1990, according to Eurisko's statistics, 88.4 per cent of all households had a television set, 88 per cent a car and 94 per cent a refrigerator and a washing machine. In addition, forms of consumption not included in this standard package, but rather centred on the self and its maintenance and presentation, increased throughout the decade. During the second half of the 1980s, the percentage of Italians who, when asked by Eurisko, claimed to 'Regularly use facial creams', 'Make use of dietetic products', 'Spend a lot of money on clothes', 'Only buy fashion clothing' and 'Wear valuable jewellery' increased steadily. Similarly, those who clamed to 'Dress as it happens without worrying too much' or 'Dress as practically as possible' decreased.[16] The excluded groups were, furthermore, rendered more or less invisible by the transformation of the media system, where, at variance with the years of the economic miracle when a social realist style of journalism had been popular, poverty, deprivation and squalor was no longer an area of interest.

But this growing presence of consumer goods in the worlds of Italians was less the consequence of a sudden break with the austere and crisis-ridden 1970s, than is commonly believed. Despite a staggering economy and much talk of austerity and limits to growth, private consumption grew steadily all through that decade. With two sharp drops, in 1974–75 in the aftermath of the oil crisis, and in 1980–83 as the global slump at the end of the 1970s played out, the annual increases in private (family) consumption during the 1970s *and* 1980s averaged around 20–30 per cent. The reorientation of consumer practices also had more the nature of a gradual transformation than a sudden break. It is significant in this respect that in ISTAT's consumption statistics, the space occupied by kinds of consumption not captured by their categories elaborated in the 1950s showed a significant increase during both the 1970s and the 1980s, from 2.2 per cent in 1974 to 14.0 per cent in 1990.[17] The image, put forth by observers like Alberoni, of a radical shift from a decade of austerity and anticonsumerist ideology to one of unprecedented consumer affluence thus probably has less to do with a radical change in the actual distribution of consumer goods, than with the self-representation of society. Indeed, journalists, intellectuals and sociologists would now begin to take the social centrality of consumption for granted. This assumption was replicated in a whole range of surveys and opinion polls like those of Censis that had a wide public acclaim, in what Rinauro calls the 'republic of polling' (*la repubblica dei sondaggi*).[18] This was particularly evident as psychographics began to have an impact outside the realm of market research proper. These surveys tended to draw a picture of the social as made up of different lifestyles of 'behaviours' rather than as united by a single logic of structural determination. Thus the 1983 Censis survey on consumption in Italy, for example, claimed that:

> today our society is made up of different kinds of behaviour and consumption (which is the most widespread and articulated form of behaviour), can represent the strategically most interesting sector for

> understanding the basic logics that drive social behaviour on an individual, collective and mass level.[19]

In a similar vein, Fabris and Mortara's influential work on lifestyles in Italy claimed that:

> today the position of an individual in relation to the means of production tells us ever less about his or her behaviours, values, and ways of conceiving of existence generally. [We have seen] a fragmentation of social class into multiple strata and segments that express the particular interests of the subjects of which they are composed, in opposition to the general interest of class.[20]

Whether such statements are true or not, they testify to the fact that it was now 'in the truth' (*dans le vrai*), as Foucualt said, to claim that the traditionally dominant reference for the self-representation of society, class, was no longer relevant. Now such statements could be accepted as a matter of course, without the need for further arguments.[21] They had become part of the hegemonic common sense.

Consumption, class and politics

As chapter 3 has illustrated, mass consumption constituted an important political issue, at least from the 1920s on. To the Fascist regime mass consumption posed a serious challenge. As seen in the US, mass consumption risked producing a mass culture of atomized, empty individualism, and it did so without any apparent subject or agent driving it. At the same time, this potential for capillary, almost subversive, social transformation made up its real promise. The (moderately successful) policies of the regime thus tried to use the medium of consumer goods to promote a new, modern national mass culture. Fascist consumer culture would help Italians leave their particularistic alignments of region or class behind to identify with the collective body of the nation. This potential of turning class into mass also lay behind much of Christian Democrat attitudes to consumption in the post-war years. Admittedly, the marriage between American-style consumer culture and Catholic Christian Democracy had been difficult from the start. But as many arranged unions, it worked out its kinks as it went along. Given the obvious popularity of modern consumer goods, detergents, bouillon cubes, canned foods, cosmetics and their media – women's magazines, Hollywood films and, in particular, television (which began transmitting in 1954; television advertising began in 1957) – the DC had to accept its fate. It was no longer possible to maintain the visions of a profoundly religious, frugal, pre-industrial and rural Italy, a *civiltà contadina*, which had dominated many factions of the DC in the immediate post-war years. From the economic miracle onwards the DC came to embrace implicitly a social model where the formation of popular motivations was left to consumer culture (implicitly because, as Achille Ardigò recognized in his famous 1962 speech at San Pellegrino, the party really did not have any coherent ideology). Cultural cohesion and social integration was left to consumer culture, and the role of politics was limited to steering and administering overall developments towards the self-evident goal of economic growth and hence increased possibilities for consumption. On the level of political strategy, the DC had made a shift away from the church and its mass organizations during the 1950s and begun to expand and cultivate the support of the middle classes by enhancing their possibilities for consumption. The exclusion of the Communists could similarly be legitimized by framing their resistance to the predominant model of mass consumption as an aversion to consumption, prosperity and comfort in general (apart, of course, from pointing at their alliance with the Soviet Union, an argument that, however, grew weaker with the development of Euro-Communism).

This very tendency to replace class with mass stood at the heart of PCI aversion to mass consumption. The ethic of status competition this promoted was not only antithetical to class consciousness, but also altogether artificial and alienating. Consumer culture, as promoted by the DC, risked replacing a genuine popular culture, dear to the Gramscian tradition, with a manufactured mass culture. As the economic miracle progressed, the party was increasingly afraid that workers might fall for the 'FIAT myth' (*il mito FIAT*).[22] This threat became particularly pressing as a series of processes set in motion a restructuring of the Italian working class. Older, politically active workers were sacked in the wake of the DC victory of 1948 and replaced with migrants, first from the northern countryside and then from the south. At the same time Italian industry began to implement scientific management and the assembly line seriously. To the PCI it appeared that these new workers would accept consumer goods as a substitute for real influence over the production process and political agency more generally.

Such a strategy of replacing class consciousness with 'individualized integration' was embraced by the Catholic trade union CISL. Influenced by the example of the American trade unions, the CISL pursued a strategy of depoliticization. A weakened influence over the production process, through new forms of machinery, new ways of organizing the production process, continuous speed-ups, and other measures to enhance productivity, would be compensated by the increasing space for individual consumption made possible by higher wages. According to Mario Romano, one of the ideological founding fathers of CISL who was active at the Catholic University in Milan, the trade union was to constitute itself as a partner to capital in the project of promoting 'a coordinated and rapid industrialization of Italian society'. In so doing, it was essential to separate 'union struggles from political struggles' and to strive for negotiated solutions that kept the 'common goal' of increased productivity in mind.[23]

Other factors also worked against the formation of class consciousness among migrant workers. Urban restructuring of the northern cities, in particular Milan, tended to destroy a working-class culture that had been strongly rooted in the social relations and everyday life of local neighbourhoods. The working class was moved from inner-city neighbourhoods to suburban housing complexes. These were often quickly constructed concrete slabs, the fruit of real-estate speculations, underserviced and with little or no space for the development of neighbourly relations. In the northern cities, and in particular Turin, migrant workers met with hostility, xenophobia and 'ethnic' discrimination from the locals. In addition, newly arrived migrants were prone to side up with Catholic organization. This was partly on account of a pre-existing Catholic culture and partly because the DC, in cooperation with local parishes, was in control of the job market through a system of letters of recommendation form priests to Catholic employers of trade union officials.[24]

To a large extent, however, such fears were exaggerated. The transformation of class conscious workers into 'mass workers' through scientific management and passifying mass consumption was not as sweeping as contemporary debates would often indicate. The kinds of urban restructuring mentioned before were largely isolated to Milan; Turin maintained both traditional working-class neighbourhoods and 'ethnic' migrant enclaves. In addition, newly arrived southerners were quickly radicalized, contrary to more pessimistic PCI outlooks (which had feared that the passage from 'bread and onions to bread and sausage' would render them passive and docile).[25] Some, no doubt came with fresh experiences of the fierce and frequently violent peasant struggles of the 1950s. Even if they came without a political consciousness, however, the level of exploitation in the factories, the frequent encounters with 'ethnic' discrimination and the general lack of public services soon produced one. For the younger generation the object of contestation was not only exploitation, but also the authoritarian practices of bosses and the police, as well as of union stewards themselves whose mediating interventions in petty everyday conflicts were not as easily accepted as they were by the worker generation of the 1950s. It could be argued that consumer culture actually contributed to giving their political outlook such an anti-authoritarian twist. Younger, migrant workers from the south, who lacked the austere production ethic of an older generation of workers, were presented with the consumerist prospect of an immediate realization of desire. In many cases they appropriated the alternative forms of consumption and self-presentation offered there. (The proportion of young migrant workers among the 'Teddy boys' was high.)[26] Consumer goods – scooters, blue jeans juke-boxes – created a new youthful sociality with values that came into conflict with the traditional morality of austerity and moral rigour that had prevailed in Communist as well as Catholic tradition. The new 'hedonism' that came with consumer culture, then, contributed to creating a new political language in which the self and its private pleasures became a political issue. Thus the struggles of young workers were framed not only in terms of a conflict between labour and capital as abstract historical actors, but also of one between concrete subjective desire and constraining, moralistic social expectations. As Communist organizer Ninetta Zandegiacomi commented on the successful strikes at the Lanerossi factory in 1960:

> The younger generations refuse the submission and sacrifice of their mothers. They want cinema, dances, weekend getaways, a house with a refrigerator and a television set. One of our claims that met the strongest support was for longer holidays, for the right to enjoy 15 whole days spent in the mountains or at the seaside. [27]

This new political generation (the youth with striped shirts, as they were known to the press, *giovani con le magliette a strisce*) entered the political scene during the manifestations against the conference of the Fascist party MSI in Genoa in 1960. There they showed little respect for authority, whether that of the police or that of PCI stewards, who had difficulty controlling their readiness to respond to police provocations as well as their use of wildcat strikes and other spontaneous forms of factory protest. These young, frequently migrant, workers were to form a new generation of organizers to lead the massive increase in strikes and social protests that began with the piazza Statuto manifestations in 1962, and climaxed with the 'hot autumn' of 1969.[28] Together with the student movements they formed a carrying subject for an Italian New Left, endowed with alternative vision of modernity. Both students and workers came to further political demands for social justice and equality as well as an anti-authoritarian 'politics of the subject'. Both put forth demands for the liberation of the world, for the creation of spaces for self-realization and for hedonist enjoyment, against the artificial rigours of mass society. Both framed their alterity in the symbolic language of consumer goods. It seems, then, that mass consumption was not only, or even primarily, conducive to political passivity. Rather, it contained a dialectic of its own. Based on their experiences as members of an emerging consumer society, the social movements of mass workers and mass students (women would emerge during the 1970s) articulated a vision of modernity different from that harboured by exponents of the old left as well as the old right. This would be increasingly evident in the 1970s as the second-generation youth movement of 1977 put the right to enjoyment and pleasure, and the refusal of the traditional discipline of work, high on their political agenda.[29]

The PCI was not particularly enthusiastic about this turn of events. While they had attempted to absorb the student movement through the Communist youth organization FGCI, the older generation of Party militants tended to equate many of the expressions of the emerging New Left with the decadent hedonism and individualism of consumer culture. Indeed PCI's attitude to the student movement of 1968 was uncomprehending enough to make the Party appear as a representative of what the students were contesting.[30] This identification of the 'alternative modernity' presented by the New Left with the individualism, hedonism and general decadence of consumer culture – very understandable given the close similarities and interconnectedness of the two phenomena – was fully expressed in the ideological vision that guided the 'historical compromise' of the mid-1970s. (The PCI decided to support a DC-led government in exchange for some influence, without actually entering into government as a coalition partner.) This move, shortly after Pinochet's Chilean coup in 1973, was motivated by fears of a similar development in Italy and by the threat of an overall economic crisis in the wake of the OPEC manoeuvre in the same year. It was also informed by an ideology of austerity that in many ways can be read as a resurrection of the old 'producer ethic' of the generation of resistance militants. This ethical vision is perhaps best summarized by the personal philosophy of Berlinguer, in journalist Enzo Forcella's words:

> He is, as we know, rigorous. He is not an admirer of lax customs and he is convinced that the students should go back to their studies, take them seriously just as an older generation did. He detests deviance and the idea that life is a game, purely a source of pleasure. [31]

It can well be argued that the ideology of austerity was a moral project, rather than any rationally motivated political strategy. It was an attempt to resurrect the values of the Old Left against what seemed to be a general dissolution of morality. In Aurelio Lepre's words, it was a defence against the 'rampant particularism and senseless consumerism' that seemed to be on its way to dominate Italian society.[32] Such a project was in many respects alien to the political structure of feeling of the New Left, and it led to a growing cleavage between the old and the young. The latter's aversion to this new moralism of the left was expressed in events like the fight between PCI stewards and the students occupying the university of Rome in 1977, as well as the frequent ironic use of PCI slogans on the part of youth movements of the 1970s. PCI's decision to ground its political strategy in the resurrection of a, to a large extent, mythological, old working-class morality was a strategic mistake.

First, it alienated much of the New Left. The Party was reluctant to take on their agenda and to deal with issues like civil rights as exemplified in its exaggerated prudence in the context of the divorce referendum of 1974 (see chapter 6, note 48). As the 1970s progressed, the PCI more and more appeared to be part of the establishment. As it became evident that the historical compromise was failing, and as the Red Brigades put the final nail in its coffin, the Party had largely exhausted its credentials among the New Left and among the new middle class that had supported it. Second, the old-fashioned working class that the PCI tried to resurrect was rapidly disappearing. The Italian social fabric had gone through a restructuring during the second half of the 1970s, similar in its scope to that of the 'economic miracle'. Between 1974 (when it stood at its peak) and 1989 the working class had declined from 45.9 per cent of the labour force to 35.4 per cent. At the same time the share of white-collar strata had increased from 20.2 per cent to 32.4 per cent, thus reaching almost the size of the working class. In addition, there was a substantial recomposition of the working class, spurred, on the one hand, by the emergence of small family firms and, on the other hand, by internal restructuring and automation inside the larger factories. Taken together, these processes tended to replace the homogenized mass worker of the 1960s and 1970s (himself in part, of course, a myth) with a much more geographically, socially and ideologically differentiated working class, much less prone to form any unified ideological subject. Rather, other sources of identity, like regional alliances would resurface. It was becoming increasingly evident that 'to be a worker in Turin and in Bassano del Grappa is not exactly the same thing'.[33]

The 'final defeat' of the old working class took place in Turin in October 1980. The last grand strike against the planned massive lay-off at the FIAT Mirafiori factory – the consequences of a massive restructuring and automation of production – ended in a march of some 40,000 white- and blue-collar workers demanding to go back to work. In that moment, as journalist Gad Lerner dramatically put it, 'the logos around which the identity of the left had been centred all through the post-war years, the centrality of the workers, died'.[34] While an important symbolic event, the 40,000-man march was the outcome of a *long-duré* trend of class recomposition. On the one hand, this process was driven by the restructuring of Italian industrial production that went on during the 1970s. On the other hand, it resulted from the inability of the workers movement to accommodate a new generation of workers. At the FIAT Mirafiori factory the workers still active in the unions Fiom, Cisl and Cgil were getting old, while the unions had continuous difficulty attracting young workers, frequently hired on short contracts. For them, to be working class was ceasing to be an identity. Nicoletta Bosco summarizes their condition:

> The newly employed are disillusioned, isolated and distanced from their work. Their situation makes them very distant from participating in the 'culture of work' that embraced an older generation of workers, a generation that saw the factory as a locus of unity and of a common identity.[35]

The hegemony of consumer culture that marked the 1980s was, then, in part a result of the successful work of market mediation, in which the value revolution of the 1960s was translated into a new cultural formation with a general, mass appeal. It was also a result of the lack of serious alternatives. The actor most likely to provide this, the PCI and the active alternative civil society it controlled, failed to take the political dialectic of consumer culture seriously.

Berlusconi

The failure on the part of the PCI to deal with the new 'politics of the subject' that had been articulated by the New Left meant that marketing was without competition in appropriating its message. Marketing transformed the value revolution of the late 1960s into a new kind of consumer culture, marked by self-expression and the diversity of lifestyles. It created a new ideological formation to fit the reconstructed, post-Fordist, society to come out of the crisis of the 1970s. Virtually no other actor was there to offer an alternative version – the social movements of the New Left had exhausted themselves during the preceding decade. This meant that consumer culture now could achieve an almost complete hegemony over public culture. The collective project of the late 1960s had been translated into an individualized logic of self-expression channelled through branded consumer goods. Style and 'the look' prevailed. In 1994 this hegemony of consumer culture had its direct political expression in the electoral victory of Silvio Berlusconi's Forza Italia party.

This was in many respects a spectacular triumph for Mr Berlusconi and his company, Fininvest. From the official inauguration of the political branch of the movement on 18 January 1994 to the parliamentary elections of 27 March – in a period of little more than two months – Forza Italia managed to capture 21 per cent of the (active) Italian electorate. This unexpected event depended on a complex set of factors. One was, of course, the so-called 'Fall of the First Republic' and the end of the old party system.[36] The end of Communism had unravelled the whole Italian political system. After the events in Turin in 1980 and after the years of terrorism, the PCI lost its sense of direction and identity. With that, the DC lost *its* main *raison d'être*, anti-Communism. Consequently, during the 1980s, votes for both the DC and the PCI declined, and absenteeism and political apathy increased.[37] The succession of Craxi-led coalition governments during the 1980s increased the use of the state budget to generate consensus, and already endemic tendencies to clientelism and corruption accelerated. Finally, in 1993, in the wake of the worldwide economic slump, and the last final symbolic blow to Communism, the system crumbled in the Tangentopoli affair. The political system was no longer able to block judicial investigations into illicit party financing. As a result virtually the whole political class of the so-called First Republic was prosecuted, jailed and publicly villified on television.[38] Both the DC and the PCI disappeared, virtually overnight (to resurface as a number of new constellations).

In the void that followed, Berlusconi moved in. Primarily, Berlusconi was anxious to protect his own interests in the media business against the dire consequences of a victory of the Left alliance (which seemed probable given their success in the local elections of 1993). In order to achieve this, he made use of the most sophisticated marketing techniques. His political party, Forza Italia, was built around his company Fininvest, or more precisely a marketing and market research firm, Diakron, created for the purpose. Its political ideology as well as its general image was elaborated through market research, qualitative focus-group analysis as well as large-scale surveys. The resulting product was then sold as membership in a Forza Italia club, building on the organizational model of the supporters clubs organized around Berlusconi's successful football team, AC Milan.[39] (Membership was literally sold, in order to set up a club one needed to acquire *kit presidente* from Diakron, consisting of a number of Forza Italia items, a pin, a pen, a tie, a briefcase, a flag, etc. at the cost of 250,000 lire.)[40] The clubs had, however, no influence over party ideology, tactics or even the selection of candidates. There was virtually no communication in these matters between the clubs and the party. Rather, the clubs served as a simulacrum of political participation: they enabled members to feel as if they were part of a new, general political effervescence, almost a revolution, and enabled the party to represent itself as founded on a grass-roots social movement. Forza Italia was a political product, elaborated and sold according to the New Marketing model first pioneered in Italy by Mulino Bianco.[41]

As in the case of commercial salesmanship, excellent marketing does not guarantee success. There also has to be a clientele ready to buy. Outside the Left, Italians embraced the new product eagerly. In part because there was little else to choose from apart from the former Communists. (And anti-Communism was still a strong card, as Diakron's surveys and Berlusconi's own constant pondering about the Communist threat indicated.) In part, however, Forza Italia expressed the values of the consumer culture with which they had come to identify. To some extent this had to do with the political programme, lower taxes, economic growth, a 'million new jobs'. More than anything else, however, it had to do with its style, look and image. Berlusconi himself, Mr Broadcasting (*Sua Emittenza*) as he was called, had given Italy private television, incessant advertising and new shopping malls. 'His channels had educated millions of viewers in the values of postmodern society', which he now drew upon.[42] He and his party represented the revolt of the 'Italy of consumers', of the middle classes socialized into the values and aspirations of a new postmodern consumer culture, against the outdated ideologies of 'politics'.

Marketing and modernity

In Italy, as in most of the industrialized world, the 1970s were a crucial period of transition. At the economic level Fordism now began to dissolve under the pressure of automation, industrial reconstruction and the impact of information technology. The most important result was the dissolution of the old working class: the disappearance of the mass worker who had been the main political subject of Western modernity during most of the twentieth century. On the cultural and social level, the 1960s and 1970s witnessed a 'silent revolution' in the realm of more abstract values as well as that of everyday personal relations and forms of life. The 'New Left', a broad coalition of diverse actors and social movements, gave a political expression to this. But, as we have seen, the 1970s also saw the beginning of an institutionalization of these new forms of life as consumer culture. During the 1980s the new, postmodern consumer culture came largely to replace the political as the purveyor of the ideological cement that kept a new, post-Fordist social model together. This book has argued that – at least in Italy – this new, postmodern 'dominant ideology' has grown out of the mediating labour of advertising: its interpretation of and engagement with the modernization process. This genealogy is marked by two important turning points.

During the 1930s the Italian advertising profession came under the influence of American advertising and marketing thought. This led to its articulation of a particular anthropological vision where the *self*, rather than the nation was central, which meant that advertising developed an interest in the psychological and, above all, sociological condition of actual consumers. As chapters 5 and 6 have shown, the instruments necessary actually to follow up this interest were largely missing until the early 1960s. Instead, advertising tended to impose an American model, with supposedly universal relevance and appeal. During the 1960s, however, advertising acquired such instruments. The period of 'Americanization' of the 1950s was now succeeded by an increased emphasis on empirical engagement with consumers and their existing worlds. At the same time those worlds, or at least the ones advertising professionals considered most relevant and interesting, changed dramatically. With its empirical orientation and its openness to the reality of the social, advertising was able to transform the social effervescence that marked the 1960s into a new postmodern consumer culture for the 1980s. This move was, however, also triggered by factors within the discourse of advertising itself.

The advertising industry did not hook on to these new cultural expressions because of their quantitative importance. Rather, they were ideologically predisposed to regard them as an important precursor of things to come: of a new post-materialistic and post-conformist age. There was a fit between the counter-culture of the 1960s, or at least the ways in which it appeared to advertising professionals, and the, however incoherent and superficial, vision of modernity that had been articulated within the discourse of advertising itself. Rather than a mere reflection of social values or, conversely, the source of a genuinely false and manipulated culture, advertising interacted with its social environment in complex and multifaceted ways. This (relative) autonomy of advertising was significantly strengthened in the 1960s with the development of a series of empirical techniques. Advertising and its theoretical vision now became a key agent that, 'like a switchman', could guide the course of the modernization process.

In Italy, then, advertising has been a key agent in the modernization process. Its consumer ethic has equalled and eventually surpassed the political in importance as a reference for the articulation of identity and, more mundanely, for the formation of a meaningful coherence to everyday life. More crucially, with the fall of Communism and the rise of Berlusconi, it has come to supply the very basic assumptions on which political discourse builds. The Italian case might quite possibly be particular in this respect, if nothing else for its absence of a strong state and a firmly rooted national political culture. Recent social theory, however, suggests a similar development for Anglo-Saxon countries: from politics to 'the market' as the key purveyor of ideology and subjectivity. There the argument, at least from a Marxist (or 'post-Marxist' perspective) is usually that the shift from political to consumer culture is linked to a shift from production to consumption and distribution as the main determining instance of the economy. Post-Fordist restructuring has done away with well-established cultures of production, most notably the working class, and at the same time expanded the role of the 'sphere of circulation': of commodities and commodified signs and symbols, of advertising and marketing as economic activities. While this model certainly applies to Italy as well, the Italian case might suggest one addition: the crucial mediating role of the advertising industry. It was there, in advertising's active engagement with the modernization process, in its use of social theory and research methods to produce the necessary knowledge of society, that a cultural model coherent enough to work as an ideological cement for an emerging post-Fordist order was first articulated. While much social theory has concentrated on the state as the key actor in the constitution of modernity, this book suggests that in looking for the roots of postmodernity, advertising and marketing might also be fruitful spheres of investigation.

Notes

1 Introduction

1 Slater N., 'The Food of Italy', in *Gastronomic Guide to Italy*, Sainsbury's, *The Observer*, 2001, p. 5.
2 Malossi, G., *Liberi tutti: 20 anni di moda spettacolo*, Milan: Mondadori, 1987, p. 86.
3 Abruzzese, A., *Metafore della pubblicità*, Milan: Costa & Nolan, 1988, p. 64.
4 Gramsci, A., 'Americanism and Fordism', in Hoare, Q. and Nowell Smith, G. (eds), *Selections from the Prison Notebooks*, New York: International, 1971. For a summary of the literature around consumer culture and postmodernity see Slater, D., *Consumer Culture and Modernity*, Cambridge: Polity, 1997. For a strong claim to the central place of consumption in contemporary societies see Bauman, Z., *Globalization: The Human Consequences*, Cambridge: Polity, 1998.
5 Ferrarotti, F., 'Dalle ideologie all' individualismo gregario', in Aa. Vv., *La vita privata nel Novecento*, Rome–Bari: Laterza, 1988, pp. 431, 445.
6 Almond, G. and Verba, S., *The Civic Culture*, Princeton: Princeton University Press, 1963. For Almond and Verba such a strong identification with political parties did not mean a strong involvement in politics generally. On the contrary they considered Italian political culture to be 'parochial', characterized by an excessive identification with the party itself and a low interest in politics, conceived as a field for the discussion and struggle over national concerns. A parochial political culture corresponded to a weak national political culture. It should be added that Almond and Verba's interviews were undertaken in a particularly politicized period: right after what Ginsborg has termed the 'cold civil war' of the mid-1950s. Nevertheless, their ideas of a largely 'parochial' Italian political culture have been repeated by others: see, for example, Galli, G. and Prandi, A., *Patterns of Political Participation in Italy*, New Haven: Yale University Press, 1970. For a critique: Sani, G., 'The Political Culture of Italy, Continuity and Change', in Almond, G. and Verba, S. (eds.) *The Civic Culture Revisited*, Boston: Brown, 1980.
7 DeRita, G., 'Il consumo come soggetività sociale: Il caso dell'Italia', Aa. Vv., *Consumo delle famiglie e Credito al consumo*, Rome: Bancaria Editoriale, 1995, p. 16.
8 The literature here is too vast to summarize. For prominent examples see Giddens, A., *Modernity and Self-Identity*, Cambridge: Polity, 1991. Or in the field of political theory, Laclau, E. and Mouffe, C., *Hegemony and Socialist Strategy*, London: Verso, 1985.
9 On Grand Narratives and their epistemological role see Jean-François Lyotard's classic work *The Postmodern Condition*, Manchester: Manchester University Press, 1984.
10 'Subjectivity' is a term that is as frequently used as it is generally loosely defined. If identity refers to the self-representation of an individual, his or her meaningful

idea of the proper self, subjectivity refers, in my use, to the social and existential conditions in which the articulation of such a meaningful identity takes place. The meaning of the term is further complicated by its appearance in two rather opposed traditions. In the structuralist tradition 'subjectivity' refers to the ways in which social structures 'locate' and thereby largely determine individuals. For the Hegelians, on the other hand, 'subjectivity' means something like 'agency'. I will indicate, usually with a footnote, if I use the term in any of these particular senses.

11 Giddens, op. cit., p. 198. See also Bauman, Z., *Intimations of Postmodernity*, London: Routledge, 1992, p. 189. For the term 'rationalization of the lifeworld' see Habermas, J., *The Theory of Comunicative Action* (2 vols.), Cambridge: Polity, 1995, 1997. On 'reflexive modernity', Beck, U., *Risk Society*, London: Sage, 1992.

12 See, for example, Riesman D., Glazer, N. and Denney, R., *The Lonely Crowd*, New Haven: Yale University Press, 1951; Horkheimer, M. and Adorno, T.W., *The Dialectics of Enlightenment*, New York: Seabury, 1972 (1944); Marcuse, H., *One-Dimensional Man*, Boston: Beacon, 1991 (1964).

13 Coolidge, C., 'Speech to the American Association of Advertising Agencies', 1926, as cited in Twitchell, J.B., *Lead Us not into Temptation: The Triumph of American Materialism*, New York: Columbia University Press, 1999, p. 50.

14 See also Berman, M., *All That is Solid Melts into Air: The Experience of Modernity*, London: Verso, 1987.

15 George Ritzer uses the term 're-enchantment' in his analysis of what he calls the 'cathedrals of consumption', i.e. shopping malls, theme parks, cruise ships and such. See his *Enchanting a Disenchanted World: Revolutionizing the Means of Consumption*, London: Pine Forge, 1999. Little does it matter for the sake of this analysis that this re-enchantment is often a fake or a 'simulacrum'. Indeed, as we learn from contemporary management thought, the simulation (or 're-engineering') of community is an important parallel to its conscious destruction through 'rationalization'. See Rose, N., *The Powers of Freedom*, Cambridge: Cambridge University Press, 1999.

16 See Luhmann, N., *Social Systems*, Stanford: Stanford University Press, 1995; Wagner, P., *Theorizing Modernity*, London: Sage, 2001.

17 See Levi Martin, J., 'The Myth of the Consumption Oriented Economy and the Rise of the Desiring Subject', *Theory and Society*, 28, 1999, pp. 425–453. The 'overproduction thesis' is argued in Stuart Ewen's classic work *Captains of Consciousness: Advertising and the Social Roots of Consumer Culture*, New York: McGraw-Hill, 1976.

18 On the early history of American advertising see Fox, S., *The Mirror Makers: A History of American Advertising and its Creators*, New York: William Morrow, 1984; Lears, T.J., *Fables of Abundance*, New York: Basic, 1994; Fox, R.W. and Lears, T.J., *The Culture of Consumption: Critical Essays in American History, 1880–1980*, New York: Pantheon, 1984; Boorstin, D., *The Americans: The Democratic Experience*, New York: Random House, 1973. On twentieth-century US consumer culture there are two recent edited volumes, Strasser, S., McGovern, C. and Judt, M. (eds), *Getting and Spending*, Cambridge: Cambridge University Press, 1998; and Glickman, L. (ed.), *Consumer Society in American History, a Reader*, Ithaca: Cornell University Press, 1999. On Britain see McKendrick, N., Brewer, J. and Plumb, H.H., *The Birth of a Consumer Society*, London: Europa, 1982; McClintock, A., *Imperial Leather: Race, Gender and Sexuality in the Colonial Contest*, London: Routledge, 1995, chapter 5; and, more generally, McCracken, G., *Culture and Consumption*, Bloomington: University of Indiana Press, 1988.

19 On the term 'form of personhood' see Hacking, I., 'Making Up People', in Heller, T., Morton, S. and Willerby, D. (eds), *Reconstructing Individualism*, Stanford: Stanford University Press, 1986.

20 In my use, the term 'consumer culture' refers to the meaning systems that are constructed around commodities in advertising and the media. My use of this term is therefore slightly different from what is common (see, for example, Slater, op. cit.). In general, although by no means always, this term is used to refer to the meanings that people make of commodities in their everyday practice, the 'webs of significance' that they spin around them, as Clifford Geertz would have said. I use the term 'consumer practice' to refer to this level of everyday meaning-making.

21 Schudson, M., *Advertising: The Uneasy Persuasion*, New York: Basic, 1984. On mythology, Barthes, R., *Mythologies*, Paris: Seuil, 1957.

22 See Williamson, J., *Decoding Advertisements: Ideology and Meaning in Advertising*, London: Boyars, 1978; Leiss, W., Kline, S. and Jhally, S., *Social Communication in Advertising*, London: Routledge, 1986; Goldman, R., *Reading Ads Socially*, New York: Routledge, 1992.

23 Colin Campbell uses a variety of this term: he emphasizes how the romantic ethic served to legitimize the daydreaming imaginative hedonism that in his view is central to contemporary consumer culture. In my use of the term I locate the consumer ethic to the discourse of consumer culture rather than to the *mentalité* of consumers. On a similar approach to the sociology of consumption that stresses the importance of legitimation see Sassatelli, R., 'Tamed Hedonism: Choice, Desires and Deviant Pleasures', in Gronow, J. and Warde, A. (eds), *Ordinary Consumption*, London: Routledge, 2001. Or, more generally, Boltanski, L. and Boltanski, Thévenot, L., *De la justification: Les économies de la grandeur*, Paris: Gallimard, 1991.

24 For an overview of these techniques see, for example, Twitchell, J., *Lead Us not into Temptation: The Triumph of American Materialism*, New York: Columbia University Press, 1999. These degrees of freedom probably vary in different circumstances.

25 Miller, D., *A Theory of Shopping*, Cambridge; Polity, 1998, p. 6. For the people Miller studied shopping on a north London street, 'the activity in which they were engaged on an almost daily basis made no impression whatsoever upon their conformity to a discourse about shopping that rested upon a fantastic vision which most of them rarely, if ever, realized', pp. 71–72.

26 Here the literature is best developed in the case of Britain: see, for example, Abercrombie, N. and Keat, R. (eds.), *The Enterprise Culture*, London: Routledge, 1991.

27 See Arrighi, G. (ed.), *Semiperipheral Development: The Politics of Southern Europe in the Twentieth Century*, London: Sage, 1985.

28 Ortoleva, P., 'I Mezzi di Comunicazione', in Aa. Vv., *Guida all'Italia contemporanea*, vol. 4, *Comportamenti sociali e culturali*, Milan: Garzanti, 1998.

29 Pasolini, P.P., 'Gli italiani non sono piu quelli', *Corriere della sera*, 10/6, 1974, republished as 'Studio sulla rivoluzione antropologica in Italia', *Scritti corsari*, Milan: Garzanti, 1995 (1975).

30 See, for example, Galli della Loggia, E., *L'identità italiana*, Bologna: il Mulino, 1998.

31 Alberoni, F. and Baglioni, G., *L'integrazione del immigrato nella societa industriale*, Bologna: il Mulino, 1965.

32 Bocca, G., *Miracolo all'Italiana*, Milan: Edizioni Avanti, 1962, p. 5.

2 From unification to the Fascist takeover: the first developments of mass consumption

1 Let me once again stress that these should be taken as ideal types. An ideal type, as Weber makes clear, is a map of reality. It should not be confused with reality itself. Both American (meaning US) and European modernities are much more

complex than what the simple model that follows will suggest. There are obvious borderline cases like the UK and, indeed, Italy. It would be more accurate to say that in each national case the two ideal typical trajectories have combined, in harmony or in conflict to various degrees. (For Weber's discussion of the ideal type see the first volume of *Economy and Society*, Berkeley: University of California Press, 1978; for the term 'organized modernity', Wagner, P., *A Sociology of Modernity: Liberty and Discipline*, London: Routledge, 1994.)

2 For an expansion of this argument see the various essays in *Getting and Spending: European and American Consumer Societies*, eds. Strasser, S., McGovern, C. and Judt, M., Cambridge: Cambridge University Press, 1998, in particular Charles McGovern's essay 'Consumption and Citizenship in the United States, 1900–1940'; and Marchand, R., *Advertising the American Dream: Making Way for Modernity, 1920–1940*, Berkeley: University of California Press, 1985.

3 For Eisenhower see 'The Congressional Record, House of Representatives', 6 June 1947, White Plain Public Library, White Plains, New York, p. 6540, as cited in Levy, A., 'Projecting America: The Impact of American Modernity in Great Britain 1945–60', MA thesis, London: Royal College of Art, 1991. On American soldiers in Europe see Ellwood, D., *Rebuilding Europe: Western Europe, America and the Post-War Reconstruction*, New York: Longman, 1992.

4 This ideal type is perhaps best developed in the theoretical writings of 1970s Marxists like Luis Althusser (see his *Essays on Ideology*, London: Verso, 1984) and Nicos Poulantzas, *State, Power and Socialism*, London: New Left, 1978. For empirical case studies see, for France, Weber, E., *Peasants into Frenchmen: The Modernization of Rural France*, London: Chatto & Windus, 1977; for Nazi Germany, Koontz, C., *Mothers of the Fatherland: Women, the Family and Nazi Politics*, New York: St Martins, 1987; for Fascist Italy, Falasca-Zamponi, S., *Fascist Spectacle*: Berkeley University of California Press, 1997; Ben-Ghiat, R., *Fascist Modernities: Italy, 1922–1945*, Berkeley: University of California Press, 2001; for Sweden, Pred, A., *Recognizing European Modernities: A Montage of the Present*, London: Routledge, 1995; for the UK, Maguire, P. and Woodham, J., *Design and Politics in Postwar Britain: The Britain Can Make It Exhibition of 1946*, London: Leicester University Press, 1997. *Getting and Spending*, op. cit, contains a number of essays on Eastern Europe, as does Passerini, L. (ed.), *Across the Atlantic: Cultural Exchanges between Europe and the United States*, Brussels: Pieter Lang, 2000.

5 See Seton-Watson, C., *Italy from Liberalism to Fascism 1980–1925*, London: Methuen, 1967; and Mack-Smith, D., *Modern Italy: A Political History*, New Haven: Yale University Press, 1997 (1959). Both stress the lack of a strong sense of nationhood in Italian history. In his 'Notes on Italian History' Gramsci also laments the lack of popular involvement in the unification process: see Hoare, Q. and Nowell-Smith, G. (eds.), *Selections from the Prison Notebooks*, New York: International, 1971. Some recent scholarship has instead stressed the popular diffusion of nationalist discourse: see, for example, Banti, A.M., *La nazione del Risorgimento: Parentela, Santità e onore alle origini dell'Italia unita*, Turin: Einaudi, 2000. Even so, the inability of the state to set in motion a profound transformation of popular orientations and to overcome the fragmented nature of the peninsula remains one of the key themes in the contemporary debates on Italian national identity: see, for example, Galli della Loggia, E., *L'identità italiana*, Bologna: il Mulino, 1998.

6 By comparison, in the 1870s to 1880s 26.9 per cent of the population had the vote in France, 20.6 per cent in Germany and 8.8 per cent in the UK: see Hobsbawm, E., *The Age of Capital, 1848–1875*, London: Weidenfeld & Nicolson, 1975, p. 43.

7 See Federico, G., 'I fattori della distribuzione', in Romano, R. (ed.), *Storia dell'economia italiana*, vol. 3, *L'età contemporanea*, Turin: Einaudi, 1991.

8 Castronovo, V., *Storia economia d'Italia*, Turin: Einaudi, 1995, pp. 11, 175.

9 See Livolsi, M., 'Consumi e vita quotidiana', in Aa. Vv., *Guida all'Italia contemporanea*, vol. 4, *Comportamenti sociali e culturali*, Milan: Garzanti, 1998; Pivato, S. and Tonelli, A., *Italia vagabonda: Il tempo libero degli italiani dal melodramma alla pay-tv*, Rome: Carocci, 2001; Malatesta, M., 'Il caffé e l'osteria', in Isnenghi, M. (ed.), *I luoghi della memoria: Struture ed eventi dell'Italia unita*, Bari: Laterza, 1997.

10 Federico, op. cit.

11 In 1875 Italy had an illiteracy rate of 52 per cent, to be compared with 17 per cent for England, 2 per cent for Germany, 18 per cent for France and 1 per cent for Sweden (all figures based on conscripts except that for England, based on bridegrooms: Hobsbawm, op. cit., p. 43. cf. Forgacs, D., *The Industrialization of Italian Culture*, Manchester: Manchester University Press, 1990).

12 Castronovo, V., *Stampa ed opinione pubblica nell'Italia liberale*, Bari: Laterza, 1979, p. 66; cf. Ortoleva, P., 'I Mezzi di Comunicazione', in Aa. Vv., *Guida all'Italia contemporanea*, op. cit.

13 Castronovo, V., *Stampa ed opinione*, op. cit.

14 See Amatori, F., *Proprietà e direzione: La Rinascente 1917–1969*, Milan: Franco Angeli, 1989; Caizzi, B., *Il commercio: Storia della società italiana dall'Unità a oggi*, vol. 3, Turin: Utet, 1975; Morris, J., *The Political Economy of Shopkeeping in Milan, 1886–1922*, Cambridge: Cambridge University Press, 1993.

15 On the consumer tastes of the nineteenth-century Italian professional classes see Melograni, P. and Scaraffia, L. (eds.), *La famiglia italiana dall'ottocento a oggi*, Bari: Laterza, 1988. Livolsi, op. cit., shows how the urban professionals, while comparatively wealthy, would still spend 50–60 per cent of their earnings to satisfy primary needs.

16 On the 'industrialization' of worker and middle-class leisure see Forgacs, op. cit.; on the emergence of a middle-class national cusine, Melograni,. op. cit.; La Cecla, F., *La pasta e la pizza*, Bologna: il Mulino, 1998; on sports and leisure, Pivato and Tonelli, op. cit., pp. 56 ff.

17 On the early history of the Italian advertising poster movement, see Ceserani, G.P., *Storia della pubblicità in Italia*, Milan: Edizioni del Sole 24 ore, 1988; Menegazzi, L., *Il manifesto italiano*, Milan: Electa, 1995; Valeri, A., *Pubblicità Italiana: Storia, protagonisti e tendenze di cento anni di comunicazione*, Milan: Edizioni del Sole 24 ore, 1986.

18 Castronovo, V., *Storia economica d'Italia*, op. cit.

19 Zangheri, R., Galasso, G., Castronovo, V., *Storia del movimento cooperativo in Italia*, Turin: Einaudi, 1987.

20 See Castronovo, V. (ed.) *La stampa Italiana nel neocapitalismo*, Bari: Laterza, 1976, p. 102.

21 Caizzi, op. cit.; Zamagni, V., *La distribuzione commerciale in Italia fra le due guerre*, Milan: Franco Angeli, 1981.

22 Scaraffia, L., 'Essere uomo: Essere donna', in Melograni, P. and Scaraffia, L. (eds.), *La famiglia italiana*, Bari: Laterza, 1988, p. 244.

23 See Salvati, M., *Il regime e gli impiegati*, Bari: Laterza, 1992; Montroni, F., 'La famiglia in Italia', in Melograni, P. and Scaraffia, L. (eds.), *La famiglia italiana*, op. cit.

24 On the 'mediatization' of middle-class lifeworlds see Berezin, M., 'Created Constituences: The Italian Middle Class and Fascism', in Koshar, R. (ed.), *Splintered Classes: The European Lower Middle Class in the Age of Fascism*, New York: Holmes & Meier, 1990; Falasca-Zamponi, S., op. cit. Meldini, P., *Sposa e madre esemplare: Ideologia e politica della donna e della famiglia durante il Fascismo*, Florence: Guaraldi, 1975; cf. Mosse, G., *The Nationalization of the Masses: Political Symbolism and Mass Movements in Germany from the Napoleonic Wars to the Third Reich*, New York: Fertig, 1975.

25 Messina, N., *Le donne del Fascismo: Massaie rurali e dive del cinema del ventennio*, Rome: Ellemme, 1987.

26 The ratio of state employees per inhabitant more than doubled between 1911 and 1936: see Ferraresi, F., *Burocrazia e politica in Italia*, Bologna: il Mulino, 1980. While GDP per capita grew by 34 per cent between 1896 and 1913, the corresponding figures for subsequent periods were 1913–22, 12 per cent; 1922–29, 10 per cent; and 1929–38, 7 per cent. Overall private consumption grew by 20.9 per cent between 1894 and 1913; between 1920 and 1939 the rate of growth was half of that (11.1 per cent). In 1938 one-half of the average middle-class family's income was spent on food; in the US the corresponding figure was 25 per cent; and in the 1930s average family income was roughly half of the French average and one-third that of the UK and the US (33 per cent and 31 per cent, respectively). Indeed, average per-capita private consumption in 1936–40 was lower than in 1926–30: see Zamagni, V., *The Economic History of Italy, 1860–1990*, Oxford: Clarendon, 1997; Qurino, P., 'I Consumi in italia dall'unità a oggi', in Romano, R. (ed.), op. cit. Only very few, Castronovo claims, maintained their standard of living all through the Fascist *ventennio* (*Storia economica d'Italia*, p. 324). Few middle-class households would attain the 'comfortable life' guaranteed by the proverbial income of 'a thousand lire a month' (from the title of a popular song) and, as many testimonies indicate, middle-class life was frugal and parsimonious: see for example, Innocenti, M., *Parlami d'amore Mariú: Come eravamo negli anni trenta*, Milan: Mursia, 1998; Vené, G.F. *Mille lire al mese: Vita quotidiana della famiglia nell'Italia Fascista*, Milan: Mondadori, 1988.

27 On the development of mass consumption during the 1930s see Cavallo, P. and Iaccio, C., 'Ceti medi emergenti e immagine della donna nella letteratura rosa degli anni trenta', *Storia Contemporanea*, 15, 1984, pp. 1149–1170; de Grazia, V., *How Fascism Ruled Women*, Berkeley: University of California Press, 1992; Aa. Vv., *L'economia italiana tra le due guerre, 1919–30*, Milan: Ipsoa, 1984.

28 Prezzolini, G., *L'arte di persuadere*, Florence: Lumachi, 1907, p.47; Lancelotti, A., *Storia aneddotica della reclame*, Milan: Dott. Riccardo Quintieri editore, 1912, p. 10. Prezzolini's connection between, on the one hand, moral and epistemological relativism and, on the other, modern commerce, is very similar to that proposed by Simmel in his 1904 *Philosophie des Geldes* (Eng. trans. *The Philosophy of Money*, London: Routledge, 1978). On Prezzolini see also Adamson, W.L., *Avant Garde Florence: From Modernism to Fascism*, Cambridge, Mass.; Harvard University Press, 1993.

29 For figures on the influence of American films see Hay, J., *Popular Film Culture in Fascist Italy*, Bloomington: University of Indiana Press, 1987, Appendix C; cf. Brunetta, G.P., *Storia del cinema italiano*, Rome: Editori uniti, 1979; de Grazia,V., 'La sfida dello "star system": L'Americanismo nella formazione della cultura di massa in Europa, 1920–65', *Quaderni Storici* 58, 1, 1985, pp. 95–133. On the avant-garde and the 'international commodity culture', Adamson, W.L.,' 'Avant-Garde Modernism and Italian Fascism: Cultural Politics in the Era of Mussolini', *Journal of Modern Italian Studies*, 6, 2, 2001, pp. 200–241.

30 For a summary see Gentile, E., *La grande italia: Ascesa e declino del mito della nazione nel ventesimo secolo*, Milan: Mondadori, 1997.

31 Cannistraro, P.V., *La fabbrica del consenso: Fascismo e mass media*, Bari: Laterza, 1975; Monteleone, F., *Storia della radio e della televisione in Italia*, Venice: Marsilio, 1992. On the radio and social control see Thompson, D., *State Control in Fascist Italy*, Manchester: Manchester University Press, 1991.

32 For this argument see Falasca-Zamponi, op. cit.; cf. D'Attorre, P.P., 'Sogno americano e mito sovietico nell'Italia contemporanea', in D'Attorre, P.P. (ed.), *Nemici per la pelle*, Milan: Franco Angeli, 1991.

3 Bourgeois into Fascists? Mass consumption and the regime

1 Villani, D., 'Ringiovanito un dentifricio con cinque mila lire per il sorriso', *L'Ufficio moderno*, 4, 1984; see also, Villani, D., *Come sono nate le undici Miss Italia*, Milan: Domus, 1957.

2 On the Motta campaign see Villani, D., 'Come si è messa a volare la colomba Motta', *L'Ufficio moderno*, August 1982; Valeri, A., 'La campagna per il panettone Motta', *L'Ufficio moderno*, 2, 1950; *Pubblicità Italiana: Storie, protagonisti e tendenze di cento anni di comunicazione*, Milan: Edizioni del sole 24 ore, 1986, pp. 79 ff.; *Dino Villani, una vita per la pubblicità*, Milan: Motta, 1978. On American cosmetics advertising and the construction of a modern beauty ideal see Piess, K., *Hope in a Jar: The Making of America's Beauty Culture*, New York: Henry Holt, 1998.

3 On the law against beauty contests see Villani, D., *Come sono nate*, op cit., p. 15; on conflicts over the representation of women, Aspesi, N., *Il lusso e l'autarchia: Storia dell'eleganza italiana, 1930–1944*, Milan: Rizzoli, 1982, p. 49; Vené, G., *Mille lire al mese: Vita quotidiana della famiglia nell'Italia Fascista*, Milan: Mondadori, 1988.

4 These additions were soon done away with as the initative developed into the 'Miss Italy' beauty contest in the post-war years. See Gundle, S., 'Feminine Beauty, National Identity and Political Conflict in Post-war Italy, 1945–1954', *Contemporary European History*, 8, 3, 1999, pp. 359–378.

5 Pellegrini, A., 'La propaganda e il suo ambiente recettore', *L'Ufficio moderno*, 7, 1938. Walter Benjamin articulates his theory of aura and mass production most clearly in his essay 'The Work of Art in the Age of Mechanical Reproduction', in Arendt, H. (ed.), *Illuminations*, London: Fontana, 1970.

6 For an analysis of Fascist mass politics in similar, Benjamin-inspired terms see Falasca-Zamponi, S., *Fascist Spectacle. The Aesthetics of Power in Mussolini's Italy*, Berkeley: University of California Press, 1998.

7 De Grazia, V., *How Fascism Ruled Women*, Berkeley: University of California Press, 1992, pp. 130 ff.

8 On the shift in popularity away from the Italian *dive*, see Messina, N., *Le donne del Fascismo: Massaie rurali e dive del cinema del ventennio*, Rome: Ellemme, 1987. On the 'White Telephone' films, Brunetta, G.P., 'Il cinema', in Isnenghi, M. (ed.), *I luoghi della memoria: Strutture ed eventi dell'Italia unita*, Bari: Laterza, 1997; cf. idem, *Storia del cinema italiano*, Rome: Editori Riuniti, 1979; on the women's magazines, Arvidsson, A., 'The Pleasures of Renunciation: Young Women and Mass Consumption in fascist Italy', Hurd, M., Olsson, T., Åker, P. (eds.), *Storylines. Media, Power and Identity in Modern Europe*, Stockholm; Hjalmarson & Högberg, 2002. . . .; on the notion of non-place see Augé, M., *Non-Places: An Anthropology of Supermodernity*, London: Verso, 1995.

9 On the history of the symbolic connection between trousers and female empowerment see Luck, K., 'Trousers: Feminism in Nineteenth Century America', in Kirkham, P. (ed.), *The Gendered Object*, Manchester: Manchester University Press, 1996; on the campaigns against modern dances, Pivato, S. and Tonelli, A., *Italia vagabonda: Il tempo libero degli italiani dal melodramma alla pay-tv*, Rome: Carocci, 2001, pp. 79 ff.

10 Grillenzoni, G., 'I caratteri del fisico e del vestire considerati come fattori demografici', *Atti del convegno internazionale per gli studi sulla popolazione*, Rome, 7–10 September 1931, Rome: Istituto poligrafico dello stato, vol. 2, pp. 261–269, as cited in de Grazia, op. cit., pp. 212, 327; cf. Horn, D., *Social Bodies: Science, Reproduction and Italian Modernity*, Princeton: Princeton University Press, 1994. On *il Selvaggio* and the Florentine 'strapaese' see Adamson, W.L., *Avant Garde Florence: From Modernism to Fascism*, Cambridge, Mass.: Harvard University Press, 1993.

11 'Estetica e figli', *Donna Fascista*, 7, 5/4, 1935.

12 'Il discorso dell'ascensione' (26/5, 1927), in *Opera Omnia* di Benito Mussolini, Florence: la Fenice, 1951–1963, vol. 22, p. 390.
13 Falasca-Zamponi, op. cit., p. 126.
14 Mussolini, B., 'Dottrina del Fascismo', in *Scritti e discorsi*, Milan: Hoepli, 1934–39, vol. 8, p. 79, as translated in Falasca-Zamponi, op. cit., p. 121.
15 Luchin A. and D'Amico, S., 'L'America', *Critica Fascista*, 3, 1928; cf. Nacci, M., *L'antiamericanismo in Italia negli anni trenta*, Turin: Bollati Boringhieri, 1989; D'Attorre, P.P., 'Sogno americano e mito sovietico nell'Italia contemporanea', in D'Attorre, P.P. (ed.), *Nemici per la pelle*, Milan: Franco Angeli, 1991.
16 Piccoli, V., 'Babitt, o l'uomo standard', *Critica Fascista*, 23; Nacci, op. cit. Compare the essay on the culture industry in Horkheimer, M. and Adorno, 1932, T.W., *The Dialectic of Enlightenment*, New York: Seabury, 1971 (1944).
17 See Adamson, W., 'The Culture of Italian Fascism and the Crisis of Modernity: The Case of *il Selvaggio*', *Journal of Contemporary History*, 30, 1995, pp. 555–575.
18 Gentile, E., *The Sacralization of Politics in Fascist Italy*, Cambridge, Mass.: Harvard University Press, 1996.
19 Herf, G., *Reactionary Modernism*, Cambridge: Cambridge University Press, 1984.
20 Bigazzi, D., *La grande Fabbrica: Organizzazione industriale e modello americano alla Fiat dal Lingotto a Mirafiori*, Milan: Feltrinelli, 2000. On the impact of scientific management in the inter-war years see also Sapelli, G., *Organizzazione, lavoro e innovazione industriale nell'Italia tra le due guerre*, Turin: Rosenberg & Seller, 1978.
21 On the revisionists see Acquarone's classic work *L'organizzazione dello stato totalitario*, Turin: Einaudi, 1965; Guerri, G.B., *Giuseppe Bottai: Un Fascista critico*, Milan: Feltrinelli, 1976; on the competence committees, Salvati, M., *Il regime e gli impiegati*, Bari: Laterza, 1992.
22 Gar was a discussion group with close ties to *L'Ufficio moderno* that met at the modernist restaurant *La penna d'oca* in Milan (also the place to savour Marinetti's futurist cooking) beginning in 1931. In 1933 Gar was absorbed within the centre for corporativist economic studies (Centro studi di economia corporativa). Gar, together with Iri formed an important breeding ground for the cadres of the 'economic miracle'. It counted among its members Adriano Olivetti, Gugliemo Tagliacarne, Roberto Tremelloni and Agostino Gemelli. See Valeri, A., *Pubblicità italiana: Storia, tendenze e protagonisti di cento anni di comunicazione*, Milan: Edizioni del sole 24 ore.
23 The 'Quota 90' announced in 1926 referred to a deflationary policy designed to restore the value of the lira to its 1922 value (90 lire to one pound sterling). It was pursued through a general credit squeeze and largely paid for by a compression of middle- and working-class wages. On its impact on the rationalization of sales and distribution, see Sapelli, G., 'La razionalizzazione della vendita: alle origini del marketing e della pubblicità in Italia', *Quaderni di sociologia*, 2–4, 1978, pp. 134–151.
24 This aspect of Taylorism has been amply theorized in the Marxist literature: see Braverman, H., *Labor and Monopoly Capital*, New York: Monthly Review, 1974; Aglietta, M., *A Theory of Capitalist Regulation*, London: New Left Review, 1978; Negri, A., 'Keynes and the Capitalist Theory of the State', in Hardt, M. and Negri, A. (eds.), *The Labour of Dionysos*, Minneapolis: University of Minnesota Press, 1994.
25 Editorial *L'Ufficio moderno*, 5, 1928; 'La lotta contro lo spreco', *L'Ufficio moderno*, 1, 1927; Passaretti, R., 'Sulla Razionalizzazione del lavoro', *Critica Fascista*, 5, 1929; Crespi, P., 'Cosa ci insegna l'America?', *Critica Fascista*, 10, 1929.
26 'Primo: sapere' (editorial) *L'Ufficio moderno*, 5–6, 1927. The reference to the novels of Guido di Verona, a popular author of middle-brow romantic fiction, connotes a particular aversion to the culture of the literate middle classes, or as Gaetano Salvemini called them, the 'illiterate intellectuals'.

27 Bottai, G., 'Razionalizzazione italiana', *L'Ufficio moderno*, 7, 1930; Bottai, G., 'Capitale, tecnica, lavoro', *Critica Fascista*, 2, 1929.
28 'L'Europa o L'America? La necessità di razzionalizazione' (editorial), *L'Ufficio moderno*, 3, 1928.
29 'Secondo: Organizzare', *L'Ufficio moderno*, 7, 1927.
30 'Terzo: Aggredire', *L'Ufficio moderno*, 8, 1927.
31 Cederaschi, E., 'Il terzo tempo della pubblicità statale', *La pubblicità d'Italia*, 7, 1937.
32 See de Grazia, V., *The Culture of Consent*, Cambridge: Cambridge University Press, 1981.
33 See Ponti, G., 'La casa all'italiana', *Domus*, January 1928; cf. Branzi, A., *Introduzione al design italiano: una modernità incompleta*, Milan: Baldini & Castoldi, 1999; Sparke, P., *Italian Design, 1870 to the Present*, London: Thames & Hudson, 1988.
34 Advertising leaflet for La Rinascente, Collezione Dino Villani, Centro di Documentazione SIPRA, Turin, fascicolo 100, miscellaneous material; Amatori, F., *Proprietà e direzione: La Rinascente 1917–1969*, Milan: Franco Angeli, 1989.
35 De Grazia, V., *The Culture of Consent*, p. 50.
36 Vené, op. cit.; cf. Innocenti, M., *Parlami d'amore Mariù: Come eravamo negli anni trenta*, Milan: Mursia, 1998.
37 See Hardyment, C., *From Mangle to Microwave: The Mechanization of Household Work*, Cambridge: Polity, 1988; Ferris-Moltz, M. and Browne, P. (eds.), *Middle Class Women and Domestic Material Culture*, Bowling Green, Ohio: Bowling Green State University Press, 1988; cf. Nolan, M., *Visions of Modernity: American Business and the Modernization of Germany*, Oxford: Oxford University Press, 1994.
38 Salvati, M., *L'Inutile salotto: L'Abitazione piccolo-borghese nel Italia Fascista*, Turin: Bollati Boringheri, 1993, p. 112.
39 H.S. 'La donna consumatrice', *Casa e lavoro*, 4, September, 1932; Magliocco, V., 'La donna, l'economia nazionale e i prodotti italiani', *Casa e lavoro* 4, November, 1932.
40 Diez Gasca, M., 'La donna e il Fascismo', *Casa e lavoro* 6, June 1934.
41 Berasconi, U., 'La donna nella casa decorosa', *Donna Fascista*, 6, 1935.
42 Quaglia, F., 'La rivoluzione in cucina: L'uso del gas nell'abitazione moderna', *Contemporanea*, 1, 2000.
43 'La massaia moderna: Intermezzo sul galateo in tavola', *Cucina italiana*, 15/1, 1931; 'I pasti delle dive del cinematografo', *Cucina italiana* 1/7, 1936.
44 See Hirdman, Y., *Att lägga livet tillrätta: Studier i svensk folkhemspolitik*, Stockholm: Carlsson, 1989.
45 Autarchy (*autarchia*) was a catchword for an economic policy of self-sufficiency proclaimed by Mussolini in 1936 as a response to the economic sanctions imposed by the League of Nations following Italy's invasion of Ethiopia the preceding year.
46 Pini, G., 'Corporazioni, autarchia e pubblicità collettiva', *La Pubblicità d'Italia*, 11–12, 1938, XVI, 'Programma di lavoro' (editorial), *La Pubblicità d'Italia*, 1, 1937.
47 Notari, U., 'La pubblicità come strategia', *La Pubblicità d'Italia*, 1, 1937; Pini, G., 'Funzione autarchica della pubblicità collettiva', *La Pubblicità d'Italia*, 7–8, 1938.
48 Cederaschi, E., 'Il terzo tempo della pubblicità statale', *La Pubblicità d'Italia*, 1, 1937; Notari, U., 'La pubblicità come strategia', *La Pubblicità d'Italia*, 1, 1937.
49 Pini, G., 'La pubblicità, il giornalismo Fascista', *La Pubblicità d'Italia*, 2–3, 1937; 'L'osservatore' "Stile" ', *La Pubblicità d'Italia*, 9–10, 1938.
50 Grego, E., 'Un libro Italiano di pubblicità e l'ignoranza di un giornalista', *L'Impresa moderna*, 4, 1920; Cavalli, P., *La Spada d'America*: Milan; Fratelli Traves editori, 1919.

51 Mazzali, G., 'Modi e forme della pubblicità italiana', *L'Ufficio moderno*, 4, 1930; 'Il nostro referendum sulla pubblicità', *L'Ufficio moderno*, 12, 1927.
52 These debates raged in *Printer's Ink* in the mid- to late 1920s as the European poster style began to have an influence in the US: see Kastner, K.J., 'Modernistic Modes in Montana', *Printer's Ink*, 4/4, 1929; 'A Commercial Art Manager'; 'Futuristic Monstrosities are all the Rage', *Printers Ink*, 12/11, 1925.
53 On the artisic policies of the Fascist regime see, for example, Ben-Ghiat, R., *Fascist Modernities: Italy 1922–1945*, Berkeley: University of California Press, 2001; Stone, M.S., *The Patron State: Culture and Politics in Fascist Italy*, Princeton: Princeton University Press, 1998; Malvano, L., *Fascismo e politica d'immagine*, Turin: Bollati Boringheri, 1988. On Fascism and 'style' see Falasca-Zamponi, op. cit; and, more generally, Hewitt, A., *Fascist Modernism: Aesthetics, Politics, and the Avant-Garde*, Stanford: Stanford University Press, 1993.
54 On the career of the futurists, Salaris, C., *Artecrazia, l'avanguardia futurista negli anni del Fascismo*, Florence: La Nuova Italia, 1992.
55 Depero, F., 'Il futurismo e l'arte pubblicitaria', in *Numero unico futurista Campari*, Milan: 1931; cf. Salaris, C., *Futurismo e arte pubblicitaria*, Turin: Bollati Boringheri, 1986.
56 Marinetti, F.T., 'Estetica della pubblicità', *Artecrazia*, 11/2, 1938.
57 'Tre domande agli artisti Italiani', *L'Ufficio moderno*, 11, 1927.
58 'Arte pubblicitaria, 1900–1933', supplement to *L'Ufficio moderno*, 9, 1933.
59 Pinkus, K., *Bodily Regimes: Italian Advertising under Fascism*, Minneapolis: University of Minnesota Press, 1995.
60 Mazzali, G., 'La campagna di pubblicità collettiva per la birra Italiana', *L'Ufficio moderno*, 1, 1930; 'La pubblicità collettiva in Italia, l'esperimento dei produttori di birra', *L'Ufficio moderno* 9, 1931.
61 See Aspesi, op. cit.; de Liguoro, L., *Le battaglie della moda, 1919–1930*, Rome: Società tipografica Luzzati, 1934; White, N., *Reconstructing Italian Fashion: America and the Development of the Italian Fashion Industry*, Oxford: Berg, 2000.

4 The American influence

1 Dalmonte, L., 'Un colpo d'occhio in una grande casa di pubblicità americana', *L'Impresa moderna*, 10, 1920.
2 Fox, S., *The Mirror Makers: A History of American Advertising and its Creators*, New York: William Morrow, 1984, p. 79; Pope, D., *The Making of Modern Advertising*, New York: Basic, 1985, pp. 18 ff. On the early developments of advertising and its connection to American national identity see also Marchand, R., *Advertising the American Dream: Making Way for Modernity 1920–40*, Berkeley: University of California Press, 1985; Lears, T.J., *Fables of Abundance*, New York: Basic, 1994; Strasser, S., McGovern, C. and Judt, M. (eds.), *Getting and Spending: European and American Consumer Societies in the Twentieth Century*, Cambridge: Cambridge University Press, 1998. On the early history of marketing, Bartels, R., *The History of Marketing Thought*, Columbus (Ohio): Grind, 1976; Tedlow, R., *New and Improved: The Story of Mass Marketing in America*, New York: Basic, 1990. The traditional account has been that the growth of American advertising and marketing was driven by the rapid development of mass production (see, for example, Even, S., *Captains of Consciousness: Advertising and the Social roots of Consumer Culture*, New York: McGraw-Hill, 1976). More recent accounts tend to point at the significance of new distributive systems instead: see Levi-Martin, J., 'The Myth of the Consumption Oriented Economy and the Rise of the Desiring Subject', *Theory & Society*, 28, 1999, pp. 425–453.
3 On J.W. Thompson's foreign expansion see Merron, J., 'American Culture Goes Abroad: J. Walter Thompson and the General Motors Account, 1927–33', PhD

thesis, Chapel Hill: University of North Carolina, 1991. On American advertising in Europe in the inter-war years see also de Grazia, V., 'The Arts of Purchase: How American Publicity Subverted the European Poster, 1920–40', in Kruger, B. and Mariani, P. (eds.), *Remaking History*, Seattle: Bay, 1989.

4 Pierce, R., *Gringo-Gaucho: An Advertising Odyssey*, Ashland (Ohio): Southern Cross, 1991, p. 38.

5 'When Carmen Goes Shopping', *J. Walter Thompson Newsletter*, 15/1, 1928; Mazur, P.M., 'Can the European Philosophy of Consumption be Changed?', *Printer's Ink*, 10/4, 1930; Fellows, C., 'The Advertising Approach to the French Market', *Export Advertiser*, 1, 1930; *Beauty from Bangor to Bangkok*, Sidney Bernstein papers, client files, box 5, J. Walter Thompson Collection, Special Collections Library, Duke University.

6 Wakeman, F., *The Hucksters*, New York: Rinehart, 1946.

7 'J. Walter Thompson Company', *Fortune*, November 1947: see also Kreshel, P., 'Towards a Cultural History of Advertising Research: A Case Study of J. Walter Thompson, 1908–1925', PhD thesis, Urbana-Champaign: University of Illinois, 1989.

8 On JWT in Milan see *JWT Italy, the first attempt*, Information Centre Records, box 10, JWT Collection. The document indicates that JWT had to withdraw from Milan on account of a decree that foreign agencies could no longer operate in Italy. Whether such a decree did in fact exist or not, it is also probable that the agency left their relatively marginal operations in Italy as a part of their general withdrawal during the depression. (In the early 1930s JWT also withdrew from Warsaw and Alexandria (1931), Madrid (1932), Berlin (1933), Stockholm (1934) and Copenhagen (1935): see Merron, op. cit.)

9 These kinds of laments had been with the profession since the very beginning. Already in 1914 writers in *L'Impresa moderna* complained about rampant chaos and clientelism in the advertising business: see 'La scelta dei periodici in pubblicità', *L'Impresa moderna*, 1, 1914; and similar complaints were frequent all through the 1920s: Favilla, P., 'Novanta per cento non sanno vendere', *La Pubblicità*, 2, 1925; Balzaretti, P., 'Il fallimento del empirismo', *L'Impresa moderna*, 2, 1920.

10 Cassola, C., *La reclame dal punto di vista economico*, Turin: Fratelli Bocca, 1909, pp. 17 ff.

11 Lancelotti, A., *Storia aneddotica della reclame*, Milan: Dott. Riccardo Quintieri editore, 1912, p. 10.

12 Cases, F., 'L'Arte della vendita', *L'Impresa moderna*, 1, 1914, 'Cercasi piazzista', *L'Ufficio moderno*, 9, 1927; see also Sapelli, G., 'La'razzionalizzazione della vendita: alle origini del marketing e della pubblicità in Italia', *Quaderni di sociologia*, 2–4, 1978, pp. 134–151.

13 'L'arte di vendere: del fumo', *Il pugno nell'occhio*, 1/3, 1923; 'La pubblicità parlata', *Il pugno nell'occhio*, 1, 3, 1923.

14 Ramo, L., *L'Arte nella recalme*, Milan: Biblioteca de L'Impresa Moderna, 1917, p. 56.

15 Beale, M., 'Advertising and the Politics of Public Persuasion in France, 1900–1933', PhD thesis, Berkeley: University of California, 1991, p. 47.

16 Cassi, cited in Cunsolo, F., *Il potere della pubblicità*, Milan: OTIP, 1954, p. 89; see also Cassi, G., 'I miei trent anni di lavoro', Milan, 1940 (private imprint).

17 'Arte Pubblicitaria' 1900–33, supplement to *L'Ufficio moderno*, 9, 1933.

18 Emilio Grego had written a book on war propaganda, *Come si lancia un prestito di guerra*, with the subtitle *Studio di psicologia applicata* ('A Study in Applied Psychology'), Milan: Edizioni L'Impresa moderna, 1918.

19 Roggero, E., *Come si riesce con la pubblicità*, Milan: Hoepli, 1920, p. 151.

20 'La pubblicità come arte e scienza: C'è la crisi', *L'Ufficio moderno*, 1, 1927; 'Uso e valore della lettera reclame', *L'Ufficio moderno*, 1, 1927; 'L'Affiche', *L'Ufficio*

moderno, 6, 1927; 'Secondo Incinsa', *L'Ufficio moderno*, 2, 1929; 'Psicologia pubblicitaria', *L'Ufficio moderno*, 1, 1930.

21 'Arte Pubblicitaria 1900–33', supplement to *L'Ufficio moderno*, 9, 1933. On the activities of Octave-Jacques Gérin in French advertising see Beale, op. cit.; Chessel, M., 'L'emergence de la publicité: Publicitaires, annonceurs et affichistes dans la France de l'entre-deux guerres', PhD thesis, Fiesole European University Institute, 1995; on the psychology of the Salpetière school see Nye, R., *The Origins of Crowd Psychology: Gustave Le Bon and the Crisis of Mass Democracy in the Third Republic*, London: Sage, 1975.

22 Gérin, O.J. and Espinadel, C., *La publicité suggestive*, Paris: H. Dunod & E. Pinad, 1911, p. 46.

23 Ibid., p. 47.

24 Cavalli, P., *La Spada d'America*, Milan: Fratelli Traves editori, 1919, p. 173.

25 Aurelio, A., 'Psicologia e pubblicità', *L'Impresa moderna*, 8, 1920.

26 Gérin and Espinadel, op. cit., p. 55. 'Millions of people' is of course an exaggeration. However, Gérin's experience as a researcher in psychology suggests that this statement has some empirical foundation.

27 Ibid., p. 61; Jona, G., 'Il potere della pubbliticà', *L'Impresa moderna*, 1, 1914; 'Il successo nel metodo', *La pubblicità*, 2, 1925.

28 'L'Arte di vendere', *L'Idea*, May 1917. *L'Idea* began as a journal of advertising technique but rapidly turned into an organ of patriotic propaganda.

29 'Come fare un annuncio', *L'Ufficio moderno*, 11, 1927; 'Arte pura, arte applicata', *L'Ufficio moderno*, 11, 1927.

30 Lancelotti, op. cit., p. 55.

31 Brivio, C., 'Il manifesto e la sua funzione', *La Pubblicità*, 4–5, 1925.

32 On the FIAT 509 Balilla campaign see Castronovo, V., *Fiat: Un secolo di storia italiana*, Milan: Rizzoli, 1999, p. 467; on Santa Vittoria, Balzaretti, L., 'Dietro le quinte di una grande campagna pubblicitaria', *La pubblicità*, 3, 1925; 'La campagna di Santa Vittoria', *ACME – Rivista di Pubblicita e di organizazione tecnica per lo svilluppo delle vendite*, April 1924, Collezione Dino Villani, Fascicolo 100 (not catalogued).

33 The 'Mostra della rivoluzione Fascista' celebrated the tenth anniversary of Fascism's foundational event, the march on Rome in 1922. It was generally regarded as a chief achievement of Fascist art and propaganda: see Stone, M.S., *The Patron State: Culture and Politics in Fascist Italy*, Princeton: Princeton University Press, 1998. The Continental Advertising Association resulted from the split of the International Advertising Association in 1928. It represented European advertising professionals, as opposed to the other half, the Advertising Federation of America: see Chessel, op. cit., p. 42. On the consolidation of the Italian advertising professsion see Valeri, A., *Pubblicità italiana: Storia, portagonisti e tendenze di cento anni di communicazione*, Milan: Edizioni del sole 24 ore, 1986; Falabrino, G., *Effimera e bella: Storia della pubblicità italiana*, Turin: Gutenberg, 2000 (1989).

34 *Atti del congresso internazionale della pubblicità*, Rome–Milan 17–21, 9, 1933, Milan, 1933; Dalmonte, L., 'Alla viglia del congresso', *L'Ufficio moderno*, 7–8, 1933. Estimates are highly unreliable. While Vera Zamagni (*La distribuzione commericale in Italia fra le due guerre*, Milan: Franco Agneli, 1981, p. 121) estimates total expenditure on advertising to be 400 million lire for 1932, there was no standardized measurement available until 1962, with the foundation of an institute for the certification of newspaper circulation and advertising expenditure. Similarly, the 802 'companies' probably included a large number of individual, freelancing technicians and artists. While the comparison with 1949 might seem surprising, it is worth remembering not only that average standards of living in 1951 were actually slightly below those of 1938, but also that the real take-off of Italian advertising occurred in the second half of the 1950s: see chapter 5.

35 H.J. Rand, 'Il governo degli affari', *L'Ufficio moderno*, 1, 1927; Jones, L., 'Come preparare e lanciare un nuovo prodotto', *L'Ufficio moderno*, 5, 1928; W.H. Frickner, 'Come faccio il direttore generale della Palmolive Italia', *L'Ufficio moderno*, 1, 1931; Cassoon, H., 'Principi essenziali della pubblicità', *L'Ufficio moderno*, 2, 1935; *Mille opere sulla pubblicità*, Rome: Enios, 1936.

36 Link, H., *The New Psychology of Selling and Advertising*, 1932, as cited in Kreshel, P., 'Towards a Cultural History of Advertising Research: A Case Study of J. Walter Thompson, 1908–25', PhD thesis, Urbana-Champaign: University of Illinois, 1989, p. 114. On J.B. Watson see also Kreshel, P, 'John B. Watson at J.W. Thompson: The Legitimation of Science in Advertising', *Journal of Advertising*, 19, 1990; Wren, D.A., *The Evolution of Management Thought*, New York: John Wiley, 1994.

37 Watson, J.B., 'Influencing the Mind of Another', speech delivered to the Montreal Advertising Association, as cited in Merron, op. cit., p. 64.

38 Goffman, E., *The Presentation of Self in Everyday Life*, London: Penguin, 1971. On the emergence of the problematic of the self in American public culture in the inter-war years, and its relation to advertising and mass consumption, see also Susman, W., *Culture as History: The Transformation of American Society in the Twentieth Century*, New York: Pantheon, 1984.

39 While Stephen Fox (op. cit) argues that 'hard sell' and 'soft sell' approaches have taken turns throughout advertising history, and while there were of course exceptions, the literature generally agrees that the self, its presentation, protection or enjoyment, became a central concern for North American advertising during the 1920s. Leiss et al., in their vast quantitative study of some 10,000 Canadian advertisements, identify a clear shift from what they call 'goods as satisfiers' to 'goods as communicators', from an emphasis within advertising discourse on 'Information-Utility' to one on 'Symbolism–Personal Use', around the mid-1920s. Richard Pollay, in a similar quantitative study, identifies a shift from 'utility' to 'vanity' as the central principle of advertising arguments. Similarly, Merle Curti, in his seminal article, identifies a shift in the 'concept of man' in advertising theory, from a 'rationalistic image of man' to an 'irrationalistic conception of human nature' around the First World War. The shift, Curti argues, correlates with an increasing use of scientific terminology and an increasingly positive attitude to science. Lears (op. cit.) makes similar observations; see Leiss, W., Kline, S. and Jhally, S., *Social Communication in Advertising*, London: Routledge, 1986; Pollay, R., 'The Subsidizing Sizzle: A Descriptive History of Advertising', *Journal of Marketing*, 49, 1985, pp. 24–37; Curti, M., 'The Changing Concept of Human Nature in the Literature of American Advertising', *Business History Review*, 41, 1967, pp. 335–357.

40 Marchand, op. cit., p. 76; Schudson, M., *Advertising, the Uneasy Persuasion*, New York: Basic, 1984.

41 Lazy, P., 'Il linguaggio pubblicitario', *L'Ufficio moderno*, 9, 1932; 'Tecnica del annuncio', *L'Ufficio moderno*, 9, 1934; 'L'incontentabile', 'Grammatica e psicologia', *L'Ufficio moderno*, 1, 1931.

42 Pomé, R., *Concezione moderna della pubblicità-Lezioni tenute al Politecnico di Milano per il Corso dei Dirigenti di Aziende Industriali (aprile–maggio 1936-XIV)*, Rome: Edizioni della federazione nazionale Fascista dirigenti aziende industriali.

43 Pomé, R., 'Il consumatore-bersaglio passivo o giudice autorevole?' *L'Ufficio moderno*, 4, 1936.

44 Helin, M., 'Le basi psicologiche della pubblicità', *L'Ufficio moderno*, 6, 1936.

45 See Baudrillard, J., *Pour une critique de l'economie politique du sign*, Paris: Gallimard, 1972.

46 Helin, M., 'La suggestione in pubblicità', *L'Ufficio moderno*, 5, 1933; Pluriventi,

N., 'Psicologia del service', *L'Ufficio moderno*, 4, 1933; Cassoon, H., 'Principi essenziali della pubblicità', op. cit.

47 Pellegrini, A., 'Il marchio', *L'Ufficio moderno*, 11, 1938.

48 Pellegrini, A., *Manuale di scienza della propaganda e della pubblicità: Teoria e tecnica*, Rome: Enios, 1938.

49 Dalmonte, L., 'Rapporto fra cinema e pubblicità', *La Pubblicità d'Italia*, 1–2, 1939.

50 Mazzali, G., 'Preferite i prodotti Italiani!' *L'Ufficio moderno*, 11, 1931; for a similar argument see 'Sanzioni e controsanzioni', *L'Ufficio moderno*, 12, 1936.

51 'Tecnica dell'annuncio', *L'Ufficio moderno*, 10, 1934.

52 Pellegrini, A., 'La propaganda', op. cit.

53 *Ti Prendo al volo*, advertising leaflet, ACME Dalmonte, 1934, fascicolo 100, Collezione Dino Villani.

54 Dalmonte, L., 'Presente e futuro della pubblicità italiana', *L'Ufficio moderno*, 7–8, 1943.

55 Dalmonte, L., 'Basta l'automobile per farla correre: grandi campagne pubblicitarie fra le due guerre mondiali', *L'Ufficio moderno*, 6, 1946.

56 Dalmonte, L., 'Presente e futuro . . .', 'La rinascita della Rinascente', *L'Ufficio moderno*, 9, 1949.

57 Advertisements, La Rinascente, *Donna Fascista* 1, 1937; *Critica Fascista*, 22, 1932.

58 Advertisment, Cirio, *Critica Fascista*, 2, 1931.

59 Dalmonte, L., 'Il segreto di Cirio', *L'Ufficio moderno*, 2, 1930.

60 Dalmonte, L., 'Presente e futuro', op. cit.

61 On the early history of market research in Italy see Rinauro, S., 'L'indagine di mercato in Italia tra primo e secondo dopoguerra: alle origini della razionalizzaszione della distribuzione', *Impresa e storia*, 21, 2000, pp. 13–60.

62 Pellegrini, A., 'La Propaganda e il suo ambiente recettore', *L'Ufficio moderno*, 7, 1938; for similar lists see Helin, M., 'La psicologia della pubblicità', *L'Ufficio moderno*, 2 1934; Augier, L., 'Definzioni psicologici per la vendita e la pubblicita', *L'Ufficio moderno*, 1, 1934; Parillaud, R., 'Il piano di vendita', *L'Ufficio moderno*, 2, 1937.

63 Dalmonte, L., 'A dir le mie virtu basta un sorriso', *L'Ufficio moderno*, 4, 1947.

64 Dalmonte, L., 'Presente e futuro della pubblicità italiana', *L'Ufficio moderno*, 5–6, 1943.

65 Advertising leaflet, *Gazzetta dello Sport*, 1934, Collezione Dino Villani, Centro di Documentazione SIPRA, Turin (uncatalogued).

66 See, for example, De Felice, R., 'Aspetti politico-diplomatici delle relazioni culturali tra Italia e Stati Uniti', in Aa. Vv., *Italia e Usa: Giudizi incrociati*, Turin: Fondazione Agnelli 1979; cf. D'Attorre, P.P., 'Sogno americano e mito sovietico nell'Italia contemporanea', in Attorre, P.P. (ed.), *Nemici per la pelle*, Milan: Franco Angeli, 1991.

67 Aspesi, N., *Il lusso e l'autarchia: Storia dell'eleganza italiana*, Milan: Rizzoli, 1982, p. 147; Butazzi, G., *1922–1943, Vent'anni di moda italiana*, Milan: Museo Poldi Pezzoli, 1980.

68 Salvati, M., *L'inutile salotto: L'Abitazione piccolo borghese nel Italia Fascista*, Turin: Boringhieri, 1993, p. 53. The results of the inquiry originally appeared in *Almanacco della donna*, 1939, Florence, 1938.

69 'Autarchia e pubblicità', *La pubblicità d'Italia*, 1, 1937.

5 The economic miracle: mass consumption and modernization

1 On JWT and its dominance in the Italian advertising world during the 1950s see Valeri, A., *Pubblicità italiana: Storia, protagonisti e tendenze di cento anni di comunicazione*, Milan: Edizioni del sole 24 ore, 1986.

2 'Emma Rosati parlando di bucato crea in Italia le relazioni umane', *Grazia*, 30/6, 1957.
3 See Gundle, S., 'Feminine Beauty, National Identity and Political Conflict in Postwar Italy, 1945–1954', *Contemporary European History*, 8, 3, 1999, pp. 359–378; Foot, J., 'Mass Culture, Popular Culture and the Working Class in Milan', *Social History*, 2, 1999; cf. Brunetta, G.P. and Ellwood, D. (eds.) *Hollywood in Europa*, Florence: Usher, 1991.
4 For a typical diagnosis of advertising as 'Americanization' see Sardi, F., 'La grafica', *Il Contemporaneo*, 37, 1955.
5 See Burke, T., *Lifebuoy Men, Lux Women: Commodification, Consumption and Cleanness in Modern Zimbabwe*, Durham: Duke University Press, 1996; Andersson, M., *Madison Avenue in Asia: The Politics of Transnational Advertising*, London: Associated University Presses, 1984.
6 'Magazine Advertising and the Housewife: A Summary Statement', Agency memo, October 1957, Information Centre Records, box 12, JWT Collection. Compare Talcott Parsons' sociological legitimation of the housewife-role in Parsons, T. and Bales, R., *Family, Socialization and Interaction Process*, Glencoe, Ill.: The Free Press, 1955. On the 'demonstration effect' see Duesenberry, J.S., *Income, Savings and the Theory of Consumer Behaviour*, Cambridge, Mass.: Harvard University Press, 1949.
7 De Grazia, V., 'Changing Consumption Regimes in Europe 1930–1970: Comparative Perspectives on the Distribution Problem', in Strasser, S., McGovern, C. and Judt, M. (eds.), *Getting and Spending: European and American Consumer Societies in the Twentieth Century*, Cambridge: Cambridge University Press, 1998.
8 Gundle, S., 'L'americanizzazione del quotidiano: Televisione e consumismo nell'Italia degli anni cinquanta', *Quaderni storici*, 62, 1986, pp. 561–594.
9 There are no official statistics on the turnover of the advertising industry until the institutionalization of an institute for controlling media circulation, IAD (Istituto Accertamento Diffusione), in 1962. I have relied on figures stated in isolated articles and speeches: see Lombardi, G., 'Premesse e promesse', *L'Ufficio moderno*, 9, 1950; and Andreoli, L., 'Pubblicità – fenomeno di suggestione e realtà economica', *L'Ufficio moderno* 1, 1960; James, D., *Talk Given to Senior Executives of J. Walter Thompson (Italia)*, 21/6, 1963, Wilson Papers, folder 13, J. Walter Thompson Collection. While there is no guarantee for the reliability of these figures, they might be helpful in indicating the direction of a general trend.
10 On the Marshall Aid and the spread of American business methods see Carew, A., *Labour under the Marshall Plan: The Politics of Productivity and the Marketing of Management Science*, Manchester: Manchester University Press, 1987; Ellwood, D., 'Gli stati uniti e la modernizzazione dell'Europa', *Contemporanea*, 3, 1999.
11 On the traditional function of women's magazines as a kind of 'transition belt' between production and consumption, as well as the recent critique of this model, see MacDonald, M., *Representing Women: Myths of Femininity in Popular Media*, London: Edward Arnold, 1995; McCracken, E., *Decoding Women's Magazines: From Mademoiselle to Ms*, London: Macmillan, 1993; Williamsson, J., *Consuming Passions: The Dynamics of Popular Culture*, London: Boyars, 1996.
12 Pasqualini, A., 'La pubblicità la vendita e la donna', *L'Ufficio moderno*, 7, 1957.
13 Benelli, G., *Cifre e idee per la pubblicità*, Milan: Edizioni *L'Ufficio moderno*, 1951, p. 43.
14 Lilli, L., 'La stampa femminile', in Aa. Vv., *La stampa italiana nel neocapitalismo*, Bari: Laterza, 1976.
15 Benelli, op. cit.; for similar discoveries see also Rezzara, A., 'La pubblicità dei settimanali', *L'Ufficio moderno*, 8, 1950.
16 Vettori, I., 'Budgets pubblicitari e controllo delle tirature-un problema che

aspetta una soluzione', *L'Ufficio moderno*, 9, 1947; Rossi di Montelera, M., 'Verso una disciplina della pubblicità', *Panorama della Pubblicità*, 8, 1949; Bottino, U.M., 'Problemi editoriali e pubblicitari: Tiratura, diffusione e tariffe', *L'Ufficio moderno*, 2, 1955; Weiss, I., 'Ancora due parole sulla tiratura e diffusione dei mezzi', *L'Ufficio moderno*, 4, 1955.

17 Doxa, founded by the statistician Per-Paolo Luzzatto Fegiz, was originally conceived as an opinion-polling company. The low demand for opinon polls, however, forced the company to take on an increasing amount of market and audience research. On Doxa see Rinauro, S., 'Il sondaggio d'opinione arriva in Italia, 1936–1946', *Passato e presente*, 9, 1, 2001, pp. 41–66.

18 On the low-brow romantic 'comics' or *fumetti* see Vetrone, A., 'Grand Hotel e l'Italia degli anni 50', *Rivista di storia contemporanea*, 4, 1988, pp. 603–631.

19 Zampieri, U., 'Il giornale di provincia strumento di pubblicità', *L'Ufficio moderno*, 7, 1955; advertisement, *Domenica del Corriere*, *Panorama della pubblicità*, 6, 1954.

20 'Un inchiesta sulla composizione dei lettori di Grazia', *Panorama della pubblicità*, 7, 1950; 'I lettori di Grazia', *Panorama della pubblicità*, 10, 1954.

21 See Arvidsson, A.,'The Pleasures of Renunciation: Young Women and Mass Consumption in Fascist Italy', in Hurd, M. (ed.), *Storylines: Media, Society and Identity in Modern Europe*, Stockholm: Hjalmarson & Hogberg (2002). For similar observations in the case of Nazi Germany see Koontz, C., *Mothers in the Fatherland*, New York: St. Martin's Press, 1987.

22 Advertisement, Durban, *Annabella*, 13/6, 1954.

23 See Arvidsson, op. cit.; on the romantic idea of love in general see Luhmann, N., *Love as Passion: The Codification of Intimacy*, Cambridge: Polity, 1986.

24 'Ditelo pure a me', *Grazia* 3, 3, 1951.

25 'La Pigrizia', *Grazia*, 9, 6, 1951.

26 'Un po' di buon senso', *Cucina Italiana*, July 1955.

27 'Stile della donna d'America', *Grazia*, 3/3, 1951; 'Ragazze che hanno un hobby', *Grazia*, 6/1, 1951; 'Una villetta per i vostri sogni', *Grazia*, 21/4, 1951; 'Una valigia per le vacanze', *Grazia*, 9/6, 1951; on the rising interest in camping and excursions see also Lepre, A., *Storia della prima repubblica*, Bologna: Il Mulino, 1995.

28 'La casa ha carattere', *Grazia*, 7/8, 1948.

29 Banfield, E., *The Moral Basis of a Backward Society*, Glencoe, Ill.: The Free Press, 1958.

30 Forte, G., *I Persuasori rosa*, Naples: Edizioni Scientifiche Italiane, 1966. Doxa did many surveys on newspaper and magazine readership during the early 1950s, which were published in *Bolletino della Doxa*. Most of them are gathered in Luzzatto-Fegiz, P.P., *Il volto slonosciuto d'Italia*, Milan: Giuffre, 1966 (1956).

31 Alassia, F. and Montaldi, D., *Milano, Corea: Inchiesta sugli immigrati*, Milan: Feltrinelli, 1960; Fofi, G., *L'immigrato a Torino*, Milan: Feltrinelli, 1964; Lopreato, J. and Locolo, D., 'Stefanaconi: Un villaggio agricolo meridionale in relazione al suo "mondo"', *Quaderni di Sociologia*, 34, 1959, pp. 239–260; Anfossi, A., Talamo, M. and Indovina, F., *Ragusa, comunità in transizione*, Turin: Taylor, 1959; for the example from *Rinascista* see Bellassai, S., *La morale comunista: Pubblico e privato nella rappresentazione del Pci, 1947–1956*, Rome: Carocci, 2000, pp. 129 ff.

32 Parca, G., *Le italiane si confessano*, Florence: Parenti, 1959.

33 'Lineamenti psicosociologici della lettrice di Gioia', Misura, 1963, unpublished audience study, Centro di Documentazione Sipra, RAI, Turin, pp. 41, 58, 28.

34 Camusso, G., 'Un Esperimento di applicazione di metodi motivazionali a ricerche di readership', in Fabris, G. (ed.), *Le ricerche motivazionali*, Milan: Etas kompass, 1967, pp. 483–484. The examples cited by Camusso refer to 'Chi sono, cosa fanno, come vivono i lettori di Famiglia Cristiana?' Misura, 1962 (unpublished audience research).

35 Crainz, G., *Storia del miracolo economico italiano: Culture, identità, trasformazioni*, Rome: Donzelli, 1996, p. x. The term mediazation comes from John B. Thompson's *The Media and Modernity: A Social Theory of the Media*, Cambridge: Polity, 1994, p. 46. On the development of the Italian media system see Ortoleva, P. 'Mezzi di comunicazione', in *Guida al Italia contemporanea 1861–1997*, Milan: Garzanti, 1998.

36 Pizzorno, A., *Comunità e razionalizzazione*, Turin: Einaudi, 1960, p. 190.

37 Ibid., pp. 80, 194.

38 On the development of a distinct youth culture during the years before and after the 'economic miracle' see Piccone-Stella, S., *La prima generazione: Ragazzi e ragazze nel miracolo economico italiano*, Milan: Franco Angeli, 1993; Capussotti, E., 'Perduti, Teddy Boys e Ninfette: La Costruzione della Gioventù e la cultura di massa in Italia durante gli anni cinquanta', PhD thesis, Fiesole: European University Institute, 2001.

39 Pizzorno, op. cit., pp. 206 ff.

40 *Bolletino della Doxa* 19–20, 1957, 5–6, 1960; Piccone-Stella, op. cit.

41 Baglioni, G., *I Giovani nella società industriale: Ricerca sociologica condotta in una zona del'Italia del Nord*, Milan: Vita e Pensiero, 1962; Ardigò, A., 'La condizione giovanile nella società industriale', in Aa. Vv., *Questioni di sociologia*, vol. 1, Brescia: La Scuola, 1966; for similar conclusions see also Dursi, M., *Giovani soli*, Bologna: il Mulino, 1959.

42 'Inchiesta sulla miseria in Italia 1951–52', in Braghin, P. (ed.), *Materiali della Commissione parlamentare*, Turin: UTET, 1978; Luzzatto-Fegis, P., *Il volto sconosciuto dell'Italia*, Milan: Giuffré, 1966, pp. 1589 ff.; cf. Lanaro, S., *Storia dell'Italia repubblicana*, Venice: Marsilio, 1992, pp. 166 ff.; Ginsborg, P., *A History of Contemporary Italy*, London: Penguin, 1990; Zamagni, V., *The Economic History of Italy, 1860–1990*, Oxford: Clarendon Press, 1997.

43 Luzzatto-Fegis, op. cit., pp. 1589 ff.

44 Crainz, op. cit., pp. 34 ff.; Petrillo, G., *La capitale del miracolo: Sviluppo e lavoro a Milano, 1953–1962*, Milan: Franco Angeli, 1992, pp. 102 ff.; cf. Salvati, M., *Economia e politica in Italia dal dopoguerra a oggi*, Milan: Garzanti, 1984.

45 *Bolletino della Doxa*, 23–4, 1964; ISTAT, *Anuario Statistico Italiano*, 1965, pp. 361 ff.

46 On the 'affluent workers' at Ivrea see Gallino, L., 'Aspetti economici, sociali e sindacali delle transformazioni interne del mondo operaio: I loro rapporti con il resto delle singole comuità', in Aa. Vv., *Aspetti e problemi dello sviluppo economico in italia, atti del IV Congresso mondiale di sociologia*, Bari: Laterza, 1959. Gallino observed that househhold budgets for workers at Ivrea were 32 per cent above that of average working-class families.

47 Franzina, E., 'L'America', in Isnenghi, M. (ed.), *I luoghi della memoria: Simboli e miti dell'Italia unita*, Bari: Laterza, 1996.

48 Calvino, I., 'La televisione in risaia', *il Contemporaneo*, 3/4, 1954; DeRita, L., *I contadini e la televisione*, Bologna: il Mulino, 1964; Calamandrei, M., 'La città in campagna', *L'Espresso*, 25/4, 1958.

49 DeRita, op. cit., pp. 96–97.

50 De Mauro, T., *Storia linguistica dell'Italia unita*, Bari: Laterza, 1963.

51 On television programming in the 1950s see Monteleone, F., *Storia della radio e della televisione in Italia*, Venice: Marsilio, 1992; on il carosello, Dorfles, P., *Carosello*, Bologna: il Mulino, 1998.

52 Alberoni, F. and Baglioni, G., *L'integrazione del immigrato nella società industriale*, Bologna: il Mulino, 1965.

53 Loperato and Locolo, op. cit., p. 257; Anfossi et al., op. cit., p. 169.

54 See, for example, Gundle, S., *I comunisti italiani fra Hollywood e Mosca*. Florence: Editori Riuniti, 1995.

55 'Il modo di vita sovietico', *Vie Nuove*, 44, 1953, as cited in Bellassai, S., *La morale comunista: Pubblico e privato nella rappresentazione del Pci, 1947–1956*, Rome: Carocci, 2000, p. 177.
56 Ibid., pp. 174, 133, 143.
57 Alassia, F. and Montaldi, D., op. cit., p. 101; see also Petrillo, op. cit. The term 'Coree' derived from the misery and poverty shown in television images from the Korean war.
58 Alassia and Montaldi, op. cit., pp. 105–106.
59 Bocca, G., *La Scoperta dell'Italia*, Bari: Laterza, 1963, p. 78.
60 Ibid., pp. 36 ff.
61 'L'Italiano s'annoia e lo sa', *L'Espresso*, 17/5, 1959.
62 Ginsborg, op. cit., p. 117.
63 See Pombeni, P., 'I partiti e la politica dal 1948 al 1963', in Sabatucci, G. and Vidotto, U. (eds.), *Storia d'italia vol V, la Repubblica*, Bari: Laterza, 1997, p. 138.
64 Acquaviva, S., *L'eclissi del sacro nella civiltà indutriale*, Milan: Edizioni di Comunità, 1961. On the trajectory of the DC see Allum, P., 'The Changing Face of Christian Democracy', in Duggan, C. and Wagstaff, C. (eds.), *Italy in the Cold War: Politics, Culture and Society, 1948–1958*, Oxford: Berg, 1995; Giovagnoli, A., *Il partito italiano: La Democrazia Cristiana cal 1942 al 1994*, Bari: Laterza, 1996, pp. 71 ff.
65 'Ornella vuol la mamma', *Famiglia cristiana*, 3/10, 1954; see also Gundle, S., 'Cultura di massa e modernizzazione: Vie nuove e Famiglia cristiana dalla guerra fredda alla società dei consumi', in Attorre, P.P. (ed.), *Nemici per la pelle*, Milan: Franco Angeli, 1991.
66 For a critical review of this concept see Compagna, F., *Terroni in città*, Bari: Laterza, 1959.
67 On Fanfani see Pombeni, P., La democrazia del benessere, *Contemporanea*, 4, 1, 2001, pp. 14–46.
68 'Lo spettro del neocapitalismo', *Passato e presente*, 1, 1959.
69 'La stuttura sociale: Aspetti e problemi di una società in trasformazione', Aa. Vv., *La Società Italiana: Atti del secondo convegno nazionale di studio della democrazia cristiana*, Rome: Edizioni 5 lune, 1962, p. 108; on Ardigò's speech see also De Felice, F., 'Nazione e sviluppo: Un nodo non sciolto', Aa. Vv., *Storia d'Italia repubblicana*, Turin: Einaudi, 1995.
70 Ardigò, op. cit., p. 111.

6 The new ethic of consumption I: the new housewife

1 Campari, R., 'Stasera canta Mina', in Aa. Vv., *Barilla: Cento anni di pubblicità e comunicazione*, Parma: Archivio Storico Barilla, 1994. On Mina see also Donaldio, F. and Giannotti, M., *Teddy-boys, rockettari e cyberpunk: Tipi, mode e manie del teenager italiano dagli anni Cinquanta a oggi*, Florence: Editori Riuniti, 1996; Liperi, F., ' "Il problema più importante": Canzioni e politica da "Volare" a "Marinella" ', in Aa. Vv., *Giovani prima della rivolta*, Rome: Manifestolibri, 1998.
2 In Alain Touraine's thought, modernity is conceived as a two-tiered movement of *rationalization* and *subjectivation*. With rationalization he refers, in a Weberian key, to the application of means to ends, with subjectivation the construction of 'man' as a conscious actor. Rationalization and subjectivation stand in a complex dialectic relationship. Rationalization is, on the one hand, often antithetical to subjectivation by aiming to substitute human agency for objectively valid rules or technological imperatives. Rationalization, on the other hand, subjectifies, by denaturalizing, by rendering contingent given and unquestioned ways of doing things and by thus forcing actors to consult their own mental facilities to refer to themselves, to acquire 'agency'. See Touraine, A., *A critique of Modernity*, Oxford: Blackwell, 1995.

3 Several historians have pointed to a similar link between mass consumption and female 'subjectivation': see Passerini, L.'The Ambivalent Image of Woman in Mass Culture', in Duby, G. and Perrot, M. (eds.), *A History of Women*, vol. 5, Cambridge, Mass.: Harvard University Press, 1994.
4 Ceserani, G.P., *Storia della pubblicità in Italia*, Milan: Edizioni del sole 24 ore, 1988.
5 On FIAT's advertising see Fasce, F., 'Voglia di Automobile: Fiat e pubblicità negli anni del dopoguerra', *Contemporanea*, 2, 2001.
6 Sparke, P., 'Industrial Design or Industrial Aesthetics: American Influence on the Emergence of the Italian Modern Design Movement, 1948–58', in Duggan, C. and Wagstaff, C. (eds.), *Italy in the Cold War: Politics, Culture & Society, 1948–58*, Oxford: Berg, 1995; Spark, P., *Italian Design: 1870 to the Present*, London: Thames & Hudson, 1988; cf. Branzi, A., *Introduzione al design italiano: Una modernità incompleta*, Milan: Baldini & Castoldi, 1999.
7 James, D., 'La moderna pubblicità chiave dei mercati', *Panorama della pubblicità* 3, 1952.
8 See Ellwood, D., 'Il piano marshall e il processo di modernizzazione in Italia', in Aga-Rossi, E. (ed.), *Il piano Marshall e l'Europa*, Rome: Istituto dell'enciclopedia italiana, 1983; Del Pero, M., *L'alleato scomodo: Gli USA e la DC negli anni del centrisom, 1948–1955*, Rome: Carocci, 2001.
9 Benelli, G., 'La pubblicità e lo studio di mercato', *L'Ufficio moderno*, 12, 1948; Norbedo, E., 'Analizzare il mercato prima di lanciare un nuovo prodotto', *Panorama della pubblicità*, 1, 1948; Holleran, O.C., 'Come si lancia un prodotto industriale', *L'Ufficio moderno*, 9, 1948.
10 Gazzera, G., 'L'elaborazione del testo pubblicitario', *L'Ufficio moderno* 10, October 1957.
11 Maso, M., 'Le applicazioni delle ricerche di mercato nelle aziende alimentari statunitensi', *L'Ufficio moderno*, 7, 1955; 'Pubblicità, prezzo, marca', *L'Ufficio moderno*, 6, 1957; 'L'immagine, la marca e il consumatore', *Panorama della pubblicità*, 38, 1957.
12 'I fattori della personalità di un magazzino', *Panorama della pubblicità*, 54, 1960.
13 Coerten, A., 'Il ruolo economico e sociale della pubblicità', *L'Ufficio moderno*, 11, 1959.
14 Spinetti, S., 'Nuovo capitalismo, relazioni pubbliche e pubblicità', *Produttività*, 12, 1957.
15 Italian translation: *I persuasori occulti*, Turin: Einaudi, 1958.
16 Bellavista, M., 'Un esempio di propaganda elettorale che grida vendetta', *Panorama della pubblicità*, 15, September 1953.
17 Pesavento, G., 'Lo scrittore in pubblicità', *L'Ufficio moderno* 2, 1952; 'In Memoriam Nino Caimi', *Panorama della pubblicità*, 9, 1952; Allen, A., 'Il direttore di ricerche, uomo chiave della moderna agenzia di pubblicità', *L'Ufficio moderno*, 2, 1959; 'Il consumatore, questo sconosciuto', *Panorama della pubblicità*, 2, 1949.
18 'Le ricerche di mercato nell'azienda moderna', *L'Ufficio moderno*, 7, 1956; Pasqualini, A., 'Lo studio di mercato', *L'Ufficio moderno*, 2, 1956; 'Ancora sul analisi dei lettori', *L'Ufficio moderno*, 1, 1957.
19 Advertisment, *Selezione*, *L'Ufficio moderno*, 9, 1957; Visconti, M., 'Come Selezione svoglie indagini di mercato nel interesse dei suoi inserzionisti', *Produttività*, 3, 1955. On the function of *Selezione* as an 'ambassador of America' see also Campo, C., 'L'america in salotto', in Attorre, P.P. (ed.), *Nemici per la pelle*, Milan: Franco Angeli, 1991.
20 'Analisi dei lettori di *Epoca*', *Panorama della pubblicità*, 45, 1958; advertisment, Cirio, *L'Ufficio moderno*, 1, 1961.
21 Dichter, E., 'Before and After Motivation Research', *Motivations*, April 1957.
22 Advertisment, Misura, *Studi di mercato*, 1, 1959.

23 On Dichter in Italy see 'La ricerca dei motivi in pubblicità', *L'Ufficio moderno*, 1, 1958; advertisement, E. Dichter Associati, *Studi e Ricerche*, 2, 1962.
24 Some studies of this were done, mostly on the initiative of the research companies themselves or that of AISM, but they were all isolated and fragmentary. Thus a survey from 1956 states that 50 per cent of the companies *asked* used motivation research, the larger ones more so than the smaller ones. In 1963 the figure is 61 per cent. The two surveys are, however, not comparable and say nothing about the extent to which market research was generally used, nor which companies were asked. A survey by *Misura* from 1961 found that 10 per cent of all the companies asked used Motivation Research (50 per cent used market research in some form). The problem is still that we do not know which companies they asked. See Ratti, G., 'Le ricerche di mercato nelle aziende italiane', *Studi di mercato*, 4, 1957; Fabbrizi, C.', Invervento: Evoluzione ed orientamenti delle ricerche di mercato', Convegno AISM, Rome 25/11, 1966; *Studi di mercato*, 1, 1967; *La Misura dell'opinione pubblica*, 1, 1961; Fabris, G.-P., Introduzione alle ricerche motivazionali, in Aa. Vv., *Le ricerche motivazionali*, Milan: Etas Kompass, 1967, p. 74.
25 Calvi, G., 'Un contributo psicologico alla scelta fra due linee pubblicitari', *Le ricerche motivazionali*, 1, 1964.
26 A. Restinco, 'Preindagine sul mercato italiano delle auto', *L'Ufficio moderno*, 1, 1961; 'Consumo di carne in scatola a Como', *Studi di mercato*, 4, 1958.
27 On margarine see 'Che cos'è una ricerca motivazionale', *Studi di mercato*, 1, 1959. On bouillion cubes, 'Tre ricerche di mercato', *Studi di mercato*, 1, 1956.
28 On such food scares see Lanaro, S., *Storia del Italia repubblicana*, Venice: Marsilio, 1992, pp. 203 ff.
29 Unpublished motivation studies by Misura, cited in Alberoni, F., *Consumi e società*, Bologna: il Mulino, 1964, pp. 170–171.
30 Calvi, G., 'Gli attegiamenti psicologici nei confronti dei prodotti dietici', *Misura*, 4, 1961. See also Arvidsson, A., 'The Therapy of Consumption: Motivation Research and the New Italian Housewife', *Journal of Material Culture*, 5, 2, 2000, pp. 251–274.
31 Calvi, 'Gli attegiamenti', op. cit.
32 See Alberoni, *Consumi e società*, op. cit., pp. 173 ff.
33 Dichter, E., 'Il consumatore del 1970', *Le ricerche motivazionali*, 2, 1964.
34 Fabris, G.-P., 'Prefazione', Martineau, P., *Motivazione e pubblicità*, Milan: Etas Kompass, 1964.
35 Gasparini, B., 'Processo alla donna moderna', *Annabella*, 21/4, 1957–7/4, 1958.
36 'La donna americana è in genere la donna moderna come consumatrice', *Panorama della pubblicità*, 35, 1957; 'Studio sulla "donna americana" ', *L'Ufficio moderno*, 10, 1960.
37 'Tecnica e proiettazione del supermarket in Italia', *Il direttore commerciale*, 1, 1959; Ravalli, S., 'Prime esperienze dei "supermarket" in Italia', *Mondo economico*, 1/7, 1961.
38 'Mercurio si meccanizza: Qui si vende senza l'ausilio di venditori', *L'Ufficio moderno*, 4, 1950.
39 Plurivento, N., 'Il supermercato', *L'Ufficio moderno*, November, 1958.
40 'Servitevi da sole', *Annabella*, 9, 1958; 'Il supermercato sta trasformando la nostra cucina casalinga', *Panorama della pubblicità*, 89, 1966.
41 Alberoni, F., 'Le motivazioni del consumatore', *Rivista internazionale di sicenze sociali*, 4, 1961, pp. 293–305.
42 Fabris, G., 'Crescente l'importanza della donna nella società dei consumi', *L'Ufficio moderno*, 12, 1968.
43 Rava, E., 'La donna e il mercato', *L'Ufficio moderno*., January, 1969.
44 'Atteggiamenti nei riguardi dei cibi conservati', *I prodotti di marca*, 2, 1968.
45 On the situation of women in the family during and after the economic miracle

see Balbo, L., *Stato di famiglia: Bisogni, privato, colletivo*. Milan: Etas, 1976; Caldwell, L., 'The Family in the Fifties: A Notion in Conflict with Reality', in Duggan, C. and Wagstaff, C. (eds.), *Italy in the Cold War: Politics, Culture & Society, 1948–58*, Oxford: Berg, 1995. The concept of 'repressive desublimation' derives from Marcuse, H., *One-Dimensional Man. Studies in the Ideology of Advanced Industrial Society*, Boston: Beacon, 1991 (1964).

46 Lilli, L. 'La stampa femminile', in Aa. Vv., La stampa italiana nell'età della tv, Bari: Laterza, 1994.

47 Advertisement, 'Amica', *L'Ufficio moderno*, 5, 1967.

48 In 1974 the DC launched a referendum to repeal the legalization of divorce. PCI had doubts about endorsing the 'no' campaign ('no' to the de-legalization of divorce) as many of its cadres believed 'the people' not to be morally evolved enough. The result, a substantial majority of 59.1 per cent, proved them wrong.

49 'Gli angeli del focolare sono calati nelle fabbriche', *Amica*, 29/11, 1964.

50 According to Doxa's investigation of the market for beauty products in 1966, 20 per cent of the women asked stated that they regularly used facial creams. In Marabelli's article from 1969 the corresponding figure was 59 per cent: see 'Diffusione dei prodotti da toaletta e di alcuni beni durevoli in Italia', *Bolletino della doxa*, 3, 1966; Marabelli, F., 'La donna e i cosmetici', *L'Ufficio moderno* 7–8, 1969; Firrao, S., 'Trasformazioni di mercato connesse alla evoluzione del ruolo della donna', *L'Ufficio moderno* 3, 1969, 'Biancheria intima femminile', *Studi e ricerche* 4, 1968; 'La donna ha sempre un bel corpo e lo valorizza', *Marketing e pubblicità*, 10, 1967.

51 On the concept of commodity feminism see Goldman, R., *Reading Ads Socially*, London: Routledge.

52 Miotto, A., 'Le motivazioni psico-sociali del consumatore', *L'Ufficio moderno*, 4, 1968.

53 Alberoni, F., 'I consumi come agire sociale dotato di senso', in idem, *Consumi e società*, Bologna: il Mulino, 1964, p. 39.

7 The new ethic of consumption II: crisis and reconstruction

1 On Mulino Bianco see Aa. Vv., *I Boom: Prodotti e società degli anni '80*, Milan: Lupettti, 1990; Aa. Vv., *Barilla: Cento anni di pubblicità e comunicazione*, Parma: Archivio Storico Barilla, 1994, pp. 282–323.

2 Francesco Alberoni, personal interview, 12/7, 1998; cf. idem, *Le sorgenti dei sogni*, Milan: Rizzoli, 2001.

3 On the concept of 'Simulacrum' see Baudrillard, J., *Simulacres et simulations*, Paris: Galilée, 1981. On the idea of contemporary subjectivity as 'set free' from the constraints of social structure see Giddens, A., *Modernity and Self Identity*, Cambridge: Polity, 1991.

4 Pizzorno, A., 'I ceti medi nel meccanismo del consenso', in Aa. Vv., *I soggetti del pluralismo*, Bologna: il Mulino, 1980.

5 Adagio, C. (ed.), *Il lungo decennio: L'Italia prima del '68*, Verona: Cierre, 1999. For an English analysis of the Italian student movement, see Lumley, R., *States of Emergency: Cultures of Revolt in Italy from 1968–1978*, London: Verso, 1990.

6 On the emergence of youth as a public category during the 1950s see Capussotti, E., 'Perduti, Teddy Boys e nimfette: La costruzione della gioventù e la cultura di massa in Italia durante gli anni cinquanta', PhD Thesis, Fiesole: European University Institute, 2001.

7 Bocca, G., *Miracolo all'Italiana*, Milan: Avanti, 1962, p. 58.

8 'A proposito dei giovani', *Rivista Piaggio*, May–June 1957.

9 A. Pasqualini, 'Parliamo del mercato dei giovani', *L'Ufficio moderno*, 2, 1958;

'Dal seme di oggi al albero di domani', *L'Ufficio moderno*, 11, 1962; Fasolo, F., 'Orientamento del indagine di merato', *L'Ufficio moderno*, 2, 1962.

10 On the teen magazines see Grispigni, M., 'S'avanza uno strano lettore: La stampa giovanile prima del '68', in Aa. Vv., *Giovani prima della rivolta*, Rome: Manifestolibri, 1998.

11 *Bolletino della Doxa*, 1964–66, passim.

12 Pasqualini, A., 'Domani è subito dietro l'angolo', *L'Ufficio moderno*, 9 1962; 'Alla scoperta dei teenagers', *Panorama della Pubblicità*, 69, 1962; 'La vendita e la pubblicità alla soperta dei giovani', *L'Ufficio moderno*, 66, 1962; 'Il mercato dei consumi sta cambiando in Ingilterra', *L'Ufficio moderno*, 4, 1964; 'Il mercato e i giovani', *L'Ufficio moderno*, 3, 1967.

13 'Attivita del club di vendite di Torino', ibid., 12, 1967.

14 'Il mercato e i giovani', *Bolletino della doxa*, 5–6, 1967.

15 On Piaggio's campaigns see Arvidsson, A., 'From Counterculture to Consumer Culture: Vespa and the Italian Youth Market, 1958–78', *Journal of Consumer Culture*, 1, 1, 2001, pp. 47–71.

16 On the early history of *antimoda* in Milan see Ruscone, A.G., 'L'antimoda: Esempi milanesi', in Aa. Vv., *La moda italiana: Dal antimoda allo stilismo*, Milan: Electa, 1987. On Beat see De Angelis, R., 'Il Beat Italiano', in Aa. Vv. *Giovani prima della rivolta*, op. cit. On the history of 1960s Italian youth culture more generally, Echaurren, P., and Salaris, C., *Controcultura in Italia 1967–1977: Viaggio nell'-underground*, Turin: Boringhieri, 1998; Balestrini, N. and Moroni, P., *L'orda d'oro*, Milan: Feltrinelli, 1997.

17 Ragone, G., *Consumi e stili di vita in Italia*, Naples: Guida, 1985, p. 43.

18 Rubin, J., *Do It! Scenarios of the Revolution*, New York: Simon & Schuster, 1970.

19 Pasolini, P.P., 'Contro i capelli lunghi', *Corriere della sera* 7/1, 1973; republished as 'Il discorso dei capelli', in *Scritti corsari*, Milan: Garzanti, 1990 (1975).

20 Malossi, G., *Liberi tutti: 20 anni di moda spettacolo*, Milan: Mondadori, 1987, p. 12.

21 'Fiorucci Story', *Amica*, 18/8, 1974.

22 Malossi, op. cit., p. 73.

23 'Messina, R., 'L'abbigliamento femminile italiano: Un prodotto industriale di successo', in Aa. Vv., *La moda italiana*, op. cit., p. 28.

24 'Femminismo e pubblicita', *I Prodotti di marca*, 2, 1972.

25 Ceserani, G.P., 'La pubblicità allo specchio', in Aa. Vv., *Barilla*, op. cit.; Balassone, S. and Gugliemi, A., *Corsari e nobiluomini: La pubblicità in italia*, Bologna: il Mulino, 1988.

26 Quoting from the gospel, 'Chi mi ama mi segue' ('May those who love me follow me'), Agenzia Italia showed a shapely female behind clad in a tight pair of 'Jesus Jeans'. More than its sexism the ad led to quite a row on behalf of its explicit blasphemy. In a famous article Pier-Paolo Pasolini saw it as a sign that Italy had finally left its pre-industrial state and entered the era of 'neocapitalism' where religion no longer fulfilled any essential ideological function. See Pasolini, P.P., 'Il folle slogan dei jeans', *Corriere della sera*, 17/6, 1973; republished as 'Analisi linguistica di uno slogan', in *Scritti Corsari*, op. cit. The creatives behind the campaign had their formative period at Young & Rubicam.

27 Ceserani, G.-P., *I persuasori disarmati*, Bari: Laterza, 1975, p. 116.

28 Ragone, G., 'I consumi in Italia tra "novità", "distinzione" e "qualità"', in Aa. Vv., *La moda italiana*, op. cit., p. 13; Schiana, G., 'Marketing: Chi consuma e perche?' *L'Ufficio moderno*, 3, 1968; 'Aspetti del futuro, VII convegno del marketing e distirbuzione a Parigi' *L'Ufficio moderno*, 6, 1968.

29 Forte, F., 'Il fenomeno della moda e i suoi riflessi sulle attività aziendali', in Aa. Vv., *Il consumatore e la moda*, Milan: 1969; Miotto, A., 'Le motivazioni della donna di fronte alla moda', ibid.

30 Stroppa, C., 'Considerazioni sul rapporto tra moda e economia', *I Prodotti di marca*, 1, 1967.
31 'La Moda come fatto sociale', *I Prodotti di marca*, 7, 1969.
32 Agneli, G. 'Nota conclusiva', *La psicologia del vestire*, 1967, p. 76; 'La moda come fatto sociale', op. cit.
33 'I figli del carosello', *L'Ufficio moderno*, 4, 1967.
34 For a summary of these perspectives, see Fattori, M., 'Una nuova lingua per i nuovi italiani', *Studi di mercato*, 3, 1972; 'Mondi di confronto', *I Prodotti di marca*, 2, 1967.
35 Musa, G., 'Non buttare via il bambino inseime all'acqua da bagno', *L'Ufficio moderno*, 6, 1972.
36 Tremelloni, R., 'Informazione sul Consumatore, XX. Convvegno IPR (sommario)' *L'Ufficio moderno*, 5, 1971; Schininà, G., 'Marketing sotto accusa?' *L'Ufficio moderno*, 4, 1971.
37 'Management e ideologia tecnocratica', *L'Ufficio moderno*, January 1971.
38 Musa, G., 'Non buttare via il bambino', op. cit.; Gambel, E., 'Il Marketing e le sue ricerche', *L'Ufficio moderno*, 2, 1971,
39 Aa. Vv., *I limiti dello sviluppo*, Milan: Mondadori, 1972. See also 'Il consumatore americano e la crisi', *Giornale di marketing*, 3, 1975, for a survey of this literature.
40 'Il marketing e la ricerca di consenso', summary in *L'Ufficio moderno*, 6, 1977.
41 'Rifondazione del Marketing', *L'Ufficio moderno*, 5, 1975, *XVIII Convegno AISM*, Verona, 1974. The ideological foundations of marketing were discussed in an exchange between Gabriele Calvi and Giancarlo Ravazzi concerning the AISM congress in Parma, 1975; Calvi, G., 'Convegno di Parma, marketing o ideologia', *Giornale di marketing*, 2, 1976; Ravazzi, G., 'A proposio di marketing e ideologia', *Giornale di marketing*, 4, 1976; 'Non buttare via il bambino', op. cit.
42 'Il consumerismo per manager', *Giornale di marketing*, 2, 1976.
43 'Uomo e società', *Giornale di marketing*, 1, 1975; 'Produzione, comunicazione, consumo, Convegno FPI, UPA, Milano 25–6/10 1974', summary in *Studi di mercato*, 9, 1974.
44 Minoia, G., 'Un compromesso storico per il marketing', *Giornale di marketing* 3, 1975. *Autoriduzioni*, 'auto-reductions', the decision to pay only a 'political' price for goods and services became a frequent instrument of struggle on the part of youth and neighbourhood militancy during the inflation of the 1970s. The 'metropolitan indians' of 1977 would decide to pay only what they argued to be 'fair' for movie tickets and food. Neighbourhood committees would decide to keep paying the old price for electricity in the face of price increases.
45 Gatti, E., 'Il ruolo del uomo di marketing', *L'Ufficio moderno*, 6, 1974.
46 Calvi, G., 'Il consumatore e post-consumista?' *Giornale di marketing*, 1, 1975. *Austerità*, 'austerity', the self-sacrifice and the voluntary acceptance of a lower standard of living on the part of the working classes as part of a strategy of corporativist responsibility, was the ideology/moral message of the 'historical compromise'.
47 Galli, G., 'Il consumerismo per manager', op. cit.; Derby, E., 'Il consumatore americano e la crisi', *Giornale di marketing*, 3, 1976; 'Un compromesso storico per il marketing?' *Giornale di marketing*, 3, 1975; D'Andrea, M. and De Ponti, M., 'Esiste il consumatore socialmente consapevole?' *Giornale di marketing*, 2, 1977; Scifo, S., 'Considerazioni sui futuri possibili', *Giornale di marketing*, 1, 1975.
48 Giovannini, A., 'Verso la civiltà anticonsumista', *L'Ufficio moderno*, 2, 1974.
49 Francesco Albeorni had been arguing this since the late 1960s. In his postscript to the second 1967 editon of *Consumi e società* he saw the youthful counter-culture as the carrier of a new kind of consumer culture where status and emulation of superiors would no longer be the central principle. Rather, consumer goods would be used as a kind of communicative medium that would stimulate creative

personalization and diversification. He formalized these observations in a 1972 article, 'L'evoluzione attuale delle strutture sociali e la teoria del consumo: Verso una reinterpretazione', *Rivista internazionale di scineze sociali*, 1972 (LXXX), V–VI, pp. 393–412.

50 Ragone, op. cit., p. 25.

51 Kotler, P. and Levy, S., 'Broadening the Concept of Marketing', *Journal of Marketing*, 33, 1969, pp. 10–15; Morello, G., 'Il Nuovo Marketing', *Studi di mercato*, 3, 1969.

52 Morello, G., 'Intervento al convegno di Firenze', *Studi di mercato*, 1–2, 1972.

53 Rovelli, N., 'Il marketing nella società in evoluzione', op. cit.; 'Crisi e ricerche di marketing', *L'Ufficio moderno*, 6, 1976.

54 Oxenfeldt, A.R., 'La nozione di domanda e la segmentazione del mercato', *Studi di mercato*, 1, 1969; Durban, J., 'La segmentazione dei mercati', *Studi di mercato*, 2, 1969.

55 *Questi i giovani*, Shell, Italy, 1970.

56 Calvi, G., 'Psicografia e stili di vita in Italia', *Giornale di marketing*, 3, 1976; *Valori e stili di vita degli italiani*, Milan: ISEDI, 1977.

57 Fabris, G.P. and Mortara, V., *Le otto Italie: Dinamica e frammentazione nella società Italiana*, Milan: Mondadori, 1987.

58 Zanchin, F., 'La pubblicità una semiologica della merce', *L'Uffici moderno*, 4, 1977; 'Abozzo di una psicologia della pubblicità', *L'Ufficio moderno*, 3, 1979.

59 Calvi, G., Valori e stili di vita, op. cit., p. 126.

60 Morello, A., 'L'evoluzione del consumatore negli anni '80', *L'Ufficio moderno*, 4, 1982.

61 Intermatrix Group, 'Scenario pasta 1983–1987' (unpublished market research), Parma: Archivio Storico Barilla.

62 Codeluppi, V., *I consumatori: Storia. Modelli. Tendenze*, Milan: Franco Angeli, 1997, p.42. On Zanussi see Sparke, P., *Italian Design: 1870 to the Present.*, London: Thames & Hudson, 1988.

63 Carloni, P., 'E io mi faccio un "amica" nuova', *Prima Comunicazione*, December 1981, cited by Lilli, L., 'La stampa femminile', in Aa. Vv., *La stampa italiana nell'età della tv*, Bari: Laterza, 1994.

64 On Armani see *I boom*, op. cit.; De Combrati, R., *Armani*, Milan: Franco Maria Ricci, 1982.

65 *I boom*, op. cit., p. 278.

66 Pilati, M., 'La pubblicità dei mezzi di comunicazione', in Aa. Vv., *La Stampa*, op. cit., p. 267.

67 In 1994 supermarkets and shopping malls were, according to GPF Associati's Monitor survey, by far the most frequent places to purchase goods, and their share of total value added in commercial distribution more than tripled. The expansion of boutiques was linked to the upsurge in fashion. Between 1971 and 1981 the number of fashion boutiques increased from 24,000 to 82,000: see Balloni, V. and Santarelli, E., 'Le attività produttive si riorganizzano', in Ginsborg, P. (ed.), *Stato d'Italia*, Milan: Il Saggiatore, 1994, p. 396; see also Barberini, I., 'La cultura dei consumatori', in Aa. Vv., *Casa e supermercato, Luoghi e comportamenti di consumo*, Milan: Coop, 1996; Badeschi, M. and Fava, A., 'Il sabato nel villagio', *Case e supermercato*, op. cit.

68 Alberoni, F. and Castellaneta, C., *Trussardi: Memorie per scrivere la storia della casa Trussardi*, Milan: Franco Maria Ricci, 1991, pp. 92, 149.

8 The triumph of consumer culture

1 *Cinesi* (Chinese) was originally the term used by the conservative daily *Corriere della sera* to designate the radical students who occupied universities in 1967. It

subsequently entered the street jargon of neo-Fascist youth gangs as an epithet for their opponents, the 'reds'.

2 The *paninaro* style went international through a shrewd marketing trick on the part of the English duo Pet Shop Boys. The *paninari* themselves originally worshipped either Duran Duran or Simple Minds. The fanzine *il Paninaro* held a public referendum for Duran Duran to play in Italy; and the most significant piece of documentation on the *paninari*, *Sposerò Simon LeBon* ('I'll marry Simon LeBon') (the lead singer of Duran Duran), by Milanese high-school student Lettizia Mottica, filmed in 1986 as *Confessioni di una sedicenne innamorata persa degli Duran Duran* ('Confessions of a sixteen year old madly in love with Duran Duran') by Carlo Cotti, was largely dedicated to the attractions of their singer. The Pet Shop Boys were, however, so impressed with the Italian *paninaro* scene that they assumed the look overnight, hoping that this would aid them in their rivalry with Duran Duran. The celebratory maxi single *Paninaro* helped them less in this pursuit, however, than their subsequent successes 'West End Girls' and 'Let's Make a Lot of Money', which firmly established them on the parnassus of late 1980s schlock, and introduced the *paninaro* style to their middle-class British fans. On the *paninari* see also Donadio, F. and Giannotti, M., *Teddy boys, rockettari e cyberpunk*, Florence: Editori Riuniti, 1996.

3 See Ardigò, A., 'La condizione giovanile nella società industriale', in Aa. Vv., *Questioni di sociologia*, vol. 1, Brescia: La Scuola, 1966; Aa. Vv., *Giovani oggi*, Bologna: il Mulino, 1984; Aa. Vv., *Giovani anni '90*, Bologna: il Mulino, 1993. On youth and consumer culture during the 1980s see also Castellani, A., 'Contaminati della merce', in Aa. Vv., *La città senza luoghi*, Genova: Costa & Nolan, 1990.

4 *Il Paninaro*, January 1987.

5 On the 'metropolitan indians' see Crispigni, M., *Il settantasettte*, Rome: Il Saggiatore, 1997; Aa. Vv., *Bande: Un modo di dire, Rockabillies, Mods, Punks*, Milan: UNICOPLI, 1986.

6 As cited in Donadio, F. and Giannotti, M. op. cit., p. 191.

7 See Hall, S and Jacques, M. (eds.), *New Times: The Changing Face of Politics in the 1990s*, London: Lawrence & Wishart, 1989.

8 Pasolini, P.P., 'Il potere senza volto', *Corriere della sera*, 24/6, 1974; republished as 'Il vero fascismo e quindi il vero antifascismo', in *Scritti corsari*, Milan: Garzanti, 1995 (1975).

9 Censis, *Consumi Italia '87*, Milan: Franco Angeli, 1987, p. 16.

10 Pilati, M., 'La pubblicità dei mezzi di comunicazione', in Aa. Vv., *La stampa italiana nell'età della tv*, Bari: Laterza, 1994, p. 252. For similar arguments see Codeluppi, V., *I consumatori: Storia, modelli, tendenze*, Milan: Franco Angeli, 1997; Dell'Acquila, P., *Verso un ecologia del consumo*, Milan: Franco Angeli, 1997; DiNallo, E., 'La nostra ipotesi di lavoro', in Aa. Vv., *Cibi simbolo nella realtà d'oggi*, Milan: Franco Angeli, 1986; Fabris, G.P., *La pubblicità: Teorie e prassi*, Milan: Franco Angeli 1997; Secondulfo, D., *La danza delle cose: La funzione comunicativa dei beni nella società post-industriale*, Milan: Franco Angeli, 1990; Sorice, M., *Le culture del consumo*, Milan: Piccola Biblioteca, 1995; Livolsi, M., 'Il cambiamento socio-culturale in Italia', in Livolsi, M. (ed.), *L'Italia che cambia*, Florence: Editori Riuniti, 1993.

11 Ragone, G., 'I consumi in Italia tra "novità", "distinzione", e "qualità", in Aa. Vv., *La moda italiana*, op. cit.; see also his *Consumi e stili di vita in Italia*, Naples: Guida editori, 1985.

12 Alberoni, F. and Castellamara, C., *Trussardi: Memorie per scrivere alla storia della casa Trussardi*, Milan: Franco Maria Ricci, 1991, pp. 116–124.

13 Ceserani, G.P., 'Una folla di spot', in Aa. Vv., *Barilla: Cento anni di pubblicità e comunicazione*, Parma: Archivio Storico Barilla, 1994; see also Ortoleva, P., *Un*

ventennio a colori: Televisione privata e società in Italia, 1975–1995, Florence: Giunti, 1995.

14 Ortoleva; cf. Abbruzzese, A., *Metafore della pubblicità*, Milan: Costa & Nolan, 1988; Mattlehart, A., *Advertising International: The Privatization of Public Space*, London: Routledge, 1991.

15 Pilati, 'La pubblicità dei mezzi di comunicazione', in Aa. Vv., *La stampa italiana nell'età della tv*, Bari: Laterza, 1994, p. 265. On the idea of a 'second economic miracle' see Turani, G., *1985–1995, Il secondo miracolo economico italiano: Istruzioni per l'uso*, Milan: CDE, 1986. During the first half of the 1980s the Italian public sector deficit increased steadily (from some 80,000 billion lire in 1980 to some 130,000 billion in 1985, at 1987 prices). Much of this accumulated deficit was financed by domestic borrowing. Consequently, state certificates that gave a return of 5 per cent above inflation became the favourite investment choice of the middle classes. These also offered a new, convenient, way of making the middle classes finance consensus-generating public spending in the South at the same time as they had an interest in supporting the system. In the medium term, however, the results became unbearable. By 1985 public debt was at 92 per cent of GDP, and at the end of the decade it was well above 100 per cent.

16 Biorcio, R. and Manieri, M., 'Consumi e società dagli anni ottanta agli anni novanta', *L'Italia che cambia*, op. cit., p. 201; see also Barile, G., 'I consumi', in Ginsborg, P. (ed.), *Stato d'Italia*, Milan: il Saggiatore, 1994.

17 ISTAT, *Annuario statistico italiano*, 1970–1990, passim; Balassone, S. and Gugliemi, A., *Corsari e nobiluomini: La pubblicità in Italia*, Bologna: il Mulino, 1988, pp. 71 ff.; Ragone, G., *Consumi e stili di vita*, Naples: Guida, 1985, pp. 21 ff.

18 On Censis see Rinauro, S., *Storia del sondaggio d'opinione in Italia 1936–1994: Dal rifiuto alla repubblica dei sondaggi*, Venice: Istituto Veneto di Scienze, Lettere ed Arti (forthcoming), Aa. Vv., *L'Italia dopo la grande trasformazione: Trent'anni di analisi Censis, 1966–1996*, Rome: Carocci, 1997.

19 Censis, *Consumi in Italia*. op. cit.

20 Fabris, G.P. and Mortara, V., *Le otto italie: Dinamica e frammentazione della società italiana*, Milan: Franco Angeli, 1986, p. 9.

21 On Foucualt's idea of statements being 'in the truth' see his 'Discourse on Language', as published in his *The Archaeology of Knowledge*, New York: Pantheon, 1972.

22 Gundle, S., *I comunisti italiani fra Hollywood e Mosca*, Florence: Editori Riuniti, 1995, p. 201.

23 Petrillo, G., *La capitale dei miracolo: Sviluppo e lavoro a Milano, 1953–1962*, Milan: Franco Angeli, 1992, p. 175. On CISL see also Del Pero, M., *L'alleato scomodo: Gli USA e la Dc negli anni del centrismo, 1948–1955*, Rome: Carocci, 2001.

24 About 800,000 people moved from the South to the industrial North between 1955 and 1961, and about 6 million moved from the surrounding countryside to the Northern cities. Between 1962 and 1971 the figures were 1.8 million and 8.9 million respectively. See Crainz, G., *Storia del miracolo economico italiano: Culture, identità, trasformazioni fra anni cinquanta e anni sessanta*, Rome: Donzelli, 1996, pp. 104 ff.; Lanaro, S., *Storia del Italia repubblicana*, Venice: Marsillio, 1992. On the sacking of politically active workers in the post-war years see Ginsborg, P., *A History of Contemporary Italy, Society and Politics, 1943–1988*, London: Penguin, 1990, pp. 186 ff.

25 Petrillo, op. cit., p. 384; Balestrini, N. and Moroni, P., *L'orda d'oro*, Milan: Feltrinelli, 1997.

26 Piccone-Stella, S., *La prima generazione: Ragazzi e ragazze nel miracolo economico italiano*, Milan: Franco Angeli, 1993.

27 Zandegiacomi, N., 'La donna in Italia', *Rinascita*, 3, 1961, as cited in Crainz, op. cit., p. 190.

28 See Tarrow., S., *Democracy and Disorder: Protest and Politics in Italy, 1965–1975*, Oxford: Clarendon, 1989.
29 Crispigni, M., *Il settantasette*, Milan: il Saggiatore, 1997.
30 See Nello, A., *Il lungo addio*, Rome: Laterza, 1997, p. 73 ff.
31 Ibid., p. 123.
32 Lepre, A., *Storia della prima repubblica*, Bologna: il Mulino, 1995, p. 269.
33 Bagnasco, A., 'Una società complessa, ma prima ancora complicata', in Ginsborg, P. (ed.), *Stato dell'Italia*, op. cit. For a classic work see Bagnasco, A., *Le tre italie: La problematica territoriale nello sviluppo italiano*, Bologna: il Mulino, 1977.
34 Lerner, G., *Operai*: *Viaggio all'interno della Fiat. Le case, le fabbriche di una classe che non c'è più*, Milan: CDE, 1988, p. 8
35 Bosco, N., 'Dove va la classe operaia?' in Ginsborg, P. (ed.), *Stato dell'Italia*, op. cit.
36 For an English survey see McCarthy, P., *The Crisis of the Italian State: From the Origins of the Cold War to the Fall of Berlusconi*, New York: St Martins, 1995; Gundle, S. and Parker, S., *The New Italian Republic: From the Fall of the Berlin Wall to Berlusconi*, London: Routledge, 1996; Gilbert, M., *The Italian Revolution: The End of Politics Italian Style*, Boulder, Colo.: Westview, 1995.
37 Absenteeism increased from 9 per cent in 1976 to 17.4 per cent in 1992, and the percentage of Italians who claimed that they 'often discussed politics' declined from 23.7 per cent in 1976 to 11.6 per cent in 1989; Biorcio, R., 'Cittadini e politica negli anni Novanta', in Livolsi, M. (ed.), *L'Italia che cambia*, op. cit.; Natale, P., 'Le tendenze elettorali degli anni Novanta: Mutamenti nei comportamenti e nelle logiche del voto', op. cit.
38 Giglioli, A., Cavichioli, S., Fele, G., *Rituali di degradazione: Anatomia del processo Cusani*, Bologna: il Mulino, 1997.
39 Porro, N., 'L'innovazione conservatirce: Fininvest, Milan club e Forza Italia', *Quaderni di Sociologia*, 9, 1994–95, pp. 6–18.
40 On Forza Italia see Gilioli, A., *Forza Italia, la Storia, gli Uomini, I Misteri*, Milan: Ferruccio Arnoldi Editore, 1994; Poli, E., *Forza Italia: Strutture, leadership e radicamento territoriale*, Bologna: il Mulino, 1994.
41 Mazzoleni, G., 'Towards a Videocracy? Italian Political Communication at a Turning Point', *European Journal of Communication*, 10, 13, p. 311.
42 Ibid., p. 310; cf. Abbruzese, A., *Elogio del tempo nuovo: Perchè Berlusconi ha vinto*, Genoa: Costa & Nolan, 1994.

Index